THE
Hidden
Masters
OF
Gurdjieff

By the same author:

Ameth: The Life and Times of Doreen Valiente

London's Mystical Legacy (with Toyne Newton)

The Psychic Jungle

The
Hidden Masters
of Gurdjieff

Jonathan Tapsell

BRUTUS MEDIA

Dedicated to
John Flores of the Rodney Collin group,
Mexico City

Acknowledgements: Michael Rosen, Muhammed Knight,
Steff Z. Odlum, Victoria LePage, Philip Heselton, Colin Wilson,
and the Sufi orders: Nashqbandi, Chishti, Malmati, Majaddidi, Mevlevi.
To Ann Devereaux, personal student of J.G. Bennett.

To the unknown 'Milk Saint' of Pashuputi, Kathmandu who told me some
of the theories related in this book regarding the masters, including the
existence of Santikar Acharya secreted underneath the Monkey Temple.

Edited and designed by Adrian Dobbie

ISBN 978-0-9574061-7-9

A catalogue record for this book is available
from the British Library.

Contents

The Great Game

"*When the Iron Birds are flying in the sky and the Iron Horses are running on the roads, we know that dharma-ending age has arrived. At this time, Tibetan Buddhism shall flourish globally.*"
Padmasambhava, 8th Century

A Fabled Land Holding a Forbidden City
A barren fastness where no Westerner dare tread for fear of body or soul, Lhasa was the most inaccessible capital city in the world, at least to medieval Europeans. This state of affairs would remain until the first years of the 20th Century.

One of the earliest visitors, surprisingly, was the Jewish explorer Benjamin of Tudela who lived in the 12th Century. He had travelled from his native Tudela in Spain and then onto Africa, Asia Minor and into the harshest terrain of Western Asia. His fantastic tales of idol-temples in a far-flung country called Tibet with its neighbouring Mongols who worshipped the wind must have blown the minds of those who could only marvel at what he must have seen.

His account had to wait several centuries to percolate into mainstream culture; Benjamin's chronicles were written in Hebrew and took a long time before being translated into Latin, the international academic language of the time. Another early name associated with the privilege of stepping just a little way into Tibet was Friar William of Rubruck, a Flemish missionary sent abroad by the King of France Louis IX in 1253 to convert the Tartars to Christianity. His tale is at least comparable to that of Marco Polo. It is understandable that his account was concerned chiefly with the religious beliefs that he encountered on his journey, with Friar Rubruck becoming the first Westerner to identify the Buddhist mantra '*Om Mani Padme Hum*'. His other religious observations were first-hand accounts of shamanic magic observed during time spent with local nomads he encountered. Rubruck recalled a practice carried out by the nomads once they had made camp and their guests had arrived. The Master of his yurt would sit below a doll called his 'brother'. His wife would likewise sit beneath a doll called her 'sister'. Men would sit on the right, women on the left of the yurt. William noted that libations were made by the head of the house to the South, East, West and North and which magical elements were apportioned to each. South (fire), East (air), West (water) and the North to the dead. Yet neither of these intrepid explorers, Benjamin nor Friar Rubruck, managed to conquer Lhasa, a capital off-limits to Westerners, or any other strangers for that matter. Entry to the mysterious city was firmly controlled by the State authorities who issued official invitations. The barren fastness, aided of course by high altitude and freezing wastelands, made it ideal for the policing of such splendid isolation.

The West had to wait a few more hundred years before Portuguese Jesuit missionary Andrade settled in Goa in 1600, to acquire any further information on the fabled city. He is acknowledged as the first European explorer to cross the Himalayas via the perilous Mana Pass and to enter Tibet. This crossing of the Mana, perched at 18,300 feet above sea level, was no mean feat and the journey proved extremely arduous. Andrade and another Jesuit missionary called Marques could not cross the pass at first due to heavy snow blocking their way, and to make matters worse there were hostile forces in hot pursuit. Marques stayed behind to put up a defence as Andrade and his team made the second attempt at the Mana Pass. Andrade and Marques survived their ordeal and in 1624 successfully went on to befriend the King of Guge in Western Tibet, bringing Christianity to the region for the first time.

The visit only lasted one month. Andrade returned to Goa with a view to revisiting Tibet as soon as he could, with ambitious plans to set up a more robust Catholic mission there. In 1625 he retraced his footsteps up through the Himalayas, this time accompanied by several other missionaries, with more funding and supplies for what lay ahead. The second mission in Tibet saw the building of a church and the conversion of the King of Guge and his wife to Catholicism, along with some of the local inhabitants. Andrade returned to Goa once more, leaving behind him a flourishing mission. A subsection of this mission in Shigatse recorded the first ever mention of the mythical land of Shambhala, at least to European ears. Andrade made plans to return a third time in 1629 to his mission in Tsaparang, but these were soon scuppered due to an invasion by a nearby state called Ladakh. The Ladahkis killed the King of Guge, overran the Tibetans and occupied Tsaparang. The new Ladakhi ruler took a dislike to the foreign mission and within a few years had successfully expelled the Catholics, along with their faith. Andrade's two accounts of Tibet were published in Portuguese and Spanish and another account found its way to Cracow, Poland. This exposition remained very much at the forefront of what was known about the mysterious mountainous Asian theocracy. As before, no one had made it anywhere near the fabled capital Lhasa.

In 1661 all of this was to change dramatically. The Jesuits sent out a new expedition this time led by a father and son. The Austrian Johan Gruber and his Belgian father Albert D'Orville started out from China with a view to making it to India via Tibet and Nepal. Their momentous journey was to take 214 days but claimed the life of D'Orville who later died in Agra due to the hardship of the trek. They entered Tibet in July 1661 and made it to Lhasa by October the same year, where they remained as guests for two months before continuing their journey towards the Indian plains. Gruber's contribution here was to constantly chart the longitude and latitude of his journey which would prove useful for future explorers. The ill-starred journey of D'Ovrville and Gruber would also underscore the importance of the Himalayan passes to trade, which would soon give birth to an episode of foreign interest in the entire expanse of the Silk Road called the *Great Game.*

During the 18th Century the Jesuits and another Christian faction known as the Capuchins sent more missionaries to Asia and some of these made it to Lhasa. Pope Clement XI gave his blessing to one such voyage and saw Italian scholar Ippolito Desideri take residence in Tibet. Desideri used his talents to master the Tibetan language, becoming the first European to do so, allowing him to grasp many facets of Tibetan culture and society. His journey into Tibet like others before him was perilous; he had already been laid up for six months with an intestinal disease but later, he and his superior reached Ladakh. Desideri thought that they should camp there and start their mission but his superior insisted they leave Ladakh and cross the wilds of the Tibetan Plateau. The pair were woefully unprepared for such an undertaking and had it not been for the generosity and protection of a female Mongolian Governor and noblewoman called Casal, the Jesuits would almost certainly have perished. Desideri owed his life to Casal who saw to it that the Europeans travelled in her armed and well-stocked caravan back to Lhasa. Desideri stayed there in Lhasa, its only European resident in 1716.

An audience with Tibetan ruler and Mongol chief Lajang gave Desideri official permission to teach Christianity and to found his mission, albeit temporarily, due to the instability of Mongol politics elsewhere. An invasion in 1717 saw Desideri leave and return another couple of times. His presence in Tibet offered Western interests the first credible understanding of the place and its people, yet his own Catholic prejudices rendered him unable to understand the concepts of Buddhism. However, the main opposition to his remaining in Lhasa came not from the insular Tibetans as one might expect, but from another Italian sect of missionaries opposed to the Jesuits, who by 1721 instigated religious-political intrigues that had him expelled from Lhasa by the Tibetan authorities. From then on, the Propaganda Fide of the Capuchin Order held the only Vatican mission in Lhasa. European politics had arrived and perhaps some might say that this incident in Tibet was the first sabre rattled in what would later be dubbed the Great Game.

The Younghusband Expedition

In 1903-04 the British Imperial forces under the command of one General Younghusband entered Tibet. The military force that rode into the ancient Kingdom in a thinly disguised invasion was diplomatically referred to as an 'expedition'. It happened to be one of the last audacious and unprovoked colonial incursions into independent lands conducted by a major European force, taking place at the latter stages of European colonisation within Asia.

The notorious 'Younghusband Expedition' belongs to a particularly colourful phase of the political rivalry between two notable 19th and 20th Century superpowers: Imperial Russia and the British Raj. Known in these far-flung lands as the Great Game, this political and diplomatic confrontation was immortalised by Kipling in his novel *Kim*. An intense rivalry, often more theoretical than actual, suspicious, even jealous, bordering on the paranoid at times, the Great Game potentially held the key to overall control of Central Asia.

Even the British Empire's India, often dubbed the 'Jewel in the Crown', was ultimately held in the balance of the Great Game, with its fulcrum in the snowladen mountain passes of the Himalayas, Pamirs and Karokorams. Behind these mountains lay the worst nightmares of Western imagination in the form of savage, unforgiving territory, religious bigotry and the harsh terrain patrolled by murderous brigands, with brutal despots observing unpredictable tribal allegiances hinged on uneasy truces and temporary pacts.

In these autonomous regions where no quarter was spared for the careless traveller, let alone interfering Europeans; beyond the Punjab and Kashmir the British could rely on very few friends or allies. The Russians too also saw a rocky road where treacherous despotic leaders could prove unreliable. Leaders in these parts could be bought, cajoled, threatened or out-manoeuvred by their scheming, well-organised European rivals, in order to change sides in a trice. Russia and Britain were so close to all-out war in a way – perhaps in the truest sense the Great Game was the first 'Cold War'. No shots were exchanged directly between the superpowers themselves as the mountainous frozen buffers and vast Asian deserts separating Russian and British outposts afforded the pair a vital distance from open hostilities, but a great many innocent peoples were drawn into the Great Game only to suffer in its wake. The more fortunate of these were only humiliated by false promises and empty diplomatic words of their colonial visitors. The least fortunate among them found only carnage, treachery and servitude. The Great Game was no place for loyalty or sentiment.

As for the Younghusband Expedition, led by a privileged dilettante who had never seen bloodshed first-hand himself, the mission became renowned as a notoriously aggressive exercise by Britain. As such, the incursion only fulfilled the Russian expectation that the true intention of the British Empire was to move further up into the soft underbelly of Asia. Undisturbed Tibet, in many respects, was the final chess piece to be moved in the Great Game; a sacrificial move in a delicate geo-political mechanism that affected the entire Silk Road and may inevitably have precipitated the fall of a number of Central Asian states, leading to a European war. Britain feared India falling into destabilisation and ultimately, anarchy under Russian influence, but Russia on her side equally feared, and was acutely aware of, the possible consequences of a Persia under the sway of the British Empire.

So lay the Great Game. Maintaining the buffer zones was the key to peace but also to pre-empt intrigues or worse still, open war. In some ways the Younghusband Expedition will be remembered as one of the more ham-fisted episodes played by either side during the Great Game. Even though ideas and tastes have changed over the last century regarding colonial history, the Younghusband Expedition was inglorious even back in its own day, being viewed only as the naked ambition of a superior power to subjugate a peaceful nation without just cause. Parallels can be drawn with attitudes towards the modern invasion of Tibet by Communist China, viewed today as equally infamous for much the same reason.

As soon as the Younghusband Expedition had early successes, the press in London, notably *The Spectator* and *Punch* reported the British engagement of the Tibetans. The column inches talked of shameful, wholesale slaughter of innocent men defending their territory without understanding why they had been invaded. The Tibetan defenders' resistance was later described by journalists as that of 'half-armed' men fighting a vastly superior army using the machine gun and supported by cutting-edge military techniques of the Victorian age. British newspaper readers, when hearing of machine guns and colonial discipline pitched against Tibetans armed with only matchlocks and clutching at prayer beads and magical amulets in the hope of avoiding slaughter acted as a long-needed wake-up call as to how Empires are forged. Jingoism was, for once, put to one side in Victorian Britain and the name of the Younghusband Expedition and its techniques were called into question. Perhaps for the first time, journalists had been allowed to report unfettered from the colonial battlegrounds.

The moral and political fallout was not to the military's liking. Today we could view this as just bad PR, but back then it may have been regarded in some quarters, particularly in Younghusband's camp, as divisive or even unpatriotic. The term 'collateral damage' had yet to be invented as a way of excusing the massacre of civilians.

It was an early example the media being caught up with the vagaries of war, with what we now call 'embedded' journalists, and for the first time men of war were caught in the cross-fire, not of the bullet, but of public opinion at home. General Younghusband's name became a by-word for uncomfortable truths regarding unprovoked incursions into foreign lands. In fairness to the British authorities Younghusband had overstepped his duties and in a sense the mission had gone way beyond its official remit, but all of that was lost on the bewildered Tibetans who had been invaded by a far superior military force. The nature of the incursion is complex and not necessarily as one imagines, which is not to justify Younghusband's actions. However, some explanation is necessary as background for what would follow.

Tibet in the Year of the Water Rabbit (1903) was one of the last remaining Himalayan bastions free from British influence. The country's ruler, the Dalai Lama, presided from within the majestic Potala Palace resting high above the Tibetan capital Lhasa. A border dispute had begun between Tibet and the mountainous semi-autonomous state of Sikkim, which lay between the Indian Raj and Tibet to the north, Nepal to the west, Bhutan to the east and India's Bengal to the south. At this time Sikkim, a former Kingdom, was a British protectorate and had been since 1890. The British had managed to cement this alliance with Sikkim through the very same means it was now using in 1903. During 1814 Sikkim entered into a border dispute with Nepal and appealed to the British East India Company which came to their aid against the common Nepalese enemy. So began the first Anglo-Nepalese War. Later, as those events concluded, Sikkim was annexed by Nepal.

In 1849 two British travellers, Dr Hooker and Dr Campbell, ventured into Sikkim without proper invitation and were taken captive, reigniting British interest in the region. The incident led to a punitive expedition and eventual British annexation of Sikkim in 1853. It was not lost on some in the Raj that as Tibet and Sikkim wrangled over their mountainous borderlands, Britain had stepped in to aid Sikkim as their ally. It must have occurred to some that this rather insignificant border incident provided a golden opportunity to extend British influence once more. The Younghusband Expedition's remit was as follows: to install a military presence to restore borders between warring neighbours, establish a diplomatic presence with the autonomous Tibetans and reinforce the ever-movable borders of the Great Game against Imperial Russia. Yet the road to hell is paved with good intentions. As the Younghusband Expedition moved towards Tibet the whole mission spiralled altogether into another proposition, becoming a notorious gambit that shamed the Raj.

The Trouble With Lord Curzon

George Nathaniel Curzon, 1st Marquess Curzon of Kedleston, is a name that will always be remembered as synonymous with the British Raj. Curzon was a quintessential product of the colonial period within an Empire where the sun never set; his appointment as Viceroy of India was the crowning achievement in a glorious career that set him apart at home and abroad.

A key player in the latter stages of the Great Game, his influence as Viceroy of India led to several historical episodes bearing his indelible mark. Much of his success and popularity was due to his experience as an administrator in the North-West Frontier fighting against the fierce Pashtun tribesmen. Curzon was a man of intense desire, whose fierce attention to detail at times bordered on an arrogant disregard for others.

Seeing himself as civilising agent working on behalf of the Crown, he held the belief that Asians were little more than savages incapable of self-governance. Set against the prevailing mindset of the Victorian age one can perhaps understand and maybe even forgive these attitudes: Curzon was, after all, no different from many others in the elite during the Raj. His record as Viceroy speaks of the Masid-Waziri Campaign of 1901. He travelled to Persia to encourage trade links in the region in 1903 and was very much a player of the Great Game, harbouring much suspicion of Russian intentions in the Asian theatre.

During his career he argued for exclusive British access to the Persian Gulf, a highly contentious policy aimed squarely at the Russians. Curzon drew borders in Eastern Europe and was a noted statesman before his death, coming close to assuming the office of British Prime Minister in the early 1920s. However, his role in India spanned a short, but pivotal, moment in time (1899-1905) and it was Curzon's hawkish view of the Tibet-Sikkim dispute that led to so many unfortunate consequences unravelling.

His initial assessment of the regional politics was to be dismissive of the Russian assurances that they had no interest or political intentions in Tibet. The Viceroy viewed the Imperial Russians as expansionists awaiting their turn to match the success of the British, with their eye on the Indian Raj.

These assurances that Imperial Russia had no interest in Tibet may have been weakened by the presence of a Russian Mongolian a man named Gombojab Tsybikov, who managed to reach Tibet during 1900-1901. He used his experiences with British explorers to infiltrate the Buddhist kingdom and secretly photograph the land. Gombojab was a Buddhist scholar who later teamed up with a Russian explorer called Norzunov. Their photographs of Lhasa dominated by the Potala Palace, home of the god-king Dalai Lama became famous, featuring in the *National Geographic* in 1905.

Curzon harboured an innate scepticism towards the Russian promises and like many other British Great Gamers, never let his guard down for so much as a minute. If the Dalai Lama had made hospitable overtures towards the Russian bear then the British lion was not to be denied. In Curzon's mind the Russian presence in Tibet had to be matched. As the Tibet–Sikkim border dispute raged, Curzon wasted no time in seizing his opportunity to ferment a British response that would be felt by the Tibetan Government, leading to the first ever bilateral relations. His aim was to equal British and Russian diplomatic acceptance inside Tibet but also to lay the foundation stone of a political dialogue between London and Lhasa.

Curzon and Younghusband had been friends for years, with Curzon frequently entertaining his younger friend in the hill stations of the Raj. Younghusband wrote to his superior regarding colonial theory, something we might today call 'political science'. A wire arrived for Younghusband, who was quartered in India, the message was from an official asking him about his journey. Completely mystified, he asked himself what journey the wire was referring to? The same day he received a letter from the Viceroy instructing him to come at once to Simla. It was here that Curzon outlined his intentions, or orders, to his younger nominee, regarding what would become known as the notorious Younghusband Expedition. In some ways it should perhaps be remembered as the Curzon Expedition, since Curzon was chief architect of the scheme. Once primed, Younghusband set off and made his arrangements for the planned invasion with strict orders that there was no need to go as far as Lhasa.

Younghusband made his way into Sikkim with horses, supplies, oil skins, ammunition and 3,000 troops augmented by 7,000 support troops. Sikkim was ruled by a British puppet leader referred to as a Maharajah by London but as Chogyal by his own people. Since the 1888 annexation by the British, he had been treated appallingly by a colonial official named White, who had been appointed to head Sikkim by London. White had both humiliated and bullied the Maharajah until he got his complete compliance. The Maharajah was a former ally of Tibet, his wife a politically astute historian who had written several important Buddhist works including a treatise on the Tibetan Book of the Dead. One evening, Younghusband was invited to dine at White's official bungalow, where he was introduced to his fellow guests, the Maharajah and his wife.

The party talked, dined and later drank a toast to the King. Younghusband was most taken by the Maharajah's consort as his diaries attest. White's pomposity was also noted in the diary: Younghusband records that the Colonial official made his servants prostrate themselves before him, but also took note of their secret amusement at having been compelled to do so.

True to his task the General rode off on horseback in the pouring rain with a retinue of Sikh soldiers, continuing his route towards Tibet. Claude White, as British political officer responsible for Tibetan frontier affairs, accompanied him. This would prove to be a mistake, as the high-handed official had never been out of Sikkim and was unused to either diplomacy or military discipline.

Upon reaching the Himalayan stop-over, en route to Lhasa, in a place called Gantok, Younghusband received a telegram not to advance into Tibet until he could be sure that Tibetan officials would be present to greet him upon entry. This suggestion was made in order to dampen the idea that this was an aggressive move on the part of the British authorities. The plan was hatched to send a forward party, led by White, to learn what status Younghusband had amongst the Tibetans and whether entry would be granted.

By the time Younghusband presented at the Tibetan border at Khamba Jong on July 18th 1903, some eleven days after White's arrival, the diplomatic damage had been done. White, in his overbearing style, had offended the Tibetan officials who were being supported in their roles by a Chinese diplomat named Ho Ksi. Younghusband wrote of White in his diary describing him as 'worse than useless in dealing with high officials of an independent nation'. The next day a conference was held between the various parties, including the Chinese official Ho Ksi.

To further complicate matters Tibet was not considered wholly independent, being under what was known as Chinese suzerainty. Curzon for one did not recognise Chinese suzerainty in this regard and some commentators relate that the Chinese resident and officials under him such as Ho Ksi were ceremonial in nature only. But to the Chinese Manchu Government all concerns regarding treaties or foreign affairs demanded protocol that they should be kept informed of all diplomatic developments. The actual treaty relating to the Sikkim-Tibet 1890 border treaty had in fact been signed by China on Tibet's behalf: hence the presence of Ho Ksi at Khamba Jong.

Communicating via the one Tibetan-speaking officer, one Captain O'Connor, General Younghusband outlined the grievances of the Indian Government, more accurately those of the British Raj, towards the border dispute, complaining also that the Dalai Lama had sent back various diplomatic letters unopened. His speech fell on deaf ears as the Tibetans refused to discuss the matter any further until the expedition crossed back onto Sikkim soil. At that comment the

Tibetans and their Chinese associate departed to their fortress and were seen no more. Frustrated Younghusband and his party were left to their own devices in the freezing wastes of Khamba Jong.

This retirement lasted several months until Younghusband finally left the area to return to Sikkim. Two jubilant Tibetan officials went off to Lhasa to report the favourable news that the British expedition had left their country. They were probably certain their strategy had worked, but then again they had never met Curzon.

Viceroy Curzon's deep concerns about the Great Game were politely listened to in Whitehall but few were willing to rise to the bait. His telegrams citing Cossacks riding to pillage India, Russian spies in Lhasa and the need for moving into Tibet were politically untimely. It was Curzon's view, one he shared with Younghusband, that their expedition might have to manufacture an incident or reason to necessitate invasion, perhaps not unlike the 'weapons of mass destruction' policy of the Bush-Blair era employed to excuse an otherwise illegal war in Iraq a century later. Meanwhile, a rather cautious Whitehall was not easily swayed and pushed aside talk of a full-scale invasion of Tibet. The Great Game had its limits.

A Buddhist Emissary

In June 1901 the *Journal de Saint Petersburg* ran an article reporting contact between an emissary of the Tsar and the Dalai Lama. To men like Curzon and other Great Gamers the presence of the Tsar's representative in Tibet significantly upped the stakes. The following summer a man named variously as Dorzhievy, Dorjiew, Dorjieff or Dorzhiev set again to cement ties between Imperial Russia and Tibet; his aim to cordially conclude a treaty between the two Kingdoms, albeit a secret one.

The name of the emissary was finally discovered to be one Agvan Dorzhiev, a diplomat, theologian, scholar of Buddhist metaphysics and, somewhat alarmingly to the British, a reputed Tsarist spy. His Asiatic, square-jawed Mongol features, intimate knowledge of Lamaism and familiarity with oriental customs, made his dabblings in Tibetan politics appear agile in comparison to his European rivals. A Buryat Mongol, Dorzhiev was born in the village of Khara-Shibir, east of Lake Baikal in 1854. He studied Tibetan Buddhism for 15 years at the Gomang College of the Gelugpa Drepung monastic university near Lhasa, before going on to become a teacher and advisor to the Dalai Lama.

He commenced in this role as far back as 1876 and was later credited with saving the Dalai Lama's life from poisoning; a favoured method among courtiers of hastening the reincarnation process should a better Dalai Lama be desired.

As a result, Dorzhiev gained significant influence in the court of the Dalai Lama. Tibet in the 19th Century was in a precarious position, with threats from hostile Chinese influence, Nepalese invasion and crippling tariffs imposed on the country by Gurkha-dominated authorities and the schemes of Great Britain.

Dorzhiev must have seemed a welcome, benign friend in comparison. For his part, Dorzhiev regularly petitioned the Tsar for more assurances towards the Dalai Lama but being in a similar position to his opposite number Curzon it seemed his entreaties received polite audience but nothing more concrete. Imperial Russia, like Great Britian, saw Tibet as a buffer state, not a possession. The Buddhist scholar's influence in the Russian court was equally appealing as he held sway over a notable courtier, Prince Esper Ukhtomsky, a self-proclaimed Buddhist and oriental scholar. The Prince, a member of the Imperial Geographical Society, was closely involved in trans-Siberian transport projects and was eventually elevated to the title 'Gentleman of the Bedchamber' to the Tsar. Dorzhiev's authority in the Russian court extended to his dissemination of the Shambhala myth and his teaching of the Kalachakra Tantra, and it was he, aided by the likes of Prince Ukhtomsky, that encouraged a comparison between the 'White Tsar' and the myth of the White Tara mentioned in Buddhism.

Author Jamie Bisher in his *White Terror: Cossack Warlords of the Trans-Siberian* says of the Dorzhiev's activities in and around the Romanov dynasty at that time, "Buryat Buddhists venerated the Tsar and his Romanov predecessors as incarnations of the White Tara, a merciful Buddhist deity. A tract distributed by Dorzhiev glowingly describing Nicholas II as an 'emanation of the King of Shambhalla."

Much has been said about the influence of the mystic healer Rasputin inside the Imperial Russian court, but Dorzhiev himself is rarely mentioned. Dorzhiev's fostering of an implied link between the Tsar and a Buddhist deity was a subtle, yet powerful tactic designed to appeal those in Tsarist circles. The Buddhist connection had political benefits, in promoting the idea of a pan-Asian empire ruled over by a Tsar who was the living incarnation of a Bodhisattva. To these ends Dorzhiev covered some ground returning to Lhasa, journeying to St Petersburg, travelling to both Paris and London.

His influence gained him audiences with the Tsar who was said to be pleased by the reports he heard about his Eastern Empire and progress on the Russian end of the Great Game. However, like his opposite number Viceroy Curzon, Dorzhiev found that few politicians were willing to back him with military assurances. The Tsar may have looked upon his emissary favourably but was nevertheless unwilling to sign up to a military assistance treaty with Tibet. Dorzhiev was granted permission to build a Buddhist temple in St Petersburg, the first of its kind in Europe. The building of the Datsan Gunzechoinei, which Dorzhiev hoped would go on to house the first Buddhist ruler of Russia, attracted a great deal of attention, both positive and negative. While the Russian Orthodox Church objected to the construction of a 'pagan' temple in St. Petersburg, it attracted others such as the painter and theosophist Nicholas Roerich, who helped decorate its interior and was later to play a great part in mystical expeditions, as we shall learn. Despite his efforts, however, Dorzhiev's political ambitions for a Tsarist-Lamaist state were never realised. His machinations between St Petersburg and Lhasa aroused British suspicions, unwittingly setting off visions of imagined plots, Cossack invasions and the loss of the ultimate prize, 'The Jewel in the Crown' – the Indian Raj. Lord Curzon had to act and act fast.

The new Secretary of State for India, St John Broderick, took office at this time. He was a friend of the Viceroy and more disposed to the idea of a timid advance into Tibet on the grounds of establishing diplomatic dialogue with Lhasa. Younghusband was briefed never to admit to his paymasters in London that Dorzhiev was the primary motive for invading Tibet, instead using a cover story that settling the border dispute for their ally the Maharajah of Sikkim was the true reason.

The expedition set off once more with funding for a more robust advance – 5,000 yaks, 5,000 bullocks, 3,000 ponies, camels, the Royal Artillery Mountain Battery, 1st Battalion Norfolk Regiment, 2nd company Sappers, 23rd Sikh Pioneers, military police, surveyors, postal officers, telegraph engineers, civil engineers, medics manning field hospitals and bringing with him the deadly Maxim machine gun, all under the banner of the Union Jack.

By 13th December 1903 General Younghusband had reached Dzelap La, the last pass from Sikkim into Tibet. It was this same pass that the British and Tibetans had first crossed swords in the original Sikkim border dispute, the Tibetans being routed by the superior might of their foe. Had no lessons been learnt since 1888? As Younghusband advanced, the Russian emissary Dorzhiev advised the Dalai Lama to flee to safety, with appeals to the Tsar for military assistance against the British falling on deaf ears. In the summer of 1904 the Dalai Lama and his aide escaped to Mongolia, while Younghusband forced entry into Tibet then headed towards Lhasa – the Forbidden City.

The Younghusband Expedition had been bloody but it was also one of the first colonial episodes that incorporated journalists, who reported back from the ground. Back home the invasion lacked support, and reports of massacres of 'half-armed' men under Maxim machine gun fire did nothing to improve the overall image of the expedition. Like its distant cousin the Iraq War, the Younghusband expedition had little justification, attracting much criticism in papers and magazines back home, particularly *Punch* and *The Spectator*. The now infamous skirmish at Guru, which became known as the massacre of Chumik Shenko, saw 3,000 Tibetan soldiers mown down by Maxims with hardly any British, Sikh or Gurkha injuries. The differing accounts seem to follow what we might call collateral damage, shifting the blame from Younghusband, were it not for a telling quote from one of his machine gun commanders: "I got so sick of the slaughter that I ceased fire, though the general's order was to make as big a bag as possible", wrote Lieutenant Arthur Hadow.

There were suggestions in some cases of the British conducting bogus negotiations with the opposition and using the temporary cessation in hostilities to launch treacherous surprise attacks on the Tibetans.

A survivor of the massacre Tseten Wangchuk recounts, "While we were waiting at the wall during the discussions, a hail of bullets came down on us from the surrounding hills. We had no time to draw our swords."

Some historians disagree, blaming Tibetan soldiers who blew the jaw off a Sikh after a struggle therefore inviting the attack. In any event, the Tibetans armed with match-lock rifles were completely out-gunned by the invaders, although they continued to harry them from the hills inflicting low-level but continued resistance. Time and time again the Tibetans were routed despite spirited defences from mighty palaces high on rocky terrain or futile attempts by monks to block roads while hiding behind walls of stones. Defeat was inevitable, with the British marching from Gyantse into Lhasa to impose a new treaty as they saw fit. The people of Lhasa jeered the conquering army as they entered the capital, wishing rain on the unwelcome foreigners by clapping at them, but the British mistakenly thought this was a sign of approval for their invasion. Rather shambolically Younghusband did not find any evidence of Tsarist military advisors nor stashes of Russian ammunitions proving a point that the denouement had been nothing more than a tournament of shadows just as those in Whitehall had long suspected. It is said history repeats itself and it did a century later in the Blair-Bush non-existent 'weapons of mass destruction' debacle. That said, his Holiness the Dalai Lama, and the man who acted as a catalyst for the invasion, Dorzhiev, remained out of reach of Younghusband in Outer Mongolia.

One Russian observer, a man of Greek-Armenian extraction, had witnessed the destructive expedition, having been present in Tibet at the time. According to his own testimony he was there on the 'Roof of the World' to seek out enlightenment. This young man, near to thirty years of age, was the enigmatic George Ivanovitch Gurdjieff. Owing to his witnessing of the Younghusband expedition and its butchery of the innocent Tibetans, Gurdjieff would remain harshly critical of all warmongers throughout his extraordinary life.

His main accusation levelled at the British was the killing of a certain Lama G, an enlightened monk who he claimed held all the ancient knowledge. Lama G it is believed, from the scant records and accounts that remain, was a disciple associated with the lineage of Padmasambhava from the Nyingmapa tradition or 'red hat' Lamas. Gurdjieff insisted that the knowledge lost in this one unfortunate death would have dire cosmic consequences for the whole of humanity.

The Harmonious Circle of Humanity

Decades later, Gurdjieff would pen the curiously named *Beezlebub's Teachings to His Grandson*. Subtitled 'An Objectively Impartial Criticism of the Life of Man', the book, part allegory, part cosmic teaching, has remained highly arcane to this day, due to its use of obscure meanings, humour, strange terminology and language. According to Gurdjieff one must read the book three times in its entirety, the first time in an impartial manner as one would a newspaper, and only on the third reading would the gems of wisdom within become apparent. Gurdjieff did not intend the book to be easily digestible, requiring a significant effort on the part of the reader in order to understand the deeper meanings within.

One section of *Beelzebub's Tales* makes reference to Gurdjieff's sojourn in Tibet, at the time of Younghusband's arrival at Guru, massacring the troops and monks he found there. He references the slain Lama G, introducing the esoteric concept of the 'harmonious circle of humanity', said to be the force governing the fate of planet Earth.

This concept, although arcane, is by no means unique to Gurdjieff; the idea of benevolent higher beings guiding the affairs of humanity is a well-worn theme among seekers treading lightly upon the road to enlightenment. In Gurdjieff's case, this concept posits the existence of an 'inner school' that guards the conscious practices and teachings of humanity. These are then transferred to an 'outer circle' of associates who, in turn, transmit them to ordinary men and women for the facilitation of personal development. In his book *Views from the Real World*, Gurdjieff states, "Great Knowledge, which has existed from the most ancient times, has never been lost, and knowledge is always the same. Only the form in which this knowledge was expressed and transmitted changed, depending on the place and the epoch…"

He goes on to state that this knowledge is largely incomprehensible in its raw form, and can only be assimilated by the majority of humanity once the inner core is directly understood in a holistic manner. He insisted that there were two parallel lines of existence within civilisation at any one time; the esoteric and exoteric, or outer, reality. It is only when political or social conditions are favourable that the esoteric concept becomes consciously injected into civilisation by the secret masters of the school.

Gurdjieff cited many examples of this transmission occurring throughout history, where wise men suddenly appear to guide the leaders, an era or movement begins and extolls new ideas that take hold to improve the lot of mankind. In some cases these sacred or conscious ideas from the school last a great many years, centuries even, and underpin what we may term as 'civilised' values: the ideas of forgiveness, compassion, love and so on.

In certain examples these ideas may come to exemplify a particular way of life. It is said that the process is organised in such a manner as to minimise distortion of meaning and maximise impact. All major religions begin as crystalisations of the ideas transmitted by these higher beings, but like any organism, ideas die or degenerate and religions ossify, becoming purely exoteric versions of their former selves. While their adherents continue to pay lip service to the original teachings, they either no longer live by them or are incapable of understanding them, so the 'conscious circle' awaits the next opportunity in order to inject new ideas, which will be in a form more appropriate to the culture, time and place. Gurdjieff writes in *Beelzebub's Tales* that the ideas of Buddhism were brought to Tibet in just such a way.

Padmasambhava brought his consort Princess Mandarava and the secret teachings of Tantra to Tibet from India in the 8th Century. At that time, the Tibetans practised the folk religion known as Bon. Padmasambhava gradually combined the two systems into what became known as Tantric Buddhism or Lamaism. Padmasambhava is represented in *Beelzebub's Tales* under the fictional name Saint Lama, throwing up a silhouette of the 'harmonious circle of humanity' and their activities.

Saint Lama's teaching, Gurdjieff recounts, gradually took hold, although it was slightly adapted by the Tibetan people. The relative isolation of the 'Roof of the World' helped keep the teaching intact for many years. Gurdjieff claims the group responsible for introducing Padmasambhava to Tibet is the same school who formulated the doctrines of Buddha and before that, the Hindu Krishna. As such this esoteric school was a consummate player in the psychological and spiritual evolution of mankind, introducing enlightened teachers at key points in history, injecting their teachings into humanity when the moment was right. As time went by a group developed consisting of seven enlightened beings, whose responsibility it was to oversee the passing down of the teachings in Tibet from generation to generation. The unfortunate Lama G is said to have served as the leader of this elect body until his untimely death. When Younghusband invaded Tibet, Lama G, in his role as councillor to the Dalai Lama, insisted that all resistance to the British should be pacifist in nature and in accordance with the Buddhist Lamaist teachings, no lives should be taken. So it was that Lama G volunteered himself to be one of the first lines of non-violent defence against the invaders. *Beelzebub's Tales* gives us this account of events,

"During the year 1902 in response to the unexpected Younghusband Expedition into Tibet a gathering of all the Tibetan Chiefs was called. This assembly included amongst its number the leader of the group of seven. Their initial decision, which was to politely ask the foreigners to leave, was a complete failure and on further discussion they proposed to destroy the expedition by force. The leader of this small spiritual group persuaded them against this because in the eyes of our "Common Creator God" all life was equally precious and the death of so many would only further increase the great burden that He carried as a result of our abnormal existence on Earth. The assembly of Tibetan Chiefs were deeply moved by the words of this future Saint and decided to send out certain of their gathering to persuade the local people not to hinder the expedition by any forceful means. The leader of the seven was one of those chosen for this task and while attempting to fulfil it was shot by one of the foreigners."

There can be no doubt when one examines British military adventures in the modern era: Iraq, Northern Ireland, Afghanistan etc., it is a lamentable fact that British forces have, on rare occasions, committed outrages against innocent civilians. The wholesale slaughter by a Victorian army of pacifist Tibetan monks clutching at prayer beads, intoning mantras, or just positioning themselves as human blockades is perhaps the first example of journalistic reporting of a colonial massacre. Reports of this incident were published in London and swiftly found a wider audience across Britain. The news certainly did not sit well, not least with the alleged eyewitness G.I. Gurdjieff.

It seems that the death of Lama G impeded the conscious development of the Harmonious Circle and as a result a degenerative effect set in.

Says Gurdjieff, "The most serious consequence of his death lay in the fact that Saint Lama had laid down quite explicitly the way in which transmission of his teaching should be carried out. Certain absolutely vital and secret instructions were to be transmitted exclusively by the leader of the group and the remaining members could only be initiated when they had reached the necessary level of spiritual attainment. The six who had brought their self-perfecting up to the final degree were in fact almost ready for this final initiation and the death of their leader seemed to have destroyed this possibility."

Gurdjieff explains the cosmic consequences of the fallen Lama and his ill-starred exit from this incarnation at the hands of the British troops and cautions that there are planetary consequences for all beings as a result. Effectively the tradition of Lama G and therefore that of Padmasambhava, Buddha and Krishna, ended shortly after Lama G's death with the demise of the entire esoteric teaching. Arguments still rage over this account. Was it purely allegorical, or somehow biased by Gurdjieff's own side in the Great Game? He was after all, if we are to believe Indian colonial records, said to be a Tsarist spy. Gurdjieff spoke thereafter of the 'psychosis' of mankind being predisposed towards war and is on record as saying that this destructive impulse inherent within humanity was in opposition to the spiritual development of the species. Gurdjieff is supposed to have left Tibet in anger, shortly after the 1904 Tibetan atrocity.

In an ironic footnote to this story, General Younghusband, leader of the bloody expedition, failed to become Prime Minister as oft predicted, echoing the age-old adage 'he who wields the sword rarely wears the crown'. Younghusband went on to become something of a prototype hippy, espousing all kind of mystical theories as a result of his time spent in the East. He was a highly popular after-dinner speaker and lecturer and often talked of the aesthetics of the East, his ideas on mysticism and even went on to write the foreword of Paul Brunton's *Sacred India*. Despite his seeming devotion to the East and its spiritual teachings he was blissfully unaware that he and his invasion were possibly responsible for the killing of one of the most important and enlightened beings on the planet: Lama G.

Ten years after the death of Lama G, notable events took place, such as the mass slaughter of World War I, precipitating the eventual fall of the British Empire. Thereafter, as Gurdjieff lamented, there soon came a deterioration in human conditions; the world soon faced the rise of Hitler, Stalin, Pol Pot, Chairman Mao and Chinese Communism. The latter would eventually see the wholesale dismantling of esoteric thought including the Tibetan Lamaist culture itself inside Tibet. These regimes replaced the old teachings with the new religions of mass hypnosis, brain washing and materialistic philosophy, kept in place with the help of the twin horrors of brutal violence and genocide.

Chapter 2

Ascended Masters and Secret Schools

"I ask you to believe nothing that you cannot verify for yourself."
G.I.Gurdjieff

Sarman-Dargauh (Court of the Bees)

George Ivanovitch Gurdjieff was born circa 1870 in the Transcaucasia region, which today comprises the republics of Georgia, Armenia and Azerbaijan. Born to a Greek carpenter named Yiannis Georgiades and Evdokia, his Armenian mother, Gurdjieff spent his early years in Kars or Ghars, a city on the Turkish/ Armenian border which at the time was part of the Tsarist Empire. His Orthodox education meant that he was conversant in Russian, but Kars being a border town the young boy mixed with diverse ethnic and cultural groups, picking up several languages during this time. Blessed with an enquiring mind, he read science under the tutelage of a man called Dean Borsh, a family friend. According to his autobiography *Meetings With Remarkable Men*, later adapted for film in the '70s by director Peter Brook, the young Gurdjieff travelled extensively through Central Asia, India, Persia and Egypt. Readers are cautioned not to take Gurdjieff at face value, however. Owing to a tendency to obscure direct meaning behind layers of allegory coupled with an overriding sense of humour – often at the readers expense – the story is not always regarded as strictly factual.

According to his own account of this time in his life, Gurdjieff claims to have joined a number of secret societies in order to learn the ancient wisdom and philosophy but he gradually settled on the idea that neither science nor religion could satisfy his quest for knowledge.

While travelling with his friend Pogossian, the pair took part in the excavation of the ruins of Ani, the ancient capital of Armenia, during which a curious discovery was made. A bundle of decaying parchments they unearthed were found to contain the correspondence of a certain Father Arem relating to an ancient mystery school known as the Sarmoung Brotherhood. According to Gurdjieff, the Sarmoung had existed as far back in antiquity as Ancient Babylon, being an Aisorian (related to the Assyrian people) brotherhood operating in the area between Kursdistan and Urmia. Full of inspiration, Gurdjieff began his search for the Sarmoung but soon after in 1887 he made another discovery; this time of an ancient map of pre-sand Egypt that seemed to suggest it was from a time before the land of the Nile had been largely reduced to desert. Consumed by curiosity, Gurdjieff temporarily abandoned his search for the Sarmoung Brotherhood to look into this potential fragment of the ultimate truth, for if the map were true, it was a representation of the Nile delta predating 3000 B.C.

Some further information on what Gurdjieff termed 'pre-sand' Egypt comes from one of his most celebrated students, P.D. Ouspensky, According to Ouspensky, Gurdjieff maintained that the religion of Christianity was not so much a teaching of Christ, but one that had its origins in pre-sand Egypt, an Egypt before that which we presently know as 'ancient'. Some studies have concluded that Ancient Egypt, as we understand it, was the inheritor of a civilisation from much earlier times. Gurdjieff said of Christian ritual that all the holidays, rites and symbols had distinct meanings but these had been largely forgotten. As mentioned in Chapter 1, he believed that the inner meanings had elapsed over the passage of time and had become purely exoteric, or more accurately lifeless, being devoid of the continued supporting energies of the harmonious circle of humanity.

Gurdjieff had a distinct advantage in this arena in that his own father was an Ashohk, a word used in Asia Minor to describe a poet or storyteller. The Ashohk often recanted by rote the ancient oral tradition of their community, sang songs in competitions, recited poetry or recounted myths such as the *Epic of Gilgamesh*; stories that stretched back millennia, having been passed down through generation to generation, unchanged perhaps even from before the Great Flood. The Ashohk's role in society was similar to that of the Bard in Western culture, in that he occupied a traditional role within the community as a living repository of the shared cultural knowledge passed down from one age to another. Drawing upon these fragments of knowledge and other cross-cultural elements, Gurdjieff gradually developed a deep-seated yearning for the esoteric and believed that life was more meaningful than might otherwise be supposed. Within him grew a fire for a deeper meaning and purpose in life. From the impact of his father's Ashohk knowledge we may learn a little about Gurdjieff's own evaluation of the ancient wisdom of time past:

" [...] I was struck by the fact [...] that this legend had been handed down by ashokhs from generation to generation for thousands of years and yet had reached our day almost unchanged. After this occurrence [...] a result that crystallised in me a spiritualising factor enabling me to comprehend that which usually appears incomprehensible – I often regretted having begun too late to give the legends of antiquity the immense significance that I now understood they really have."

From the period after 1887 Gurdjieff once again travelled extensively. It may be during this time that he became involved in the intrigues of the Great Game as a means to finance his adventures. He appears to have been involved in many questionable business activities according to his accounts, although he never admitted to spying. He joined forces with the 'Seekers After Truth', an esoteric group led by a Russian nobleman Prince Lubovedsky. Members of the organisation travelled singly or in pairs, sometimes organising expeditions in search for arcane knowledge, leaving no stone unturned in their quests. It has been said that Hitler's own mentor Karl Ernst Haushofer (the father of geopolitics) was himself a member.

Once again Gurdjieff sought out the Sarmoung Brotherhood. Much of his account of the continued search is peppered with figurative stories. One such sees Gurdjieff and his companions crossing the Gobi desert on stilts in order to avoid a sandstorm. This is almost certainly an allegory employed to underscore the clarity and perspective that comes from the activation of higher centres within humanity. Likewise, his accounts of being hit by stray bullets on at least three occasions have been described by seasoned Gurdjieffians such as the late Bert Sharp, as a reference to the three stages of initiation towards awakening. Gurdjieff's autobiographical accounts have to be treated carefully and not taken literally by any means. However, there is no doubt from the many eyewitness accounts gained from those who met him that Gurdjieff possessed extraordinary powers and perceptions that set him apart from other men, lending credence to the fact that he was indeed privy to secret knowledge.

Gurdjieff's quest to find the Sarmoung Brotherhood would ultimately bear fruit. He related that after an arduous 12-day journey traversing dangerous mountainous terrain by horseback and donkey, often blindfolded so the location was not compromised, his guides brought him to the legendary Sarmoung Monastery. After crossing a perilous rope bridge across a yawning ravine he was invited into the secret place as a pupil. Once inside the monastery he discovered to his surprise that his friend the Prince from the Seekers After Truth was already there. It is said that this discovery took place in 1897 or 1898, about the same time he came into contact with the Tsarist Buddhist Emissary Argvan Dorzhiev.

Inside the Sarmoung Monastery, Gurdjieff was initiated into the ancient mysteries which had come from the times of Ancient Babylon circa 2500 B.C., as spoken of in the letters of Father Arem. The monastery was located in Turkestan which is a huge area encompassing the shores of the Caspian Sea, Aral Sea to Lake Balkash and lies between Siberia, Tibet, India, Afghanistan and Iran. Part of Turkestan lies within the 'Roof of the World'.

Sarmoung itself is an interesting Persian word as it can be translated to mean three things. The first being 'bees' and they of course produce honey, which does not perish and can survive for thousands of years. This was a direct allegorical meaning related to the function of the secret brotherhood and the transmission of their teachings. Bees store honey while the school stores knowledge to be released at the right time. A second meaning arrives in the Persian translation, giving the word 'sar' meaning 'head', both literally and in terms of a leader or distinguished one. 'Man' is the Persian word for a trait of heredity of family or race. The author and student of Gurdjieff, J.G. Bennett, said of the word, "The combination sarman would mean the chief repository of the tradition." A third slightly obscure meaning is 'he who preserves the Zoroastrian teachings'.

Gurdjieff relates how during his time at the Monastery he was introduced to carefully preserved sacred dances taught with the aid of life-sized wooden stick men. The temple dances he said were a form of cosmic language demonstrating the primordial principles of life. Here he was also introduced to the symbol of the Sarmoung: the nine-pointed 'Enneagram' which demonstrated the cosmic laws of seven and three which governed the universe. Much of Gurdjieff's later teachings are directly related to understanding the Enneagram – the laws of three (conscious) and seven (mechanical). The Sarmoung had therefore delivered what it had promised – the keys to complete spiritual transformation and all that Gurdjieff and the Prince had dreamed of finding in their quest.

To this day, arguments have raged as to whether the whole story of the Sarmoung is allegorical or factual, or a mixture of the two to obscure and protect the teachings. Even Gurdjieff's own pupils are not entirely sure on this point. From the few definitive answers he gave we only know that the Sarmoung Brotherhood had at least two centres, one called the 'Olman' monastery based in the Northern slopes of the Himalayas where the Prince spent his final days and the other being a 12-day trek from Bokhara, the latter was the unnamed monastery where Gurdjieff and the Prince met as guests of the Sarmoung. Its location, according to J.G. Bennett who studied with Gurdjieff, is in the mountains near Tashkent, in the Syr Darya and Pyansje valleys.

Le Prieure (Institute for the Harmonious Development of Man)

John Godolphin Bennett was an extraordinary man by any standards. Born on June 8th 1897 he was educated at Kings College, London and went on to the Royal Military Academy to study engineering. He was a gifted linguist speaking

50 languages, who became a scientist who specialising in fossil fuels. Also a talented mathematician, it is testament to Bennett's manifold talents that he was appointed head of the Ankara branch of MI5 in British Constantinople at the tender age of just 21.

During the First World War he was called upon to serve in the Royal Engineers. While serving in France he was thrown from his motorcycle by an exploding shell and lay in a coma for six days. His life immediately after the war speaks of tense introspective desperation; his father died on the day of his wedding on Armistice Day 1918. In his autobiography *Witness* he describes completing his Turkish course at the School of African and Oriental Studies, London, only to be dispatched to Salonika in Greece two months later and thence onto Turkey.

Here he got on and excelled in his position as Assistant Liaison Officer at the War Office. Due to the politics of post-war Turkey there was great fear of Bolshevik plots, particularly those stirring up Jihad within the British Empire. Millions of Muslims resided in huge swathes of British possessions around the world and anyone seen as fanning the flames of insurrection had to be investigated. Bennett slowly drifted into the spy business with his first job checking the Mevlevi Sufi order to assess the risks. To the layman the Mevlevi order present as the white-clothed 'whirling dervishes', nowadays seen performing spinning dances for enthralled tourists. The order was founded by the mystical Sufi poet Jalaludin Rumi in 1273. He was venerated by his supporters as second only to the Prophet being called 'Our Lord'.

Bennett recalls encountering the Mevlevis one Thursday, but far from uncovering secret plots, he found their ceremonies, music and prayers profoundly moving. Weeping and overwhelmed with emotion, he looked around and noticed others sobbing at the music also. He was invited to attend again and so began his first contact with Sufism; a life-long journey had begun.

The dervishes were happy to give their answers to his questions about life and soon enough, in another part of Turkey, he was introduced to the tradition known as the 'Howling Dervishes'. This group worshipped by intoning the names of Allah while grasping at their beards and bringing themselves to an ecstatic state. As the ritual gathered pace, one man in no more than a loincloth would beat himself bloody with a chain, while metal spikes were driven through his cheeks as he continued to chant. At the climax of the ceremony the elderly man in the loincloth lay down as two Mullahs placed a razor-sharp, curved scimitar across his chest and stood upon it. They shouted "Allahu Akhbar" as everyone awaited the inevitable slicing of the supine figure. As they released their weight from the elderly man, he took the sword and demonstrated that his body was completely unmarked by the blade. Those present remained in transfixed silence, highly elated by the death-defying exhibition of faith. Like Gurdjieff before him, such experiences caused Bennett to develop a deep yearning for the spiritual which was to grow into a lifelong quest for the truth.

During 1920 a contact who shared similar interests in matters spiritual introduced Bennett to Gurdjieff. The meeting which took place in Constantinople (Istanbul) was to become the most important of Bennett's life. Of the conversations, conducted in Turkish, Bennett later remarked that he had never met a man who understood him more than he understood himself. While this meeting left an indelible impression, the young intelligence officer was too busy with his earthly work to commit to the discipline that Gurdjieff was 'probably likely to demand'. Destiny decreed that Bennett was not to see Mr Gurdjieff again for another 25 years.

A quarter-century later Bennett visited Gurdjieff once again, this time at his 'Institute for Harmonious Development' in the Prieure, Fontainebleau, Paris in 1923. Gurdjieff had set up this private institute to showcase his ideas called variously as 'The System', 'The Work' or the 'Fourth Way'.

Bennett spent the summer months at the Prieure and was greatly impressed by what he saw. Upon arrival he was shown into the drawing room at the Prieure by Madame de Hartmann, a long-time student of Gurdjieff's 'system'. Once again, Bennett was to be greatly affected by his Russian master. To Bennett's amazement, Gurdjieff instantly picked up the thread of the conversation from all those years before in Constantinople, instantly adopting the Turkish tongue they had originally conversed in. As he returned to the very subject they were discussing a quarter-century earlier, Gurdjieff told Bennett in no uncertain terms that his mind was awake but his body and emotions were asleep. He recommended that Bennett start to work on his body by learning to separate his self from his physical form. From there his emotions would follow. Bennett was promptly set to work in the somewhat unfamiliar setting of the scullery; scrubbing floors, serving food and cleaning pots and pans. Hard physical labour came next, with Bennett being instructed to saw down trees and break rocks during gruelling 12-hour days, the like of which he was most unused to.

Discussions, music, group exercises, postures, lectures – all these followed the day's exhausting toils. Bennett fasted and observed others at the Prieure, seeing first-hand how Gurdjieff was able to create the conditions of extraordinary tension necessary to experience and see one's own limitations through practical, physical work. Bennett saw the masks slip, as raw emotion, or naked essence, began to overtake one's day-to-day persona at the Prieure, exposing what a person really was. One such individual was a man named Orage, a newspaper editor who had had come to 'talk' to Gurdjieff, but soon found that was not how things worked at the Prieure. Orage, who didn't know one end of a shovel from the other, soon found himself digging a garden. Bennett observed that before long he was tanned, with rippling muscles and the calloused hands of a fisherman or labourer. People changed here under Gurdjieff.

It was not all hard work though. Jokes were played and the famous 'toast of the idiots' was held on occasion, with sumptuous banquets hosted by 'G', as his students called him. At such feasts Gurdjieff would ask people to nominate another diner as a particular type of idiot. This was usually done after all the students had consumed a fair amount of alcohol, to ensure a degree of *in vino veritas*. Yet even so, no one was under any illusion that the toasts were anything other than a cognitive tool to observe and teach people about themselves and others. Gurdjieff also had sexual liaisons with some of his female pupils, even siring children with a few. There were those who claimed he was a master of exotic tantric practices. Critics called him a charlatan pointing to his questionable liaisons with women students.

Some of the accounts that have reached us from students who studied there leave no doubt that Gurdjieff was a highly evolved being, possessed of knowledge that ordinary men did not, or could not, have. Ouspensky, the Russian mathematician who had been studying with Gurdjieff since the days of Imperial Russia, recalls an occasion where he was about to storm out of the room following a disagreement only to hear the telepathic voice of Gurdjieff telling him to return to his seat.

Madame de Hartmann and her musician husband Thomas, who played Gurdjieff's compositions on the piano, fled the Russian revolution with their teacher. Finding themselves lost in a forest and fearing discovery by hostile revolutionary forces, Gurdjieff and the De Hartmann's uncovered a dolmen. Using knowledge that is presumably lost in our modern, GPS-reliant era, Gurdjieff was apparently able to use the dolmen as a compass to direct them to safety. Another tale tells of a person scalded by hot water in the Prieure kitchen, whose hand should have been seriously burnt, were it not for Gurdjieff's lightning reactions as he grabbed the victim's wrist, plunging the wound back into the gas flames and thereby effecting an instant cure.

The American Fritz Peters, who knew Gurdjieff towards the end of his life, spoke of his time suffering from depression brought on by shell-shock sustained during the war. Upon seeing Fritz Peters in this state, a huge spark emanated from the Russian mystic, which passed into the shattered man. Almost at once, the American felt the joys of spring as the elderly Gurdjieff left the room. Peters became convinced that that this energy transference came at a great cost to

Gurdjieff himself, who had consciously been able to pass a massive amount of vital energy at will. Peters remarked that after this act Gurdjieff looked visibly drained. Bennett was one of many who had encountered the mystic, being fully convinced that Gurdjieff was in possession of the secrets of self-transformation, both in theory and practice.

Although he was encouraged to extend his stay at the Prieure, money was pressing and Bennett chose to resume his career in England, having left Turkey and MI5 behind him. One thing is certain though: Bennett, of all the people connected to Gurdjieff, knew that the British authorities in India regarded the Russian as a Tsarist spy. This may have coloured their relationship slightly, although more charitable accounts suggest that, for Gurdjieff, spying was simply a means of furthering his esoteric mission since it facilitated access to regions otherwise out-of-bounds to ordinary travellers. Despite it all, the institiute at the Prieure lasted just a decade; the upkeep costs grew beyond Gurdjieff's entrepreneural capabilities and he was forced to sell the chateau and its grounds in 1932.

Idris Shah and the Sarmoung

Gurdjieff died in Paris in 1949. Curiously his grave inside a conventional Christian cemetery is marked by two dolmens, which makes perfect sense as we will see later in this book.

Despite the privations of war and the interruption of his international contacts, he continued to teach right up to the end of his life. Soon after the war ended his students had regrouped and J.G Bennett was among them. This time Bennett's involvement was more intensive than his previous dealings back in the 1920s. Prior to his death, Gurdjieff had given Bennett exercises to practice and had entertained he and his wife in Paris. Bennett had been deeply impressed by his time with Gurdjieff and documented some of the years of his spiritual journey in a series of books. The pair had discussed Sufism but Gurdjieff was convinced that Bennett would go on to uncover more knowledge about esoteric Christianity. Of all Gurdjieff's students who went onto to promulgate his work, none was more tireless or restless in his search to find the fount of the Fourth Way teachings than Bennett. His take, however, was regarded as unorthodox by some of Gurdjieff's retinue and being perceived as a maverick student, he drew significant ire for his experimental stance.

Madame de Saltzman, perhaps one of the more evolved acolytes, faithfully preserved what they had learnt while trying not to let the teachings become distorted, but this did not help the 'System' evolve further. Gurdjieff groups sprang up in Mexico, South America, USA, South Africa, Australia and the UK but these were first-generation efforts. What real value these groups possessed in terms of passing on the genuine teachings can be gauged by the influence they wielded. Ideas are organic; they live and yet they also become old and die unless supported by the energy of the originators in the conscious circle of humanity. According to some Sufi sources, the energy or 'Baraka' of a teacher dissipates upon his death. Kathryn Hulme, a student and friend of Gurdjieff felt, with some justification having worked directly with Gurdjieff in Paris, that it was not acceptable to follow a fellow student "having fed at the source".

J.G. Bennett was made head of the 'System' in England prior to Gurdjieff's death. The decision appeared controversial since Bennett was not as widely known in those circles; he had, after all, been absent for 25 years before his return. Bennett was unique, however, in that he strove to find new masters that might provide answers to the questions of enlightenment. After the death of his teacher Gurdjieff, Bennett once more returned to the heartlands of Asian mysticism.

It may be this restless, unrelenting facet of his personality, a vicissitudinous streak, that caused Gurdjieff to choose Bennett ahead of all others to lead the Fourth Way in England into the second half of the 20th Century. Bennett's experimental approach, always willing to give time to other spiritual teachers and to explore their paths, led to criticism from other, more purist, members of the Fourth Way who wished to keep the teachings in their original form. Bennett was adaptive in his approach to the Work while others saw no need to deviate from what Gurdjieff had taught them. Bennett went on to teach the Fourth Way at Coombe Springs, near Kingston-upon-Thames. He saw it as a place where people could learn about Gurdjieff's ideas and to this end sought to publicly promote them to a wider audience.

His project to popularise the teachings caused Gurdjieff's favourites, Jeanne de Saltzmann in France and Jane Heap in London, to distance themselves from his initiative. The animosity came to a head in 1955 after Bennett had begun construction of a nine-sided building dedicated to Gurdjieff at Coombe Springs, as a temple for the performance of ritual dance. De Salzmann and others no longer viewed Bennett as a bonafide teacher of the Fourth Way, due, they said, to his interpretation of the teachings. This spat saw traditional students of the Work ostracising him. But Bennett was a visionary and could not stand still for too long. As a scientist specialising in fossil fuels, Bennett was among the first to grasp the role of climate change and the impact on nature caused by the largescale burning of coal. He was clearly ahead of his time by some decades.

Still yearning to meet another teacher of Gurdjieff's standing, Bennett started a lengthy tour of the Middle East in search of new ideas and teachers. He met the Sufi Emin Chikou who deeply impressed him. Then in 1956 he encountered a spiritual practice called Subud. The practice, as it should be described, was first discovered by an Indonesian man called Mohamed Subohadiwidjojo but later called Pak Subuh. The exercise known as the 'latihan' involved opening up to a higher power (a life force). The latihan was not attached to religion but was considered to be guidance from God. Bennett was 'opened' at a latihan ceremony and later taught the practice to Bendictine monks in England. It was at this point that Bennett became convinced that Islam and Christianity would one day unite. Just six years later he adandoned Subud to move on once again, visiting Nepal between 1961-3 to study with a Hindu yogi. Bennett became convinced that he was uncovering kernals of esoteric truth as he had done years before in Paris and Constantinople. During this time he once again dallied with Sufism.

Meeting English-educated Afghani Idris Abutahir Shah in the early1960s Bennett connected with Sufi ideas once more. Shah was a gifted writer and publisher, who owned Octagon Press that published much of the early '60s occult books. Those occult connections extended to the founder of Wicca Gerald Gardner and Wiccan High Priestess Eleanor Bone, both of whom he counted as friends. Shah wrote under various *noms-de-plume* and if nothing else was prodigious. One such book gained notoriety: *The Teachers of Gurdjieff*, written by Shah under the pseudonym Rafael Lefort and published in 1966. In rather disingenuous fashion, the book asserted that Lefort had managed to trace the individuals who had taught Gurdjieff back in the Sarmoung monastery and in a further deceit pointed to none other than Idris Shah himself as the next possible successor to the Brotherhood's legacy in the West. If this was not absurd enough, Shah then built upon this deception by successfully persuading Bennett of the veracity of the book's claims.

Shah had first become entangled with the Fourth Way teachings of Gurdjieff in 1962 when a newspaper article surfaced announcing Shah's contact with a monastery in Asia. Bennett, who was in the midst of his search for the origins of Gurdjieff's teachings, was introduced to Shah by an intelligence contact who recommended the Afghani as genuine. Bennett's first impressions of Shah were mixed. He was at first unsure of the English-educated Afghani but in the end was happy to consider him in a favourable light and promote his document 'Declaration of the People of the Tradition'. This initial meeting resulted in Bennett being persuaded that Shah was a genuine emissary of the Sarmoung Brotherhood, who possessed the secret knowledge of the inner circle of humanity. For several years, Shah visited Bennett at Coombe Springs on a weekly basis. The Afghani's ambitions were greater than mere spiritual advancement: he wanted to influence political and business leaders in a greater mission. A susceptible Bennett, who was concerned with growing problems facing mankind, agreed. In 1965 Bennett went to the Coombe Springs Committee and in typically unpredictable fashion announced he was to give Coombe Springs to Shah. By that time Bennett was convinced that the Afghani would continue the work of the inner circle of humanity, a mission that superseded that of Gurdjieff. Things did not go as Bennett planned. Shah sold Coombe Springs to developers after a few months and set up his own charitable foundation. Many think Shah deliberately tricked Bennett, but the latter went on to say that despite the decision to sell off Coombe Springs, and the sale being 'hard to bear', Bennett considered it may have been motivated by the Sufi practice of severing all links with the past. Critics might say Bennett was in denial at an obvious dupe.

Writer James Moore claims that just a few years later Shah fooled Robert Graves and destroyed his academic credentials by pretending to offer up a genuine manuscript of 12th Century translation of the *Rubiayyat of Omar Khayaam*. Shah claimed the work had been in his family for 800 years, but upon inspection by experts in the genre, the ruse was uncovered; the document was nothing but a Victorian forgery. Graves was slated by academia for promoting the fake work, while Shah failed to deliver the 'original' book that he claimed to have access to. Graves' wife said her husband had complete faith in Shah due to their deep friendship, but he had fallen for a hoax and his reputation was in tatters.

Whatever the case for Idris Shah and his claim to be a genuine emissary of the Sarmoung Brotherhood it didn't affect his success or international reputation; he is still highly regarded to this day. The only Gurdjieffian to fully accept this tenuous Sarmoung connection was Bennett himself. Bennett, it must be said, stressed the Sufi connection in all things Gurdjieff, believing his own work to be a continuation of the original flame kindled by the teacher. Looking once more at the fanciful account of Rafael Lefort in *The Teachers of Gurdjieff*, the entire work sets out to subtly undermine Gurdjieff while at the same time keep his current followers close to the Sufi (Naqshbandi) cause. Whether Shah and Lefort are one and the same person, we will never know for sure but the seductive myth of higher masters and secret schools nearly saw three victims; in the form of the Gurdjieff legacy, the Naqshbandi Sufis and the genuine Sarmoung legend – all unwittingly hijacked by ruthless ambition on the one hand and benign credulity on the other.

Khwajagani – the Masters of Wisdom (Naqshbandi Sufis)

Khwajagani or 'the Masters' is a Persian term referring directly to the inner circle of humanity, and is now applied exclusively to the Sufism of Central Asia, during the 10th-16th Centuries. Heirs to the greatly esteemed esoteric knowledge, it is accepted within Islam that their lineage connects mankind with a higher demiurgic force governing the evolution of the planet.

Naqshbandi Sufism was founded by Baha ad-din Naqshbandi (Bahudin) and is firmly focused on conscious breathing exercises designed to increase mindfulness. The Naqshbandi employed these breathing techniques that increased awareness during the practice of the 'zhikhr' or prayers. Naqshabandis talked about the inner life of man and gave instructions or guidance on how to live by a set of principles that were those of the aim of the prayers. These approaches gave transcendent import or enhancement to the practices.

In 1048 Abu Yaqub Khwaja Yusuf was born in Hamadan (Iran). By his thirty-fifth year Yusuf was considered a teacher and had a circle of initiates around him including a Turkish master Ahmad Yasawi. Settling in Bokhara, Yusuf inherited the turban and walking stick of Salman the Persian, the first of his countrymen to convert to Islam. Salman also had connections with the older Zoroastrian religion of Persia. Theses relics were passed to the teacher of Yusuf by Sheikh Farmadi from a direct line of the Prophet's descendants.

Yusuf became a Grand Master, tolerant of all religions, who spoke of the futility of theology. According to J.G. Bennett in his erudite work *The Masters of Wisdom*, Yusuf preferred his connection with the Magi Priesthood, the Zoroastrian fire worshippers of Bokhara. Before his death, Yusuf appointed as his successor Khwaja Abd al-Kaliq Ghujduwani, a Naqshbandi master who was 'silsila' – an Islamic term meaning 'lineage', referred to as the 'golden chain', conferring a direct connection with the Prophet Mohammed. Naqshbandi Sufis claim their silsila through Caliph Abu Bakr. Ghujduwani became a key figure in this Sufi order for introducing silent invocation. Under Khwaja, the Naqshbandi incorporated earlier practices from the region, such as Zoroastrianism, into their Sufism by employing dance and music in their practices. The very essence of Islamic teaching – Khidr – the 'messenger of God', to whom truth or 'haqq' is adapted, has Zoroastrian roots. Khidr is associated with the colour green and the coming of summer. Even to this day thousands of Zoroastrians gather at the Pir-Sabz or green shrine in Yadz, Iran during mid-June.

The continued success of the Khwaja, as they became known, could perhaps be attributed to their avoidance of clashes with orthodox Muslims, who view their lack of worldly attainment or seeking of immediate political power as ultimately unthreatening. The Sufis talk of love of God, not power or material wealth.

It could be said that the type of methods used by the Khwaja are comparable to those of the Zen Buddhists. One historical case in point underscores how leaders could be influenced without the Khwaja ever seeking their favour and that involved the mighty nomadic conqueror Genghis Khan. When Khan and his warriors were sacking Bokhara they came across a small village, where they saw a humble weaver going about his work on his loom. Due to the weaver's apparent unconcern at the invading hoards all about him, the Mongols were filled with admiration. Genghis Khan himself asked the weaver why he was able to work serenely as all about him was in mayhem. The weaver Kwarja Arif answered, "My outer attention is on my work and my inner attention on the Truth."

Kwarja Arif was invited to stay close to Genghis Khan until his death and therefore became a trusted ally and adviser. Although Genghis Khan and his golden hoards enjoy an infamous reputation among historians, it is recorded that the village of the weaver was left untouched. Genghis Khan died in 1227, having established in just two decades one of the most successful and long-lasting Empires the world has ever seen. Remarkably the rule of Genghis Khan has two seemingly conflicting facets, the first being an unrelenting colonisation. Bokhara for example was sacked in vengeance for the death of an Ambassador and the city levelled. Ordering exquisite tortures such as pouring molten silver into the eyes and ears of one governor who rebuffed his attempts to establish trade links has not exactly enhanced Khan's reputation from an historical viewpoint.

What is seldom discussed though is that once the Mongols had installed themselves as the new rulers they showed religious tolerance and promoted rights for women, while the rule of law established meritocracy over tribal affiliation, perhaps for the first time. The Mongol society was therefore a socially mobile one too. The one hundred of Genghis Khan's most trusted men included Christians, Buddhists, Muslims and Animist shamans.

The influence of the Khwajagani is unknown but he may have attempted to safeguard and promote enlightened concepts within Khan's military expansion. Thanks to the religious tolerance shown by Khan, Islam was able to spread via the Silk Road and technologies were exchanged between cultures both East and West. Later, after the death of Genghis other Mongol rulers embraced Islam and a peaceful dissemination occurred, including that of Sufism.

Babur ('babr' meaning 'tiger' in Persian) was a descendent of Genghis Khan who founded the Mughal dynasty and a Muslim sultan influenced by Persian culture. Like his forebears he also encouraged religious tolerance. Babur spoke in the extinct Turkic or Chagatai tongue once spoken widely by the Tartars in Uzbekistan, Central Asia. Chagatai was the second son of Genghis Khan. Babur had joint ethnicity being descended from both Mongol and Turk.

The army of Babur headed southwards conquering swathes of what is today Afghanistan, Pakistan and Northern India and found himself in the Punjab, which partly satisfied the legacy of his Mongol ancestor Timur who had conquered the territory in times past. Writer Dina Le Gall in her work *A Culture of Sufism: Naqshabandis in the Ottoman World* claimed that, "The conquests of India by Babur in 1526 gave considerable impetus to the Naqshabandiyya Order."

The power and influence of the Sufis grew, albeit subtly, reaching its zenith in India during the 16th Century. Naqshbandi teachings brought peace, stability, culture and enterprise in society, particularly in the Indian Punjab. Their philosophy often spoke of preparing people for changes in accordance with higher laws, divine intervention, the will of Allah from a higher level. With talk of Saints in direct communion with angelic or demiurgic forces at work on Earth the Naqshbandi certainly seemed to believe that they were part of something akin to the harmonious inner circle of humanity. With this there is recognition of a concept that affects history and events, perhaps not initiating them but benignly influencing them. Take the Sarmoung, Naqshbandi, Khwajaghani, harmonious circle of humanity, Masters, and the idea of an esoteric centre where those who search and attain to a certain spiritual level are able to receive help from advanced beings or more accurately directed by a higher demiurgic mandate. Bennett certainly believed that Gurdjieff's mission was connected to a larger harmonious plan orchestrated by a divine order. Comments made by Gurdjieff himself to pupil C.S. Nott suggest that there was a greater authority that sent their representative. To another pupil, Boris Mouravieff, who asked about the source of his teachings Gurdjieff answered in a typically evasive response, "Maybe I stole it".

Footprints of the Masters

The Sarmoung monastery was found in at least two locations, it is said. The first is allegedly twelve days' trek from Bokhara by horse and donkey, and as Gurdjieff mentions two rivers on the journey seem to point towards Tashkent. Bennett placed the destination of Gurdjieff's quest and eventual encounter with the Sarmoung in the Syr Darya or Pyansje valleys, as said before.

Idris Shah and his supporter Major Martin insist the Sarmoung were located in Afghanistan. Writer Omar Michael Burke, possibly another *nom-de-plume* of Shah, offered his thoughts in the book *Among the Dervishes* published in 1973, linking the Amudari dervish order with the Sarmouni. Both this account and that of Martin suggested the Sarmoung had closed down, removing themselves to the West. We can only guess whether Shah himself had suggested this somewhat convenient story, as it seems to follow that of Rafael Le Forte very closely.

Amateur Historian Adrian Gilbert wrote in *The Magi: Quest for a Secret Tradition* his belief that the Sarmoung were once located, as Gurdjieff suggests, in Northern Mesopotamia. He specifically mentions King Antiochus I Epiphanes and Gilbert pinpoints the school to the tiny Kingdom of Commangene, today south-eastern Turkey encompassing the plains of Syria. He suggests the Persian influenced Antiochus was allied to the Sarmoung in some way but this of course is way before Gurdjieff's contact with the brotherhood.

Gurdjieff's grandson Professor Paul Beekman Taylor, who while not a student of the Fourth Way, did have contact with the mystic in the early part of his life, has this to say on the origin of the teachings:

"It isn't even all that clear to me that Gurdjieff unequivocally claimed that he had been in Lhasa or any other part of Tibet proper. What he did claim is that he received ultra-esoteric teachings (that formed the [or a] basis of his own teachings, including the well-known dances) at an almost entirely inaccessible location somewhere in the vicinity of the Pamirs from a group called the Sarmoung Brotherhood. They had yet another 'sister' monastery on the northern slopes of the Himalayas called Olman Monastery. I'm not sure if he claimed to go to this Olman Monastery, but even then I am the opposite of clear when it comes to knowing where the 'northern slopes of the Himalayas' might be."

Gurdjieff claimed to have acquired certain knowledge in Tibet and here Professor Beekman Taylor appears cautious to accept the account at face value.

Gurdjieff's highly cryptic book *Beelzebub's Tales to His Grandson* which he referred to as a 'Legominism' (a word coined by Gurdjieff to describe a message for the future hidden within a work of art to be deciphered by initiates) mentions the five major religions active in the 20th Century as Christianity, Islam, Buddhism, Judaism and Lamaism. The last religion on this list is probably more widely known as Tibetan Buddhism.

In *Beelzebub's Tales* a complex story alludes to the fact that transmission begun by both Hinduism and Buddhism in creating Lamaism was being prepared by the inner circle of humanity who had something uniquely important to pass onto mankind via a new messenger, whose teachings would be suited to the modern psyche.

This anointed messenger, the unfortunate figure of Lama G, was directly sanctioned by the enlightened beings of the inner circle until he was unexpectedly killed by the Younghusband Expedition in summer 1904. If this event was not tragically destructive enough, *Beelzebub's Tales* alludes to the looting by British and Sikh troops of the monasteries, with the obliteration of relics, sacred texts and the ransacking of records relating to the inner circle's teachings.

We must bear in mind that Gurdjieff always had the propensity to write allegorically and so accounts cannot always be relied on as being entirely factual, but in this case it does mirror events of the British Expedition which is named and shamed in his writings for its butchery of the pacifist Lamaists. The negative effects of the Younghusband Expedition on humanity cannot be underestimated if, as Gurdjieff lamented, the transmission of three major religions had been stopped in its tracks. In his account, Gurdjieff explains that due to the beliefs of the horrified inner circle they wished to ensure the divine messenger Lama

G was returned to life. It was important that what he knew as chief of the circle passed down to the other six and as he had not died consciously before giving those instructions, they endeavoured to restore him to life. The so called 'Science of Death' to decide one's next reincarnation are of supreme importance to the Lamaists and they resolved to put it to use.

As the six made their connection with Lama G their experiment did not go well. They poured their energy into his body without performing the necessary connection with his soul first. The result, it is said, was a massive explosion a mile wide which killed all six in the process. Some researchers have tried to weave in the mysterious explosion at Tunguska, Siberia into this event.

Results of the mighty Tunguska explosion, most likely following a huge meteorite striking the Earth, caused parts of Western Europe including London to be bathed in strange pink light into the early hours of the morning, so bright people could read books without lamplight in the dead of night. The explosion at Tunguska was said to be one thousand times more powerful than that caused by the atom bomb dropped on Hiroshima. The surrounding forests for miles around were devastated. The dates are four years apart however. Lama G died in 1904 while the Tunguska explosion in occurred 1908, stretching all credibility of the theory to the limit. But the Siberian connection should not be wholly dismissed even if the above story may safely be discounted.

An interesting article in the *Epoch Times* yields further to clues to people connected with Tsarist emissary Dorzhiev, who was sent to sign a treaty with Lhasa. The *Epoch Times* article tells of a Buddhist Lama linked to Dorzhiev who was in the same lineage and gives us a unique insight into the personal lives of these characters of a kind quite distinct from the usual vague historical silhouettes that are occasionally cast of the wall of events. The strange story of the death of this Lama called Itighelov is recounted below.

"The body of Hambo Lama Itighelov, who was a spiritual leader of Russian Buddhists from 1911 to 1927, was first exhumed from the grave in 1955, at the Lama's request. When after the third exhumation in 2002 after 75 years since the Lama's death, his body still showed no signs of decay, medical experts decided to examine the miracle.

The grave contained a wooden box and there was a sitting Buddhist lama in a 'lotus' position. His body was preserved as if it were mummified, however it was not. The body was covered with silk clothes and fabric. "Samples taken 75 years after the body had been buried, show that the organics of the skin, hair, and nails of the dead man aren't any different from that of a living human," a professor of history at the Russian State University for Humanities, Galina Yershova stated at a press-conference in 'Interfax' central office in Moscow, according to Pravda.ru.

"His joints flex, the soft tissues are elastic just like in a living person, and after they opened the box, where the body of the Lama lay for 75 years, there was a very pleasant fragrance," Yershova was quoted as saying.

We may presume this would have been Lama G's preferred method of exiting this plane, rather than being machine-gunned down by hostile invading forces. The article innocently provides clues to the characters surrounding the Younghusband Expedition years and the seriousness of their religious practices.

Itighelov founded the Buriat Brothers, an organisation providing humanitarian troops in the World War and was also involved in Dorzhiev's ceremony in 1913 to honour the Romanovs as White Tsars/White Taras.

As a master of Tantra, Itighelov informed his students that he would die and took up meditation in the lotus position. After a few days the students noticed their teacher showed no signs of life and they buried him as found. His last wish was that his body should be exhumed later 30 years on and his body examined.

Pathologist Yuri Tampoleev is still investigating the curiously well-preserved monk, whose elastic skin, semi-plastic blood, and still-movable joints defy explanation. With no evidence of embalming chemicals, dehydration or the presence of peat bogs, preservation of a corpse in such a way is a supremely difficult task. Combine that with the region's summer temperatures of 40°C plus and so far science has failed to offer any answer to the mystery of the preservation of Lama Itighelov, let alone how he predicted such a result.

Itighelov enjoyed close connections with Dorzhiev and the Yellow Hat sect who were involved with St Petersburg circles including Tsar Nicholas II. Couple this with his responsibility for the protection of the Dalai Lama when the Younghusband Expedition arrived and it is quite feasible that Itighelov and those around him were encountered by Gurdjieff during his time in Tibet. Like them, Gurdjieff was certainly involved in the machinations of the Great Game, as attested by British colonial records in India seen by Bennett. Were these characters involved with the inner circle of humanity or Sarmoung he spoke of in his writings and lectures? Is the mysteriously preserved corpse of Itighelov scientific proof of the supernatural powers of such people?

The chief problem with the above is there is some circumstantial evidence that Gurdjieff was involved with an entirely different sect of Lamaism called Nyingma – 'The Ancient Ones', which in itself is part of the Vajrayana ('vajra' is Sanskrit for 'thunderbolt') tradition of Tantric Buddhism. Said to have originated under the Tantric master Padmasambhava, the name Vajra is literally descriptive, since the 'thunderbolt' alludes to the fastest method towards enlightenment which can only be attained under the strict guidance of a designated lama. James Moore, biographer of Gurdjieff, suggests that he may have been an initiate of Nyingma or the Red Hat Lama sect around 1901. Moore suggests Gurdjieff was presented to the Romanov Tsar Nicholas II around this time in the guise of a Transcaspian Buddhist. Anthony Blake says that Gurdjieff went on to marry a Tibetan woman in 1902. This statement itself is pregnant with meaning if we think of Gurdjieff's Legonomism. Is this story of Gurdjieff's marriage, really an encoded message that he had taken an 'oath' to wed himself to Tibetan mysticism? It is therefore little wonder that he was so critical of the Younghusband Expedition and its massacre of the lamas? Undoubtedly the conflagration left an indelible impression on him, firstly at the futility of war but it is more understandable still, if the killings that took place at Guru were those of his own spiritual brethren.

The footprints of the masters do not end there as the obscure name of one Tibetan monastery may lead us away from the red-herrings painstakingly lain by Idris Shah and the Legonomism of Gurdjieff, to another possible location of the Masters of Wisdom.

The Old School

As mentioned above, the Nyingma tradition was translated from Sanskrit into old Tibetan in the 8th Century having arrived from India. It is not strictly Buddhist as understood in countries such as India, Burma, Cambodia or Thailand as Nyingma incorporates local deities and elements of magic and shamanism in its practice. We shall return to this in more detail later on as it presents several mysteries.

This more esoteric branch of Buddhism is found in Central Asia (Nepal, Sikkim, Ladakh, Tibet, Mongolia and parts of North-West China). The translation work was begun by Tibetan Emperor Detsen who was said to have employed 108 translators to work with the great sage Padmasambhava to complete the work. This in itself is interesting, since the number 108 in Huinduism is related to the concept of spiritual completion. For a time Nyingma was the only school of Tibetan Buddhism.

With the ascension of King Langdarma in 838 A.D., about 80 years after Detsen, the emperor decided to revert back to the old religion. Langdarma is recorded as being so bitterly opposed to Buddhism that he wished to see its wholesale destruction; an action later echoed by the 'cultural revolution' of Maoist Communism. This was not to be, however, as regicide brought Langdarma's reign to an abrupt end only four years after he ascended the throne. His killing was carried out by a Buddhist hermit who saw to it that Langdarma was 'liberated' from his unhappy existence, which in turn led to the emergence of Buddhism in Tibet. The cave-dwelling hermit Pelkyi Dorje took it upon himself to commit the ritual assassination of the Emperor as an act of compassion. In one act he would rid the Tibetan people of an unenlightened ruler and help liberate the demon-king by enabling him to reincarnate in more suitable circumstances.

To Pelkyi Dorje's Buddhist sensibilities, it was a win-win situation. Taking a reversible robe, black on one side and white on the other, he blackened his white steed with coal to evade detection and rode to the royal court to slay Langdarma, secreting a bow and three arrows as his murder weapon. Today the killing is celebrated by the Sha-Nak or Black Hat Dancers who ritually re-enact Pelkyi Dorje's slaying of Langdarma in the course of their purification rites. It is interesting to note the parallels with Langdarma and the 'sacrificial king' mythos of European paganism as espoused by Dr Margaret Murray, Gerald Gardner and others. One can only wonder whether such tales are simply universal archetypes that occur in all religions the world over, or whether, through links unknown to modern history, the witch cults of Europe may owe some debt to the far-flung lamas of the 'roof of the world'.

After the demise of King Langdarma, Tibetan Buddhism struggled for some time but eventually flourished in the 11th Century. Lamaist teachings eventually spread to areas of Nepal, Sikkim, Bhutan, Mongolia and parts of what are today China (Buryatia where Arghan Dorzhiev originated from) and as far as Kalmykia on the Volga.

We return once more to the Nyingma tradition, whose adherents are known as Red Hat Lamas. Representing the oldest lineage of Tibetan Buddhism, their teachings, like those of the Sarmoung, were characterised by their avoidance of political allegiances in favour of community-level dialogue and their lack of a singular head or leader.

Unlike other subsequent Lamaist schools who favoured monasticism, the Nyingma teaching was often disseminated by non-celibate lay householders. There is some evidence to suggest that Tibetan Buddhism was not really Buddhism as usually understood, but that it was co-opted as under Lamaism as a convenient vehicle for the continuation of far older systems of belief. Within Lamaism lay the kernel of an altogether more controversial, some might even say esoteric, teaching which the travelling Tantric sage Padmasambhava introduced without the Tibetan king's knowledge.

Gurdjieff's careful coding of his teaching to disguise its origins may, in spite of this, lead us to Tibet and the red hatted lamas of the Nyingma tradition who Gurdjieff well knew were the guardians of a sacred tradition far more ancient than Buddhism itself.

Chapter 3

Shambhala and Argharthi

*"Shambhala, sometimes referred to in the West as El Dorado or
Shangri-la, is a mythological kingdom, protected by a psychic barrier
so that no one can find the kingdom who is not meant to. For centuries
the people of Tibet and Mongolia have believed in the existence of the
mythical kingdom of Shambhala, hidden behind the distant mountains
north of the Himalaya."*
Mary Sutherland, taken from her work *The Legend of Shambhala.*

Wisdom Gone Wild

James George was born in 1918, in Ontario, Canada. A distinguished military
and diplomatic career led to his appointment as Canadian High Commissioner
to India in 1967. The posting was fortunate, since George harboured a deep-
seated interest in Eastern mysticism which he could now indulge 'in the field'.

Alongside his diplomatic duties, his time in the region was spent travelling
the Silk Road to seek the teachings for himself, retracing the footsteps of men
such as Gurdjieff. Much like J.G. Bennett before him, his unique position gave
him the perfect opportunity to further his quest for enlightenment. George had
read Gurdjieff and was greatly impressed by the teachings of the Fourth Way.
His own ideas developed in an altogether different direction, however.

His own belief was that the Sarmoung Brotherhood was not to be found
in Afghanistan, as suggested by Idries Shah, but instead much closer to India in
the Himalayas. Following in the metaphorical footprints of the masters, James
George stumbled across the name of an obscure Tibetan monastery which
led him to a startling conclusion as to the source of Gurdjieff's teachings.

Unimpressed by the red herrings lain by Idris Shah, George believed that he
had had unearthed the true location of the Masters of Wisdom. He was shocked
to learn of the existence of a monastery by the name of Zarmang, sometimes

spelled Surmang, located in Tibet. Could this be the famous Sarmoung Monastery where Gurdjieff gained the esoteric knowledge he would later go on to espouse? Were this breakthrough not significant enough, there was more to come.

James George, being conversant with many Eastern teachings, learned that this particular monastery had produced a very special student indeed; a man named Chogyam Trungpa who was believed by many, including the current Dalai Lama, to be a fully enlightened being. Trungpa's spiritual teaching method even corresponded with that of Gurdjieff, in that both men employed techniques of shocking and exerting the pupil. The similarities between Gurdjieff and Trungpa were so compelling the Canadian diplomat became convinced it could only mean one thing: that they had trained in the same system.

Fortuitously, George had the opportunity to meet with Trungpa in New Delhi, India. During their conversations, he asked Trungpa about the mythical land of Shambhala. The Tibetan sage turned and stared into a mirror, saying that he could see it there, just as he always could whenever he meditated. Trungpa described his vision to George and insisted that the mythical Shambhala was both an ethereal and a physical place. James George reflected on this, concluding that both Gurdjieff and Trungpa had sensed a psychic pendulum swing in mankind's development from a focus on the outer world back to the inner, from worldly science to experience.

Could the legend of Shambhala, generally dismissed as no more than a quaint legend or old folk tale, be more than that? George recalled Gurdjieff's term Legonomism – a coded message only understood when the consciousness of the onlooker was sufficiently developed to receive the signal it contained. Correct use of Legonomism brought the message alive as if the teacher was in the room with the pupil so that every part became a vibrant, living, talking, breathing universe; a far-cry from inert theories based purely on intellect. Intellect alone could distort, teachings could be misunderstood, whereas Legonomism activated by consciousness conveyed the whole message. Could the legend of Shambhala be one such message? James George concluded that both Trungpa and Gurdjieff were sent on a mission to the West by the mysterious brethren of the Zarmang monastery.

Oddly, both men had firmly rejected monasticism. Gurdjieff flatly condemned it, which may seem strange since it is widely assumed that his journey had truly begun in just such an institution. On closer inspection, this may not be quite the paradox it first appears.

The monastic tradition was in fact a much later addition to the Nyingma tradition, which we will recall was largely practiced by laypeople within their own communities until the 19th Century when Nyingma was reformed.

It seemed to the Canadian diplomat that Trungpa and Gurdjieff were merely acting in line with the original teachings of the Nyingma tradition.

The original Nyingma carried out their spiritual work very much in the midst of the maelstrom called ordinary life. For the original Nyingma, every problem thrown at a person during their daily comings and goings became a chance to transform, teach and overcome; a method promoted by both Trungpa and Gurdjieff. The latter called his path the Fourth Way for this very reason, as it was neither the way of the fakir, nor the monk, nor it was it the way of the yogi. According to Gurdjieff, the fakir developed his body, the monk his emotions and the yogi his intellect. Gurdjieff stressed it was important to develop all three faculties in unison to find true balance.

The Fourth Way, said Gurdjieff, was the path of the 'sly man', the man who wishes to develop and reach enlightenment quickly. Nyingma closely corresponds to the Fourth Way since it is the path to transformation and enlightenment in just one lifetime. George used his vast knowledge of Eastern scriptures, combing Tantric, Hindu and Buddhist texts to compare with the various clues in Gurdjieff's writings; for example certain comments regarding the speeding up evolution, which are taken directly from the 'Diamond Path' of the Vajrayana school. He suspected that Trungpa, as well as Gurdjieff, used the Buddhist technique of 'yeshe cholwa' (Tibetan for 'wisdom gone wild') to shock their pupils into wakefulness; everything told him that both had been trained in the style by the same school – Nyingma.

The Canadian believed that Gurdjieff had left as his legacy fresh new ideas about ecosystems of the universe, effective tools to enable man to transform world he lived in. He quoted Gurdjieff's enigmatic conversation with his pupil mathematician Peter Ouspensky: "If, by a certain time, what ought to be done has not been done, the earth may perish without having attained what it could have attained…"

He had, in his own lifetime, attempted to bring about an entire system of knowledge to enable man to transform the world in which he lived.

George began to discuss the concept of Shambhala, which he rightfully recognised as having been brought to India and Tibet in around 900 A.D. It was, however a far older concept taken from the Kalachakra (Wheel of Time) system of Tantra. James George had become convinced through his researches that the concept of Shambhala was in fact a teaching tool to enable man go in search of himself, not only externally but also internally; a journey of seeing oneself as one really is. The diplomat often quoted the Persian Sufi classic *Conference of the Birds*, an allegorical poem about a flock of birds who decide undertake a journey to the meet the mighty Simorgh of China. The Simorgh is a phoenix. After many adventures, just three members of the original flock reach their destination only to find disappointment at the mighty Simorgh. The trio of birds do however see themselves in a mirror. This classic tale is yet another template for the spiritual journey undertaken by the seeker.

The Sufi tale the *Conference of the Birds* has been interpreted as the journey to the Simorgh being the central 'I' or essence of a person, with the chattering birds the various personas or masks we all display. George wrote about Shambhala, leaving us to consider whether the mythical kingdom might be just such an allegory. His own conclusions about Gurdjieff were more complex, as he suggested that the Russian mystic had codified Shambhala with solar language. This mystical solar language, he suspected, came to Tantra from earlier sources possibly Iranian, Babylonian or even Sumerian. James George was on the right track: had he known more about Padmasambhava and the original translation of the Dharma for Tibetan King Detsen, but we shall cover this later.

The expression 'wisdom gone wild' has become better known in the West as 'crazy wisdom'. Crazy wisdom is perhaps best associated with one Tibetan more than any other in our own age and that is a man called Chogyam Trungpa. His story is so compelling for two main reasons. Firstly, because in our media-driven environment we can actually follow the thoughts of Trungpa as he reached a pivotal point of becoming enlightened, allowing others to share his thoughts and feelings within that process. Secondly, his story mirrors that of another maverick spiritual adventurer on many levels, G.I. Gurdjieff. The fact that they may have been products of the same lamasery inside Tibet, albeit in different ages, makes this fascinating tale all the more interesting. If Gurdjieff and Trungpa were in fact trained lamas from this place then it could appear to the casual onlooker as though these two masters, having both been taught at this particular monastery, did indeed have a mission to penetrate the West.

Trungpa had fled Tibet in 1959 to avoid Chinese persecution and went on to study at Oxford University. Black and white photos of the time show a smiling young man sitting among other sixties students wearing his lama's attire. Like any other university student, Trungpa enjoyed his time studying in England and also took full advantage of the usual extra-curricular activities; he chased girls and by all accounts enjoyed a drink or two.

However one day in 1969, while out driving his car, he lost control and careered through the plate-glass window of a joke shop. This accident was far from funny, however, leaving Trungpa paralysed down his left side. His teacher from University, a man named Jeremy Haywood, visited him in hospital and related later that Trungpa saw the accident as a clear message to "strip himself of all facade in the world."

During his convalescence in hospital, Trungpa decided to abandon all outward 'props' as he called them, abandoning his lama's robes so that he might present an authentic Tibetan teachings, but in a more Western manner. By 1970 he found himself married to an English woman called Diana and that same year the couple left the UK to set up home in North America.

During the heyday of the 1960s counterculture revolution, protesters railed against wars such as Vietnam, began the onset of a sexual revolution and took experimentation with drugs to new highs. The '60s had ushered in huge social change and many hungered for authentic mystic teachings. Trungpa soon found keen audiences who wanted to "see the lama" as he remarked, tongue firmly planted in cheek. He met with people like beat-poet Allen Ginsberg while the singer Joni Mitchell even became his pupil. He was no ordinary lama, however, as it became clear that his teaching methods were markedly different from those expected of a Tibetan 'rinpoche'. Female students around him became his lovers, he used profane language and could drink excessive amounts of alcohol without appearing intoxicated.

One particular incident underscores this unusual teaching method: Trungpa was appearing at a conference and was sharing a stage with an individual who pretended to know about all sorts of spiritual matters. As the man held forth, Trungpa appeared to listen intently, but gradually began displaying signs of being increasingly, embarrassingly, drunk. So much so that his followers finally had to help him off stage. Once they had managed to manhandle the lama into a lift to another floor he instantly returned to sobriety and cheerfully asked "How did I perform?" His behaviour was unpredictable, bizarre and wild – true to the name of his teaching style. On another occasion an earnest seeker asked him what he thought of Gurdjieff's exercise of self-remembering – a kind of spiritual mindfulness. One can only imagine the look of horror on the face of the enquirer when Trungpa responded, "I don't give a fucking shit about that right now. Fancy a drink?"

By 1974 the rebellious lama had founded the first ever 'Tantric University' in the States, drawing ever more celebrities into his circle, with musicians and counter-culture celebrities queuing up for a bit of the Trungpa magic. Musicians Marianne Faithful and John Cage, acid-guru Ram Dass, the writer Willam Burroughs and intellectuals such as the famed psychiatrist R.D. Laing – all fell under his spell. The community may well have espoused its Vajra teachings but this master of Crazy Wisdom was not without his scandals. Sordid tales emerged from visitors; a pacifist poet and his wife alleged they had been assaulted by a drunken, bottle-wielding mob after a dinner-dance; stripped and beaten they were thrown before the Rinpoche who mocked them as they lay at his feet.

Further insinuations of excessive secrecy, alcoholism and the abuse of the pupil-guru dynamic for sexual ends, emerged. Gurdjieff himself suffered a similar fate during the 1920s after the writer Katherine Mansfield visited him at his Prieure Institute in Fountainbleu, Paris. Suffering from incurable pulmonary tuberculosis, Mansfield was urged by Gurdjieff to remain at the Prieure and to put her final days to good use in preparation for the end.

Her eventual death caused a furore back in England and Gurdjieff had to bear the brunt of a myriad slurs and slanders as a result. Mansfield chose to stay close to her teacher, even in death, but with public perceptions driven by a hostile press, the public viewed the episode in a dim light.

There are parallels between Trungpa and Gurdjieff that do not end there, as Canadian diplomat James George began to realise. His important discovery of the Zarmang lineage may have led us to a vital clue as to the origins not only of the Fourth Way teachings but Tibetan Buddhism itself, both of which draw upon the most esoteric of systems – the Tantric Kalachakra system.

Madame Blavatsky: Fraud or Fakir?

Most superficial texts on the subject will explain that the Kalachakra system hails from Tibet, with the inference that Kalachakra is a construct of Tibetan Buddhism. To be more accurate, the Tantric Kalachakra was written in Sanskrit with origins in India, with a far more ancient provenance if the sacred texts are to be believed. The twin systems of Tibetan astrology and astronomy are drawn heavily from the Kalachakra, as is the concept of Shambhala, with it being said that Kalachakra is the 'state religion' of Shambhala. Although James George believed it was the mystic Emmanuel Swedenborg who had first made mention of Shambhala in the 18th Century, it was popularised in underground circles by the Scottish Rite Freemason Chevalier Ramsey – a known supporter of Jacobite politics. George did not delve very far into the myth and it remained very much a theoretical teaching to him in many respects. Chevalier Ramsey's own assertion was that Shambhala and Hindu Tantra were oriental equivalents of the Kabbalah, but this view may be too simple, since it does not take into account the ancient origins of the teachings themselves. It would take another unlikely character, who emerged half-way through the 19th Century, to bring the notion of Shambhala with its Masters of Wisdom back to wider public awareness.

Helena Petrovna Blavatsky (1831-91) was born in Ekaterinoslav, of Ukranian-German aristocratic descent. To this day this remarkable woman remains one the enduring enigmas concerning mystical thought on the Roof of the World and is none the less influential for it. Without her writings much of the Tibetan spiritual lineage would not have reached Europe when it did and we may never have witnessed the great occult revival that flourished in last quarter of the 19th Century. Her work in creating Theosophy and the movement that sprang up around it, rescued occult philosophy from the clutches of scientific rationalism and medieval superstition by planting the seed of psychological evolution in the Western mind. Madame Blavatsky is credited with the popularisation of many Eastern concepts, one of which being the mythical kingdom of Shambhala.

During her childhood her mother died and a young Helena grew up in her maternal grandparents' home. From the outset Blavatsky was a gifted child, no doubt inheriting some of her talents for her mother, who was herself a renowned novelist. The young Helena took to music and painting. An autodidact, she developed a strong personality with a razor-sharp intellect. As an impresario Blavatsky toured Imperial Russia and by her teenage years she had gravitated towards esotericism.

At 18 years of age Blavatsky married, but this union was never consummated; she soon used this opportunity to escape her surroundings to travel far and wide, adopting a largely bohemian lifestyle. She became involved in the circus, but took up journalism, often frequenting psychic spiritualist circles. Her biography beyond this point is one of conjecture, depending on whether it is told by a supporter or critic.

Aged 20 years, Blavatsky is alleged to have made contact with a Kashmiri mystic by the name of Mahatma Morya while staying in Hyde Park, London. Blavatsky used the term 'Mahatma' as it would have been more familiar to the colonial British. Privately, however, she would doubtless have used her preferred term, the Tibetan word 'tchanchub', meaning a reincarnated Boddisatva, to describe the being she met. Mahatma Morya is said to have mapped out her destiny in a special mission, appearing to her in numerous locations including Yokohama and New York. Blavatsky claimed to enjoy a psychic link to 'ascended' Mahatmas, and this is a common theme with those who claim to experience such encounters. She alleged that her principle guru, Morya, eventually resettled in Tibet at the court of the Panchen Lama (the second highest cleric after the Dalai Lama). Another of her spiritual Masters went under the name Mahatma Koot Hoomi, whom, it was said, hailed from the Punjab. It is worth noting that Hoomi the name for a low, throat-chanting method inherited from the Tibeto-Mongolian shamans.

Detractors of Blavatsky argue that her claims are false and that her tales of psychic contact with concealed Mahatmas are nothing but the fabrications of a fraud. Her own story runs that as a young woman she discovered the library of her great grandfather on her grandmother's side, Prince Pavel Dolgorukov. An initiate of Rosicrucianism and a Scottish Rite Freemason, Dolgorukov had been initiated in the late 1770s into the Rite of Strict Observance. This esoteric German masonic rite had been founded by one Baron von Hund, a Master Mason whose account implied that he received instruction to pass on this secret charter by certain 'unknown superiors'.

These unknown superiors were said to be a remnant of the Knights Templar who had taken refuge in Scotland many centuries before, following their dissolution and ruthless suppression under King Philip IV of France in 1307. The Rite of Strict Observance was both chivalric and subversive, being heavily linked with the Jacobite cause against the English and to the re-establishment of an independent Scotland under the rule of Bonnie Prince Charlie. It was this model of the Scottish Rite, with its unknown superiors and secret mission to effect change in society that critics suggest is the true inspiration for Madame Blavatsky's purported contact with the Mahatmas.

In the 17th Century, the German Rosicrucian Brotherhood published their teachings in a series of manuscripts in an attempt to usher in a new, enlightened age. Much of their good work in promoting science to counteract ignorance and superstition was halted by the Holy Inquisition of the Catholic Church, driving Rosicrucianism underground for many years. In the midst of this, Rosicrucianism acquired a reputation for being an 'invisible academy', while in London some openly declared this invisible college to be the precursor of the Royal Society, the body of scientists and progessive thinkers that was instrumental in the rebuilding of London in the wake of the devastating fire of 1666. The Royal Society, headed by Christopher Wren, ushered in a more civilised and scientific age, overseen by Rosicrucians and Freemasons.

While there is no doubt that Helena Blavatsky travelled widely, her accounts of living in Tibet have troubled some, with many detractors questioning whether she ever set foot there at all. By Blavatsky's own account, she visited the Roof of the World aged 25 years as part of her tour of Asia, which took in India, Kashmir and Burma between 1856-7. Her second sojourn to Tibet, which was apparently made overland from Turkey, took place at the behest of the Mahatma in 1868.

Here she remained until 1870, receiving the teachings of her masters in Shigatse at Tashi Lungpo Monastery. This monastery was the seat of the Panchen Lama and was also near to her Mahatmas Koot Hoomi and Morya who allegedly operated an independent school for adepts that operated outside the authority of the Panchen Lama. Given the suspicion of Tibetan authorities towards foreigners as attested by the severe difficulties experienced by Younghusband and others, critics of Blavatsky have cast extreme doubt on her ease of access into the remote Lamaist kingdom. One such traveller, the Englishman Henry Savage Landor wrote of his time in Tibet in his graphic tale *In the Forbidden Land: An Account of a Journey in Tibet, Capture by the Tibetan Authorities, Imprisonment, Torture &* *Ultimate Release*, published in 1898, which included photographs of the author's time spent in chains before being placed on the rack.

Yet according to Blavatsky, she faced no such opposition or privations and was instead invited by her secret masters and instructed directly in their ways; to fast, meditate and understand the various mysteries of the cosmos. There are those more aggressive opponents who view Blavatsky as the progenitor of the entire 'secret masters' myth in the modern age that gave inspiration for those who followed. Macgregor Mathers and the Hermetic Order of the Golden Dawn; Aleister Crowley; Gurdjieff; J.G. Bennett; Annie Besant; Alice Bailey and Idris Shah; all went on to claim their own contact with a directorate of 'hidden superiors' in the mould of Blavatsky's Mahatmas.

It does not help her reputation that Madame Blavatsky was prone to fits of hysteria and foul-mouthed tirades. A scandalous newspaper exposé by a former employee claimed she faked miracles at séances such as using a long white glove stuffed with cotton wool to fake the appearance of 'ectoplasm'. Accusations of plagiarism from earlier sources, including the works of French occultist Papus and Louis Jacolliot's works on Krishna and the Bible in India, abounded and leading Theosophist Annie Besant rejected Blavatsky outright as a genuine psychic. Her disillusioned follower Emma Colomb claimed in a Christian college magazine that the so-called 'Mahatma Letters' apported during seances to contact Mahatma Koot Hoomi, were simply dropped through ceiling floorboards by hidden accomplices onto the circle below.

Supporters of the Russian Theosophist point out in her defence that hostile Christians of the time, not journalists, published these attacks in an effort to undermine her work. Theosophists cite Blavatsky's assiduous research based on translations taken from complex ancient Tantric texts such as the Tibetan Kalachakra Tantra, that she did have had some contact with a higher source that acted to guide her. Writer Victoria LePage in her work *Shambhala* says of Blavatsky that there are figurative clues to the occult tradition that should not be taken as picturesque prose. One such hidden gem, says Le Page, is contained in Blavatsky's quote about the heart of Mother Earth, that "beats under the foot of the sacred Shambhala."

This obscure reference, LePage argues, reflects an old tradition; the 'beating heart of the Earth' is taken from its core inside Tibetan teachings; the most advanced of cosmic secrets concerning a current emanating from Mount Meru. It begs the question how did Blavatsky come by such knowledge? Was it simply that she had translated so much Kalachakric material in her time and if so why did she deliberately disguise and withhold some of what had been discovered?

One answer could be that the Kalachakra has an inner and outer component. The latter teachings can be openly disclosed by lamas to the world-at-large while the inner teachings are only known to initiates of the ancient tradition. By withholding or obscuring certain information in her writings Blavatsky is revealing the Kalachakra information on Mount Meru exactly as it should be taught, further suggesting she may well have been a genuine initiate. She certainly used Tibetan terms that were not widely known at the time.

Whatever the case, Blavatsky had founded Theosophy, which remained the cornerstone of her work although the Russian aristocrat was largely discredited by the end of her life. Her work was rubbished just about everywhere, even inside esoteric circles. Despite this, Theosophy continued largely unscathed and has continued to bring ancient concepts taken directly from the East ever since. If that was the mission of the Mahatmas then their disciple had been highly successful. If Madame Blavatsky was a mere fraud and faker then she had been equally successful by unwittingly triggering the genesis of today's New Age movement.

The Lost Tantra

The reputation of Madame Blavatsky has been one of scorched earth until about thirty years ago when further translation work on Sanskrit material revealed a previously unknown Tantra. It has become known as the *Lost Tantra* and is a Kalachakra masterpiece. The material from this Tantric teaching was immediately recognised as identical in nature to Blavatsky's *Stanzas of Dyzan*, leading some to conclude that Blavatsky must have been privy to these secret teachings. Her claims of meeting with an Atlantean brotherhood whose mission was to guard lost teachings suddenly takes on a whole new life. What seems impossible becomes intriguing. So much so, that the present Dalai Lama released this statement in 1989 about the work of the Russian mystic.

"I am therefore happy to have this long association with the Theosophists and to learn about the Centenary Edition: THE VOICE OF THE SILENCE which is being brought out this year. I believe that this book has strongly influenced many sincere seekers and aspirants to the wisdom and compassion of the Bodhisattva Path. I very much welcome this Centenary Edition and hope that it will benefit many more."

The Dalai Lama was not the only high-ranking Lamaist to recognise Blavatsky, as her work had already been endorsed by a former Panchen Lama back in 1925. Another noted orientalist and Buddhist scholar Dr Suzuki also heaped praise on her works. All agree that she remains an important Buddhist missionary whose knowledge of the Tantra was second to none. In recent times, a renowned Tibetologist David Reigle demonstrated the Tibetan Buddhist sources of H.P. Blavatsky's writings, including that the *Secret Book of Dzyan* originated from the lost Mula Kalachakra Tantra. This text is the root of the more exoteric Kalachakra Tantra, the latter being more widely known today. But how did she come by such information, about which those in the West were unaware before recent translation work? Dr Suzuki formed the opinion that she could have only learnt this advanced knowledge of Tantra as a result of training in a Tibetan monastery.

Blavatsky says she accompanied her master into Tibet where she became acquainted with the old language of Senzar – the most ancient form of Sanskrit. Using this ancient language she learnt the teachings, including those of the inner Kalachakra Tantra.

David Reigle has released an academic paper which suggests that the Lost Mula Tantra remains unknown largely due to the fact that we have only a series of manuscripts on a largely untranslated work called the Vimalaprabha. Reigle makes the point that although the Kalachakra teaching is usually associated with Gautama Buddha, its transmission belongs to an earlier Buddha figure. He says that although the documents were written down at the time of Gautama in India it does not necessarily follow that the knowledge was conceived in that period. Discoveries in Nepal in the 1970s showed that much of this Tantric work was preserved on palm leaves in the Newari script.

The Newari people enjoy special status when connected to preserving ancient knowledge concerning the ascended masters, so it is no surprise that they were guardians of the lost Tantra. Reigle seems to suggest that the origins of the Tantra may lie in Hinduism. He lists the Kings of Shambhala and links the transmission of their knowledge back into humanity via the Rishis of India. So perhaps Madame Blavatsky really came into contact with this knowledge while in India, which would be more feasible than her claims of travel in Tibet. If the latter were true it would make her one of the greatest travellers of her age to boot. It is more likely that Blavatsky encountered the Buddhists that existed somewhat closer to home; in all likelihood, the Buriat people of Imperial Russia. The Buriats certainly had contact with the Dalai Lama as we have seen in earlier chapters and were key players in the Russian Great Game. They were also custodians of the Kalachakra as it moved from Tibet into Mongolia and into Siberia. They would also have had access to Russian lands and been conversant with the mother tongue of the Tsarist Empire.

Due to the uncertainty surrounding her sources, maybe Blavatsky should be regarded as the precursor to Gurdjieff himself – a person who had come by high esoteric teachings and codified them in a way that was palatable to the people of their age. Both seem to have had a mission above and beyond their own lives and day-to-day responsibilities – as if they were acting under the auspices of the hidden directorate. People, you might say, on a mission.

Steps to Shambhala

Shambhala was popularised by people like Madame Blavatsky, although it was first brought to the attention of Westerners through writings on the Kalachakra system by 19th Century Tibetologist Alexander Cosmo de Koros. Some may argue that Shambhala was presented even earlier than that, firstly as a result of Catholic missionary Andrade's mission in the 1620s. Ever since then, Shambhala has remained an enduring and elusive otherworldly myth, evocative of paradise lost. The Portuguese Andrade was recorded as the first Westerner to go across the Himalayas into Tibet, having heard tales of undiscovered lands containing Christians while he was staying as a guest in India. Some fragmentary evidence points to Gurdjieff acquiring the enneagram symbol not from the Sufis or the Sarmoung, but from the inner teachings of the Jesuit order. The Jesuits in turn may have acquired knowledge of the enneagram centuries before, during their perambulations in Asia.

The myths of Shambhala had reached India, arriving at the court of Moghul Emperor Akbar the Great in Delhi in the mid-1500s. Akbar, as third Emperor in his dynasty, had married a Rajiput Princess in order to consolidate power over the course of two decades and by the 1570s was very much under the sway of the Naqshbandi Sufis. This arrangement had a huge impact on his outlook towards orthodox Islam, and to this day he is regarded as a heretic in some circles, since his rule was more tolerant towards other Islamic sects such as the Shias. Akbar built a great hall and invited theologians of all faiths to debate and this led to him establishing Din-i-llah, a sort of B'hai faith of its day.

The Moghul court continued upon Akbar's death in 1605 and his disloyal son who had once led a rebellion against his father successfully ascended the throne. Andrade became attached to the court of Emperor Jahangir as a Jesuit representative. It was here that he immersed himself in the strange tales of other guests at the royal court, who told stories of fabled lands and long-lost communities of fellow Christians. The Silk Road is a great place for storytelling. Ashohks travelled about it attached to the many trade caravans and Andrade made a ready ear for their romantic yarns. Upon hearing about such a land he readily made a map, leaving a huge blank where Tibet lies. His notes on the map show only a lake named Manasarovar Lacus – the purported place where the Christian community lay. We have recounted Andrade's arduous journey into Tibet earlier in Chapter 2 but it was from this contact that the name Shambhala (transcribed by the Portuguese missionaries as Xembala) first reached the West.

Andrade may have taken mention of Shambhala literally and his belief in its actual existence could have influenced his mission of discovery. Due to the complexities of Kalachakric Tantric teachings Shambhala may be understood in metaphysical terms or in a more Eastern mystical fashion, both far from the ken of Western materialism. Our nearest equivalent in the West may be the Grail quest of Arthurian legend.

The Shambhala legend varies according to which myth is recounted. However, the mythos unites Central Asia, and its origins are claimed by several traditions including the Lamaists, but it may be far older belonging to Tantra alone. In the Kalachakra doctrine Shambhala is both Hindu and Buddhist and is ruled over by a King. The Hindu King is called Indra, while to Buddhists the ruler is a Boddhisattva or reincarnation of the Buddha. Surrounded by his entourage, all Devas (or gods), the King of Shambhala lives in a cave, or in some variant myths a brightly shining pagoda, that gives off a diamond-sparkling radiance by both day and night from its position at the top of the main mountain – Mount Meru. The capital of Shambhala, Kalapa, is populated by saintly, enlightened beings who act as governors overseeing the outer reaches of the Kingdom.

All who live there are advanced spiritual beings seeking total perfection and enlightenment. The king, while in office, exists to emit wisdom and the teachings that will benefit the entire planet. It is from here that the Buddha received instruction and the knowledge of the Kalachakra itself first emanated. There are 96 prefectures in the Kingdom, a number of great significance as we shall see later. In essence, Shambhala is the fount of all that is enlightened, harmonious, beneficial and evolutionary for the planet.

All teachings and every single spiritual path originates here and pours forth into the world, Shambhala being the very embodiment of the inner circle of humanity's hidden directorate. To those in the West it may be regarded as nothing more than a charming myth but it is more than that to Central Asian thought; to Tibetans, Mongolians and the Chinese (prior to the Maoist 'cultural revolution') Shambhala exists in reality. Those with the Karma to find it will gain entry. Shambhala is hidden from the profane. Think again of Gurdjieff and the Legonomism – a teaching activated by consciousness.

Even when religions die out Shambhala replaces them with new teachings, its love and guidance unlimited and it is here that one realises that Gurdjieff, in his writings about the death of Lama G, might have been talking about the concept of the inner circle of humanity in a way that a Western mind would find more accessible. Lama G as mentioned at the end of Chapter 1 was mown down by Younghusband's British Expedition in 1904 and was, according to Gurdjieff, on the cusp of delivering a brand-new esoteric teaching to the Earth from Tibet. One of Gurdjieff's main pupils and his chief proponent in spreading the 'Work' was a Russian mathematician called Peter Ouspensky, who penned the famous *In Search of the Miraculous*. Ouspensky's book contains a logical, practical explanation of Gurdjieff's ideas and within it is something called the 'step diagram', which has allusions to the concept of Shambhala.

The step diagram is a picture demonstrating the upward and downward flow of universal energies. On the upper part of the diagram, at the highest end, is the Absolute or God and at the other end of the spectrum is unregenerate matter. Man rests approximately in the middle section of the step diagram. The general principle behind this measure of universal energies is, in laymans' terms, that the uppermost area called the Absolute operates under one law only, while at its lowest extreme at the bottom of the diagram, 6,000-odd laws are in play.

As the scale descends, the cosmic laws increase, taking the energies from a very light, refined state to a dense or gross state. Each level in the step diagram represents a portion of the universal food chain. Every level of life must consume energies from other levels in order to maintain itself and in turn provides nourishment as it is consumed by other levels adjacent to it. Ouspensky described it as a "psycho-physical digestive tube".

The normal laws affecting Man such as gravity, emotions, sustenance and so on are necessary for an average life, yet if he is not careful he can slide downwards to the square marked 'Invertebrates', where he increases these laws to 96 and this is where madness, violence and delusion set in. If he is wise, a man will ascend to the next step to escape such laws as gravity (think of flying yogis and levitating monks), go without food like a fakir and remain in a positive state, free of negative emotions – to live as taught by the great sages and saints throughout history. According to the step diagram, man may have higher possibilities, yet he still remains the 'food' of Angels. It is curious because as one goes up the step diagram one arrives at Angels, Planets and Archangels, leading finally to God or 'the Absolute'.

At each corresponding higher level, the laws are halved each time, and what seems impossible to the world of 48 laws is not impossible to the world of 24 laws. Look at the depressive state of 96 laws compared to the happy, well-adjusted emotional state of a man under 48 laws. See the world of 12 laws, and this is essentially where the miracles of the saints are manifested; these appear completely at odds with our understanding of normal life since they operate under the rules of a separate reality.

Looking closely again at the numbering Gurdjieff and Ouspensky ascribe to mankind within the step diagram we see that it bears a remarkable similarity to the legends of Shambhala.

The Step Diagram, or Diagram of Every Living Thing

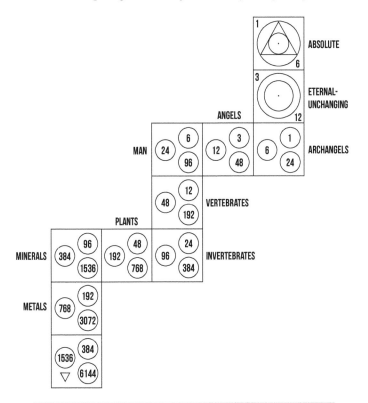

96 laws	Man in false persona or a delusional mindset	Accident
48 laws	Man in everyday persona or the Earthly body	Karma/cause & effect
12 laws	Man in essence or of the planetary body	Fate
6 laws	Man in higher intellectual or Real 'I'	True will/destiny
3 laws	The manifestation of God	

There is but one King of Shambhala: this is the Absolute operating under one law; there are 12 principalities and Shambhala has 96 prefectures; there are other numbers at work in the legends but the principle is the same. Here Ouspensky and Gurdjieff are conveying the beneficial structure and cycle of energies that not only affect mankind, but underpin the workings of the Universe itself. It must be stressed that Gurdjieff's ideas cannot be taken in isolation; his 'Work' is an holistic model and the step diagram is no exception. The cosmic laws presented here are also closely interconnected with the chakras within the human body and there is no denying that this has a most Eastern origin. To encapsulate the step diagram and its meaning, we may say that any being wishing to gain enlightenment must ascend and by doing so place themselves under the power of fewer laws to become closer to the Absolute.

Is the step diagram Gurdjieff's attempt to explain the concept of Shambhala to a 20th Century Western materialistic mind? The provenance of the step diagram is unknown, but suggests a Central Asian leaning, possibly Buddhist or Hindu. Is it then too far a leap to suggest that the source of Gurdjieff's knowledge (the Sarmoung) is indeed the Zarmang Monastery in Tibet?

Cintamani

The concept of Shambhala is not limited to Tibet, in fact in some ways it is a global phenomenon. If we think of the Grail mythos, or the fabled Xanadu, there is always time in legend to paint a picture of faraway lands that hold the promise of paradise or untold riches, for those brave enough to seek them. The crux of the matter is whether these tales are of real geographical locations or maps of the territories of inner space. Modern geographers would perhaps quickly dismiss Shambhala as fantasy or the superstition of more primitive times, but as we have said earlier, traditionally the Central Asian peoples have insisted on the physical reality of Shambhala's existence. But how?

One of those who attempted to penetrate the mystery with some success was eccentric Russian explorer Nicholas Konstantinovitch Roerich, aided by his wife Helena, both of whom were initiates of the Theosophical path. The Roerich legacy includes a work entitled *Shambhala: The Resplendent*. Born in 1874 in St Petersburg, Nicholas Roerich was something of a genius, if not a genuine polymath. A student of painting and the arts, literature, poetry, archaeology and philosophy, he was certainly something of a Renaissance man. He was, like Blavatsky and Gurdjieff, swept up in the occult revival of the last quarter of the 19th Century in Europe.

Having trained as a painter at the Imperial Academy of Arts while also studying law at St Petersburg University, he rose to some prominence in the Imperial Russian capital. He travelled widely, his influences diverse as they were arcane. His painting was well received, and he is still to this day widely noted as an important artist in his depiction of Russia's ancient past. His work was hung in the Louvre and the National Museum in Rome and was exhibited in every major European capital. He became an art director in 1906, having been hailed as something of an innovative genius in the media of the time.

In the arts he contributed stage sets for several major ballets including the Ballet Russe by Diaghilev. Interestingly, he was one of the first generation of conservationists, concerning himself with preserving architecture and places of historic interest, in a foreshadowing of later organisations such as UNESCO. He and his wife Helena developed a deep interest in Theosophy and Eastern mysticism during the early 20th Century.

During 1923 the Roerichs were recipients of a mysterious gift delivered to their hotel while staying in Paris. A wooden casket was deposited with them and within it an embroided cloth containing a finger-sized meteorite. Some accounts say it was a fragment of a larger piece and had been worked into the shape of a tortoise carapace, others say it is the shape of a human heart. Due to the cloth being embroidered with the letters IHS, a monogram of Christ, later commentators thought the talisman to be of Rosicrucian origins. Photographs later emerged of the object.

Inscriptions carved upon the fragment of meteorite were presumed to be holy, although the language they were written in was unknown. The manner in which the Roerichs came to possess the stone is shrouded in almost melodramatic secrecy and mystery. According to Russian authority Alexandra Andreyev in his work *The Myth of the Masters Revived: The Occult Lives of Elena and Nikolai Roerich*, Nicholas Roerich received notice on October 6th 1923 from an American 'bankers' trust' that he and his wife had been left a small package.

The package in question turned out to be a wooden casket containing the inscription 'de la part M.M'. Inside the heavily scented casket was a small shrine wrapped in purple-red cloth, upon which were inscribed figures, spheres and other symbols. As they took the shrine from its cloth wrappings they discovered a decorative letter 'M' adorned by leaves. The shrine emanated a noticeable heat that was felt by all present. Later the stone relic materialised, and became known to them as the 'Black Stone'. As the Roerichs were dyed-in-the-wool Theosophists the letter 'M' with its leafy adornment was taken to be indication of some link to Mahatma Morya, the ascended Master of Blavatsky fame. Other theories regarding the appearance of the artefact included the idea that high-ranking masonic sponsors of Roerich's expedition had arranged the delivery. There are others who postulate – and it seems a prosaic tale in comparison – that a Lamaist Abbot presented the holy relic of the Cintamani to Roerich while he was travelling in Asia. Roerich and his wife were determined to present the talismanic stone in Tibet.

Andreyev explores the theme of the Black Stone in some detail, quoting the historian Rosov, who recounts that the divine stone had previously passed through the hands of the Emperor Napoleon and his consort Josephine.

That the stone had also been subsequently held in safekeeping by the Parisian secret society known as the Prieure De Sion only added weight to the potential historical importance of the relic. And thus, this sliver of meteorite came into the possession of the Roerichs. Photographs of the Cintamani were taken shortly after its appearance and feature in Roerich's 1936 painting, *Treasure of the World – Chintamani*. It is interesting to note that in Tibetan mythology, the wish-fulfilling stone Cintamani rides on the back of the 'wind horse' Lung Ta. The inner mystery of Lung Ta relates to the internal winds that hold aloft the human mind, which in turn inform our actions in life (karma). Lung Ta represents the pivotal element of space.

By accounts taken from the ancient Buddhist text called the Pali Canon we are left with a description of the Cintamani being originally composed of eight facets, each of great luminosity. Other traditions, both Vedic and Hindu, ascribe the provenance of the gem to the sacred masters. Whether the stone artefact in the Roerich's possession was one and the same divine relic of myth is a matter of conjecture.

The infamous Russian monarchist Baron von Ungern-Sternberg was another notable figure who drew heavily on the Shambhala mythos, which prophesied the appearance of a general who would come to fight the forces of evil and deliver mankind to the Dharma. Known as the 'Mad Baron', thanks to his devotion to Vajrayana Buddhism and the violence meted out to enemies and his own men alike, Ungern-Sternberg believed himself to be the Kalki, the legendary general born of Shambhala whose mission was to restore enlightenment to the world. Sharing the Orientalist penchant of the time for 'going native' he often donned traditional Mongolian attire, which only added to the Baron's already colourful image.

Oddly enough, the war prophesied in the Shambhala mythos is a conflict with an overriding spiritual mission; perhaps the closest Buddhism has ever come to the Islamic concept of Jihad, or the Christian Crusaders' concept of the 'Holy War'. Ungern-Sternberg's own 'Shambhala War' was marshalled by an aristocratic cavalry officer whose views were vehemently opposed to the Communist revolution. Rebelling against the White Army he chose to use his Cossack training to lead an independent military force with the ultimate aim, equally as eccentric as anything Roerich had to offer, of restoring the Mongol empire of Genghis Khan and reinstating the Romanov Dynasty back in St Petersburg.

It was this initiative that led him to support the ascension of the Bogd Khan to the Mongolian throne. The plan was ill-starred, although it received Japanese backing with a series of Chinese warlords also being party to the plan. Eventually the Baron's forces lost ground and abandoned the region, whereupon von Ungern-Sternberg withdrew to Manchuria and curried local favour by marrying a local Princess named Ji, further fuelling the Baron's reputation for the outlandish. The marriage cemented contacts within Imperial circles, including the notorious warlord Zhang Zuolin, the one-time ruler of Beijing.

The Baron's legacy may, on one level, seem romantic, but dashing it certainly is not; though he was a Buddhist he showed no compassion for the Jews he executed in cold blood. Historians do not remember him kindly. The 'Mad Baron' was not shy about hanging his enemies from trees and roasting them alive with fires lit below. In order to dispatch a Japanese military leader he had taken a dislike to, the Baron tipped off the Chinese authorities who seized the Japanese soldier on his arrival in Chinese territory. He was arrested and summarily executed. To describe von Ungern-Sternberg as ruthless and despotic is an understatement.

His leadership came to a head in Mongolia when some among his troops decided to give up the war and join Russian émigrés in Manchuria. The Baron had ideas to retreat instead into Tibet. A mutiny occurred which saw his officers killed and an assassination attempt on his own life. Although he survived this attack, only three days later the Baron was captured by the Red Army.

In the autumn of 1921 Baron von Utegern-Sternberg finally received a taste of his own medicine; he was tried by the Communists and found guilty of 'counter-revolutionary' crimes. The next morning he was executed by firing squad. The Bogd Khan, upon hearing news of the death of the warlord-aristocrat had prayers said throughout Mongolia to honour his liberator, the dead commander.

The politics of both Tibet and Mongolia had long been beset by such turmoil, in their roles as autonomous regions with strong ties to China. At various points one of the three countries had been stronger than the other two and invaded their neighbours. Tibet was seen as a centre of spiritual affection and allegiance whereas China always seemed to take the dominant position having diplomatic envoys stationed in both Lhasa and Mongolia.

The antics of the 'Mad Baron' scarred the region and divided Inner and Outer Mongolians in the aftermath. It is no great surprise that the superior force of the Bolsheviks, being well-armed and experienced in modern warfare, overcame their opponents who were certainly no match for the new invader. Three years later, in 1924, the Bogd Khan died and his wife followed a year later. Chinese authorities prevented the installation of a successor to the Bogd Khan and as such the Lamaist rule of Mongolia, the Khaganate, came to an end. In its place the new Communist rulers of Mongolia formed a Peoples' Republic, forbidding another tulku to rule the Kingdom.

However, in 1932 the Panchen Lama launched an offensive from Tibet to attack the new Mongolian atheist state and this, in turn, became the next bloody

'Shambhala War'. It was to this offensive that Roerich gave his wholehearted support, under the auspices of a botanical expedition. What is rarely told of the Shambhala War is the reason for its inception – the roots of which lay in the secret plans of the esoteric societies of the region, particularly the Tibetan Lamaists.

During 1932 a new Bogd Khan was found in Tibet. While this event was not announced to the world at large until the fall of communism in the Soviet Republic some fifty-odd years later, the new Bogd Khan was secretly installed within Tibetan-Mongolian Lamaist circles. In 1991 after the fall of Communism and when democracy was once again restored, the ninth Jebtsundamba was formally enthroned in India by the Dalai Lama and later another coronation was performed in the Mongolian capital Ulan Bator in 1999. The discovery of the infant tulku Bogd Khan during 1932 was a tightly-kept secret known only to Tibet's highest spiritual authorities. Roerich had enough influence on the inside of the Mongolian Lamaist circle to be privy to their state secret but was he one of those informed? Given the discovery of such a prominent and important tulku, it is understandable that the Panchen Lama launched the war in Mongolia, since success against the atheist oppressors greatly increased the chances of a Buddhist Bogd Khan to ascend to the throne once more. However, it does beg the question regarding how much Roerich, a staunch supporter of the Panchen Lama, really knew about these events and why he chose to deliver the mystical relic of the Cintamani stone to Tibet around this time. Was the holy amulet a specially ordained gift to the beleaguered throne?

Questions of lineage, tulku and the myth of Shambhala are taken extremely seriously in Central Asia. A direct legacy of the Mad Baron's activities was to drive out the remaining Imperial Chinese and then the Russian Bolsheviks to support Mongolian independence in the region. Opinions on his political legacy are bitterly divided, but in a charitable sense he stood as the last bastion between the old ways of the Nomadic steppes and the horrific communist takeover which saw the wholesale dismantling of the indigenous religion in the name of Marx.

Some commentators say, however, that if the Baron had not driven out the Chinese it might have meant that today Mongolia would have remained inside the Chinese Peoples' Republic and as such, the consequences could have been far worse. The return of the Bogd Khan to his homeland with support from His Holiness the Dalai Lama in 1999 enraged the Chinese communist elite who viewed the Lamaist culture as a direct threat to their political schemes for the region.

King of the World

Besides Shambhala another such kingdom exists and was investigated by a Polish adventurer one year before Roerich managed to set foot on the Roof of the

World. The Pole was a man equally as indefatigable as any who had come before him, his name Ferdinand Ossendowski and the hidden kingdom he sought goes by the name of Argharthi. This mythical kingdom is spelt variously: Agartta, Agharta, Agartha, Agharti, Arghati, and more besides, according to diverse traditions and regional cultures of the Silk Road.

Primarily Argharthi is known as an underground realm which features in the legends and tales of the Central Asian region. It is said to reside in a vast network of tunnels, some constructed by its inhabitants, some the result of natural geological features, with parts of the structure having been swept away by past catastrophes. Argharthi is similar to Shambhala in one key respect: that it is seemingly only accessible to the initiated. One reason for this exclusivity is that Argarthi houses a vast repository of sacred knowledge that guards the very nature of mankind's origins, going back before the Great Flood.

As with Shambhala it is ruled by a king calling himself 'The King of the World'. Argharthi was first brought to public attention in 1873 by Frenchman Louis Jacolliet while in India. He spelled it as Asgartha describing it as the 'solar capital' of India. He equated this legend with the caste system of the Aryans saying that the Asgarthans had initiated the warrior caste into their rites. It was another Frenchman, Saint-Yves d'Alveydre, who wrote in *Mission de L'Inde* in 1886 that Argharthi began to capture Western interest when the Polish voyager Ferdinand Ossendowski really capitalised on the tale. His account of his journey on the Roof of the World is as curious as those that we have seen so far, but stranger still, given the great uncertainty in Western minds whether such places truly exist outside of legend of allegory. Perhaps Ossendowski is all the more audacious then to our eyes, since he claims direct knowledge of Argharthi as a real physical place.

Reading about his journey we are confronted with a travelogue in which he describes huge unexplained sources of light, with columns beaming up into the night sky in a region which had no electricity or generators and was too far south of the Northern Lights phenomenon. He talks to of a group of indigenous people called Azaras, who were tall people with long hair and beards whose aspect he likened to Hindus, that lived in the mountains with a special remit to protect Argharthi. His tale is one of charming discovery of a yet untapped resource.

Ossendowski had met with both the Mad Baron, whom he joined acting as his military intelligence officer, and the palace officials serving the Bogd Khan. His account of meeting with the Mongolian living god or Buddha is curious and he reflects a great understanding of the local spiritual allegiances and delicate politics between China, Tibet and Mongolian people providing solid evidence of the strong belief in the existence of Argharthi.

"In the great palace of the Bogdo a lama showed me a special casket covered with a precious carpet, wherein they keep the bulls of the Dalai and Tashi lamas, the decrees of the Russian and Chinese Emperors and the Treaties between Mongolia, Russia, China and Tibet. In this same casket a copper plate bearing the mysterious sign of the 'King of the World' and the chronicle of the last vision of the Living Buddha lay side-by-side." In his account of travels in the region during 1921, Ossendowski tells of being taken inside an ornately fashioned temple having one wall painted yellow. It was explained by a Mongolian lama that the yellow paint denoted a place where someone special had once lived. He was taken further inside the monastery building, seeing the opulent surroundings including a throne surrounded by four chairs.

His guide told his Polish guest that one night during winter several horseman arrived and gathered locals to the room. A stranger then mounted the throne to reveal his head from under his cap, all present fell to their knees recognising from the sacred bulls of the Dalai Lama and Bogd Khan the supreme ruler of humanity, the 'King of the World'. After blessing those present and praying according to Tibetan custom the King of the World then gave out a series of prophecies for the next half-century. This event was not dated by Ossendowski although others have stated that it took place in approximately 1890, foretelling the start of the First and Second World Wars and great suffering to come. A comforting rider being that once evil forces think they have control of the Earth, the King of the World will begin his liberation of humanity. The Mongolian lama finished his tale by saying that the King of the World and his entourage simply disappeared to those present leaving only the depression in the folds of the silk on the throne as evidence of where the enigmatic royal visitor had once sat.

It seems that men like Roerich, the Mad Baron and, to some degree, Osendowski were greatly impressed by these legends of Shambhala and Argharti and acted accordingly. Ossendowski finishes his account at the temple by saying that he had visions of his own family blending in with the incense smoke as the lama prayed for his relations. As the incense smoke visions dissipated the smoke disappeared behind a Buddha statue. His visualisation ended but Ossendowski makes the point that others present also saw the same mental images, demonstrating that his psychic experience had a level of objectivity. All three Russians above accepted the mystic faculties of the lamas as reality, while initiates like Blavatsky, Trungpa to some degree even Gurdjieff, insisting on the spiritual hegemony of the ascended masters, better known as Shambhala, to guide the destiny of mankind. All of them students of the Kalachakra system.

Suggestions as to the location of the secret entrance to the lost subterranean world of Argharthi are legion. Ossendowski related that he had been told by lamas that one entrance was underneath the Potala Palace in Lhasa, while other explorers suggesting various sites in remoter regions of Tibet. With such strict taboos on revealing its location, which include the cutting out of tongues, the precise locality of Argharthi remains as mysterious as its King. Did Ossendowski unwittingly encounter the high initiates of the hidden directorate? Were the others such as Gurdjieff, Blavatsky and Roerich all pawns in a bigger plan decreed by the enlightened schools?

The word of God is disseminated by the King of World – Hindus, Buddhists and Jains await his missive.

Chapter 4

Legends of the Immortals

"Do you have the patience to wait
Till your mud settles and the water is clear?
Can you remain unmoving
Till the right action arises by itself?"
Lao Tzu

China in the time of Gurdjieff was very different to the commercial powerhouse and communist materialist monoculture it is today. Back then it was rich in esoteric lore although the country was fragmented and often subject to strife, division or being overrun by warlords. Being steeped in ancient lore it was home to a number of traditions, some of which are now widely known, such as the *I-Ching*, acupuncture, Tai Chi, Taoism and the Shaolin fighting arts. Much of its particularly Buddhist impetus has now been lost, yet Gurdjieff drew from some of these secrets, music being one strand, medicine another.

Hsi Wang Mu – Mother of the West

If, as history suggests, Shambhala is a real place located in Tibet wherein the enlightened reside, its influence spans a wider range of territory still. The Shambhala of myth was a resplendent and luxurious kingdom, yet across the border in China the Taoists yearned for simplicity, which for them became the hallmark of their mysticism. For it is the Taoists who have pointed to the benign influence of the sublime masters more than most systems – so much so that they leave tantalising clues to its true origins, it would seem.

In the idyllic retreats of the Kun Lun (Chinese: Pin Yin) mountains, mystical stories of Immortals abound. The region is also notable for its legendary history, being intertwined with real-life Chinese historical characters who appeared to foster many unanswered questions about what the ancients believed was inspiring their civilisation. As always, these are allied to the umbilical cords of mystical dimensions. The Kun Lun is the longest chain of mountains in Asia, residing in the southern part of Central Asia, but perhaps the northernmost parts of the Roof of the World. The range extends East to West, some 1,250 miles across, touching the Pamirs of Pakistan on the westerly side and facing up the Karakorums to the south. A south-easterly aspect in the Plateau of Tibet meets one of the two sources of the Yellow River, which by ancient repute flowed directly from heaven via the Milky Way. One of China's great waterways, the Yellow River is considered a cradle of Chinese civilisation, with many expressions and myths attached to it.

The Kun Lun mountains, according to myth, are home to a magnificent jade palace frequented by a ruler called *Kuan Jin*, a goddess of mercy. In common with other Central Asian gods and goddesses, her names are many and interchangeable and she can be equated with deities bearing similar qualities according to the region or language, but her remit and location remains the same.

Her place in motifs found in ancient scripture show Kuan Jin in various guises, but the overall message is clear; she is a feminine aspect of mercy while also enjoying the honour of being the oldest deity in Chinese culture. Many of the ancient Chinese tea rituals based on a square of eight segments flowing in certain directions have connections to the goddess. Guanyin tea is named after the goddess Ganyin, an alternative form of Khan Jin. It is said that she hides in her garden concealed by clouds, in which a massive peach tree dedicated to immortality bears fruit that matures every 6,000 years. In the night skies she is associated with the constellation of the Big Dipper (known as the Plough in the UK) and according to legend she decides how long any being shall live and presides over them in the afterlife also.

Perhaps the overriding mother Chinese goddess is Wang Mu – the Sovereign Mother. She is represented within the famed *I-Ching* in hexagram #49 and is associated with both leopards and tigers. In many paintings, Wang-Mu is represented as taking the form of a tiger. The upper trigram of this *I-Ching* hexagram, Li, represents a lake or a body of water. In conjunction, the two trigrams create a hexagram whose image is that of a fire within a lake. One meaning that could be construed from hexagram #49 is that the home of Wang-Mu sits at the foot of the Kun Lun mountains close to a lake. However, in the commentary to Hexagram #35 (Easy Progress), the word Wangmu is mentioned, suggesting the grandmotherly aspect, or in a slant of meaning, female ancestors more generally. Wang-Mu was once connected to weaving and therefore she is associated with silk, needlework, sewing and dressmaking. Her crown is the loom, for she is the cosmic weaver. 'Wang' in Chinese is also a word to denote the spirit world. One of the aspects of Wang-Mu carried through various dynasties and their effects upon the populace was that Wang-Mu allowed women to separate themselves from traditional role models imposed on them: dutiful daughter, young mother or older, extended family member. Researchers such as Cahill have suggested her association with the Yunü or Jade Maidens; these Taoist goddesses are related to bawdy singers, musicians and brothel workers, also too the seducers of young boys, but this aspect was never discussed openly. As for Wang-Mu her mainstay of worship was always North-East China but her veneration gained popularity and spread to parts of the South-East also. The most auspicious time connected to the deity was the seventh hour of the seventh day of the seventh month. This was mainly due to her connection with the seven stars of the Plough constellation, which we will see has great import later in this story, for it is linked to the swastika.

It was not until the advent of the Ming period (1368-1644) that the convergence of Taoism and Buddhism gave rise to Wang-Mu proper, along with the teaching that advised adherents who sought her wisdom to seek paradise upon their death in the West. The two paths of Taoism and Buddhism did not always see eye to eye, but in this goddess they were able to find common ground; a deity representative of both teachings. In one way it demonstrates the equality of the Chinese system that female and male gods were considered on a par, echoing the Yin and Yang aspects of the universe. In the same spirit, Hsi Wang Mu, as legend has it, hosted the arrival of the first primordial beings Nu and Ku within the grounds of her wonderful jade pagoda sitting west of the Kun Lun. The pair are redolent of Adam and Eve as found in Judeo-Christian faiths, as they too were said to live in a paradise and, according to myth, Nu and Ku are the primal ancestors of all Chinese people and culture. What is interesting here is the name of their host Hsi Wang Mu, as her last name 'Mu' appears in various forms worldwide and is always associated with the Great Flood, the survival or revival of the human race and specific myths of a super race or certain gods who gave birth to mankind.

The Mu legacy features prominently in the Roof of the World sagas. This fact was not lost on a Chinese revolutionary called Tse (1872-1938) who was born in Sydney, Australia before moving to Hong Kong. Tse sought to exploit the legend of Mu to his own ends. He wrote a work entitled *The Creation, The Real Situation of Eden and the Origin of the Chinese*. To truncate the rather complex theory, Tse was convinced that the Garden of Eden had been located just north of the Kun Lun range, boxed in by Khotan and River Tarim. Tse also tried to weave into his incredible notions the age-old myth of a sunken continent. This he placed in the Pacific near Papua New Guinea, stretching almost to South America. His sketches in red ink show the landmass to be identical in shape to the mythical Mu of the Atlantis legends. Controversial this may have been, but Tse cited as evidence the story in the Biblical Book of Genesis that tells of a spring in the centre of Eden that broke out into four separate rivers. By way of illustration, his other maps in black and red ink show the River Tarim going westwards to become four distinct rivers: the Aksu, Kashgar, Yarkhad and Khotan. He placed Eden itself in what is known today as Xingjiang (Chinese Turkestan).

Tse's curious theory appeared during 1914 when the world had more pressing matters to attend to, but nevertheless he went onto become a Christian social reformer, a key figure in persuading some of his countryman to abandon the practice of foot-binding and later founded the newspaper the *South China Morning Post*.

Other researchers such as the author Andrew Tomas may not have taken the ideas of Tse literally but were willing to look at Hsi Wang Mu, Queen of the West, and the bleak frozen peaks of the Kun Lun once again. Echoing the Shambhala myths, it was said that only the virtuous and wise could reach Hsi Wang Mu and her garden, whose peach tree of immortality again has its parallels with Biblical imagery. At a prearranged time, selected individuals of high virtue would be invited to eat from the peach tree and thereby become Immortals themselves. Towards the end of his life the Chinese philosopher Lao Tzu, the father of the Taoist Way, is said to have made the perilous crossing of the Gobi desert to the peach garden of Hsi Wang Mu. Lao Tzu's legacy is perhaps the greatest of all Chinese mystical tracts, the *Tao Te Ching*. He is also closely associated with the principal of all imperial rulers, the Yellow Emperor Huang-di, patron of the esoteric arts and progenitor of Chinese civilisation.

Lao Tzu certainly spoke of the 'Ancient Ones', although whether his last sojourn to the west in search of the fabled garden of Hsi Wang Mu was successful is not recorded, as he simply falls off the pages of history. Later, other wise men and even the odd Emperor set out on this same journey to seek an audience with the Immortals. Could those same Immortals such as Hsi Wang Mu be yet another expression of the inner circle of humanity – the hidden directorate?

The Country of Satisfaction

The Chinese sages wrote of the Country of Satisfaction, which closely resembles Shambhala in every respect. Here as before, the sacred peach tree blossoms, all desires are met and peace and tranquillity reign supreme. Such was the renown of Hsi Wang Mu that even the great Taoists like Lao Tzu were drawn towards her legends and sought refuge in the fabled peach garden. Neighbouring nations also harboured tales of a fantastic realm beyond normal life which was the source of harmonious existence. The Kirghiz nation talked of Muztagh Ata, which followed a similar theme – a blissful sanctuary guarding sacred truths in which grew a sacred plum tree whose fruits, once again, dispensed longevity or even immortality. To Western sensibilities the origins of these ideas may appear merely the result of wishful thinking, somewhat akin to Grail heritage of Britain, which must firmly remain within the confines of myth. Yet the Oriental mind does not accept such rational viewpoints so readily.

Unfortunately much damage has been done to Chinese culture by successive Communist Party edicts, so it is hard now to gauge the mindset of China, but if we look to the remaining Lamaists in Mongolia, Tibet, Nepal and Ladakh we are faced with a dilemma, in that they consider these myths to be factual; they relate to real, physical places that one can actually visit. Likewise their views on the Masters of Wisdom or the hidden directorate is that this is palpable – a reality rather than a pipe dream.

Many Freemasons may concur with this idea; as we have seen, there are certain esoteric lodges and quasi-masonic groups that accept the existence of 'secret chiefs' and unknown superiors who dictate the direction of both their movement and the world at large. In Asiatic circles these places have become the thrones of the gods from which beneficial cosmic energies flow outwards towards humanity. Such was the Chinese obsession with the affairs of the incarnate gods taking human form they formed the official office of state called Li Fan Yuan which oversaw matters of foreign policy such as tulkus being born; one such was the Bogd Khan in Mongolia as discussed in the previous chapter.

Even to this day the atheist Communists of Beijing follow in a long tradition and are nervous of tulku lineages in neighbouring states whose authority may yet pose a challenge to their own. In many ways China is as Confucian as it has ever been. However the spirit of the Tao still permeates Chinese thinking, despite decades of more modern Maoist brainwashing techniques. It is said that Lao Tzu refused Confucius initiation into the Tao – perhaps to emphasise that the outward teaching Confucius sought to bring to the authorities could never become the inner emptiness so beloved of the Taoists. This is quite significant because it meant that however famous Confucius became as a result of his collecting of wisdom for use at the Emperor's court, he would remain uninitiated and therefore exoteric. Lao Tzu, on the other hand, was a master who sought out the Immortals and belongs to a very different order of knowledge.

For centuries the Chinese court of the Emperor took advice from the 'mag' – a magical adviser who wore a type of conical wizard's hat which was gold in colour. Their symbol was a four-armed cross with splayed ends, not dissimilar to that of the Knights Templar. The mags possessed a profound knowledge of the stars, attested by the fact that they knew of the 19-year metonic cycle, which predicts the recurrence of the Moon's phase on the same days of the solar year.

This same cycle was also used in the West by most ancient societies including the Druids, and is still employed in Christianity to calculate the date of Easter each year. Some researchers such as Robert Temple in his book *Crystal Sun* go further still, advancing a theory that the Ancient Chinese had come by great scientific knowledge, as found in their texts such as the *Huai-Nan-Tzu*, a collection of works on diverse matters dating to the time of the Han Dynasty and edited by Prince Han (c. 179–122BC).

Today the text has been reproduced into English but much of its information is partially lost. It is as profound in subject matter as any book found inside Asia. Documenting in part the precise nature of the material universe and its creation, the *Huai-Nan-Tzu* is a foundation work of the Taoist Way. The author Robert Temple marvels at the technology which is found within the *Huai-Nan-Tzu*, which he believes to be proof that the Ancient Chinese were capable of constructing advanced telescopes with which they observed and recorded the motion of the heavens. Of course, Temple has written another work, *The Genius of China*, in which he concludes that many so-called modern innovations had been previously invented in China in ancient times.

The author Colin Wilson in his correspondence with fellow writer John Michell considered that the ancients knew numbers represented all types of forces and motion. Numbers therefore became symbolic. It is no surprise therefore, that we should learn that the Ancient Chinese Taoists constructed the divination system called the *I-Ching*, also known as the *Book of Changes*.

This divinatory oracle consists of 64 'hexagrams' each being based on a combination of two 'trigrams'. The trigrams are made of broken lines and solid lines which represent yin and yang energies. Yes or No. Sun and Moon. Male and Female. Nobody can say for sure where the oracle came from, but it is generally ascribed to the mythical serpent king, first Emperor of China, Fu Hsi. Like its Western counterpart the Tarot, its inception is shrouded in mystery and there are some who say the *I-Ching* may not be Chinese in origin at all and is actually drawn from a far older source.

Wilson was one who began to consider the relationship between the number of hexagrams (64) and its relationship to DNA. DNA in the cells of human bodies has four chemical bases. Others may hark back to the previous chapter and the step diagram which relates to the eight-note octave. 8 x 8 = 64.

Wilson wrote in *Atlantis to the Sphinx* of a man by the name of Hayes who had also made this connection between DNA and the *I-Ching*:

"Hayes recalled that when he had studied the *I-Ching* in his hippie days, he had wondered vaguely why the number of its 'hexagrams' (each one made up of two trigrams) should be 64 – eight times eight and not seven times seven or nine times nine. And now he learned that each of the triplet units of RNA links up with another triplet in the DNA molecule. So the 'double helix' of information in the heart of all reproductive cells is made up from 64 hexagrams, as in the *I-Ching*. Could this really be just coincidence? Since his extramural course left him with time to kill, he began looking more closely into this 'coincidence'. Of course, it seemed unlikely that Fu Hsi, the legendary creator of the *I-Ching*, had stumbled upon some kind of mystical insight into the 'code of life'. But it seemed worth investigating. If it was not coincidence then, that there should be eight trigrams hidden in DNA. And when he learned that this was so, Mike Hayes began to feel that he had stumbled upon something that could be very important indeed." We shall see later how Hayes linked the *I Ching* to the octave of Gurdjieff and therefore unravelled some of his musical theories related to the universe.

Interestingly early images uncovered in the 1920s by the archeologist Sir Auriel Stein depict the legendary Fu Hsi with his sister Nu-Wa. The siblings, both inhabitants of the legendary Kun Lun mountains, are entwined by shared serpent legs in a double helix that strongly resembles that of the DNA molecule. Another singular aspect of the early painting is that they hold aloft what appear to be the tools of Masonry, the compass and the square. These implements rule the heavens and the Earth respectively. In some legends the brother and sister marry but in their shame they cover their faces with a fan, which is a wedding symbol in China to this day.

Nu-Wa is a flood deity credited with saving mankind and repairing the sacred pillar that ascends to heaven. Like the Kun Lun goddess Wang-Mu, there is yet another connection to the Plough constellation. Indeed the painting featuring the pair has the constellation in the upper most part of the frieze.

Nu-Wa is a flood goddess. Her name when spoken aloud is familiar – it sounds very much like the name of another mythical figure associated with a flood: Noah. A coincidence perhaps, but then these familiar themes will continue to present themselves as we go on. Nu-Wa, Noah. According to the Bible story of the flood, eight persons were onboard the Ark. Likewise in Chinese mythology eight persons survived the flood, including Nu-Wa, who in turn repopulated the Earth following the great cataclysm. It would appear that from Taoist sources, the inventors of the *I-Ching*, Tai Chi, acupuncture, Feng Shui and the rest of the ancient sciences, this knowledge came to us via Immortals who survived a great flood. Enter James Churchward.

Empire of the Sun

Earlier we mentioned Idris Shah and treated his claims with caution, but now we introduce a maverick anthropologist, inventor and historian called James

Churchward and it is at this juncture that we must once again exercise some prudence in assessing the information. There is no doubt that Churchward, who spent most of his life pursuing evidence for a pre-flood civilisation, made a great contribution to the swathe of books on this subject that have followed. If nothing else, his research into ancient symbolism, the remarkable similarities between cultures, their shared words and near identical myths of the Great Flood make his work both bold and ground-breaking.

Churchward's legacy as a nonconformist historian has led academia to highlight the inaccuracies in his disclosures and to dismiss his conclusions. For example, he is said to have discovered an important map, which in one book is pinpointed as being unearthed in India and in another, Tibet. However, we must also remember that such borders are prone to shift over time, as we have observed in the case of Sikkim, which is currently part of India yet was once a region of Tibet. Taking into account the sheer breadth of material from around the world, much of it visited by him in person; from Polynesia, North and Central America, India, Egypt, to Europe, some might forgive a small mistake regarding the place in which a certain map was unearthed? Detractors say that the story of James Churchward is a case of a man desperate for recognition and that he fabricated events to support his theories. Critics challenge his claims as mere pseudo-scientific ramblings saying his work is totally discredited and based on hoaxes. As for his own account of being privy to sacred texts in an unknown tongue, this has been swept aside. His tale, like others in this book, is remarkable and therefore worthy of closer inspection.

Colonel James Churchward (1851–1936) was born in Devon, England into a large family household. Possessed of a bright and enquiring mind, he turned to inventing and made an important contribution to the war effort in World War I, creating a type of steel armour for the US Navy and patenting several metal alloys. Like certain Englishmen of his day he found himself in the Colonies, in his case Ceylon (now Sri Lanka), working as a tea planter. His elder brother was the well-known masonic author Albert Churchward and it is clear that James also had a deep interest in the esoteric. He had already met with the distinguished photographer and antiquarian Augustus Le Plongeon, who had made studies of the pre-Columbian ruins in South America and the pair are said to have discussed Atlantis and Mu. Le Plongeon was convinced that evidence of Freemasonry could be found within the Mayan culture, from a period long before masonry's supposed inception in the British Isles.

In his sixth decade, Churchward found himself a married man with some land, living in Connecticut, USA. Having previously authored works on big-game hunting and fishing, he turned his attention in 1926 to the more rarefied subject of the esoteric. His third book, the first title in a series about the lost land of Mu, was entitled *The Lost Continent of Mu: Motherland of Man*. This was followed by *The Children of Mu*, *The Sacred Symbols of Mu*, and *Cosmic Forces of Mu*. He also published several other volumes supporting related theories regarding the historical origins of civilisation.

In these works, Churchward advanced the theory that a lost continent lay beneath the Pacific Ocean, having sunk many thousands of years before in a great, cataclysmic deluge. He claimed that a full half of the earth's population had been wiped out in the flood and that this event was kept alive in the folk memory by the many flood myths and legends still recounted around the globe. Churchward used his considerable fortune and his erudite knowledge of geology, metallurgy, chemistry, history and archaeology to investigate his theories. He travelled widely in his quest to prove the existence of Mu and his story begins in the East.

During 1868 while serving in the Indian Raj as a British soldier helping with famine relief he befriended an Indian priest. One day this man began to talk of a collection of old clay tablets held in the temple archive and although he claimed never to have read them himself, he alluded to the fact that they were a record of the home of mankind, a land that went by the name of Mu. Churchward was more than curious, as he knew Mu was one and the same with Atlantis. His entreaties to view the tablets fell on deaf ears; the priest refused as they were considered too sacred to be seen by profane eyes. The priest did however inform him that the tablets were written in an archaic tongue that was fast dying out. He called this language 'Nacaal', named after the people who may have created them while still living in Mu.

Six months had passed since his first request and Churchward had pretty much accepted defeat as the priest had no intention of breaking his vows to protect the relics. But then, one evening while paying the priest a visit, he was taken aback to finally see the tablets laid out in front of him for his perusal. Churchward soon became an avid student of the Nacaal langauge, learning to decipher the tablets for himself. He claims in his book *The Lost Continent of Mu* that these clay tablets written in Nacaal were the genuine records of Mu. These, we are told, were one seventh of the total collection which was dispersed between other holy sites, possibly inside Burma. His task became a lifelong passion, leading him to conclude that all ancient culture as we know it came from these antediluvian forebears and that their memory echoed down the centuries through the common myths and symbology of the Great Flood. Some of his deposition is compelling and he cites a document called the *Lhasa Record* discovered by archaeologist Paul Schliemann, grandson of the celebrated Heinrich Schliemann whose discoveries included the lost city of Troy. Paul Schliemann found the object of his fame in one of the oldest monasteries in Lhasa. The document in question was not an original but a later translation and while Churchward noted that it contained some minor mistakes he was otherwise happy to part publish it as further testimony to Mu.

> *"When the star of Bal fell on the place where now is only the sky and*
> *the sea, the seven cities with their golden gates and transparent temples,*
> *quivered and shook like the leaves in a storm; and, behold, a flood of fire*
> *and smoke arose from the palaces. Agonies and cries of the multitude*
> *filled the air. They sought refuge in their temples and citadels, and*
> *the wise Mu – the Heiratic Ra Mu – arose and said to them: did I not*
> *predict all this? And the women and the men in their precious stones*
> *and shining garments lamented 'Mu save us!' […] Flames and smoke*
> *choked the words of Mu: the land and its inhabitants were torn to pieces*
> *and swallowed up by the depths."*
> – Extract from the *Lhasa Record* featured in *The Lost Continent of Mu.*

Churchward identified that the Kingdom of Mu was known by its emblematic name the Empire of the Sun. It was located in the Pacific Ocean and populated by 64 million inhabitants. He said the existence of the continent could be determined by the correct reading of the universal hieroglyphs found around the Pacific rim and beyond. Behind the folktales and legends lay an untold story of the destruction of Atlantis and its vanished, highly advanced, seafaring civilisation.

Churchward contended that survivors of the Mu disaster established sacred centres of initiates who passed knowledge down to other less advanced humans. For example he believed the Nacaals, the writers of the clay tablets he had been shown, passed their knowledge onto the Brahmins, who to this day jealously guard their high-priestly status as the elite caste of Indian society. The legendary Nacaal who hailed from Mu were, Churchward maintained, the source of all esoteric teachings and magic including the Eastern mantra 'Aum'. The Nacaal are also equated with the Naga, legends of whom populate the Asian classics such as the Mahabharata and who are regarded as sacred deities across Asia.

But Churchward did not stop there. He spoke of the high initiates of Mu that survived the global catastrophe becoming the gods of our legends. He believed that they passed on some of their secrets, including the spiritual teachings of all religions, the methods of constructing large-scale complexes such as the Egyptian and Mexican pyramids and super-advanced technologies to enable powered flight. The unfortunate aspect of all this was that the *Lhasa Record* of Paul Schliemann was a complete hoax.

When his inconvenient fact came to light, Churchward was hopelessly undermined. Needless to say, none of this impressed his colleagues in academia. But, could there be other evidence to suggest we should not draw our conclusions too hastily in writing Churchward off?

Dmu Dag, Mu Tsag (The Cord of Mu)

The original religion of Tibet, which predates the arrival of Buddhism, is known as Bon. Considered the world's oldest continuous religion, being 18,000 years old, it is often wrongly ascribed to be a form of primitive shamanism, but it is very far from being anything of the sort. To foreign eyes it can be hard to tell where Tibetan Buddhism begins and Bon ends. Tibetan artworks and deities of both traditions take on a similar aspect, but the main difference between Bon and Tibetan Buddhism is their rival approaches to the history of Tibet. Behind Bon are several layers of belief, even different forms of the religion. Some of this is allied to the original shamanistic practices of Central Asia, but local deities such as mountain spirits and nagas are also often incorporated into practice. There is also a strain of Bon that has Lamaism within it – Bon Buddhism. There are complex differences between the Old Tibetan traditionalists of Bon-po and gshen and the later aspect of Bon practiced as an organised religion. Bon and Bon-po should be regarded as very separate terms if one is to be precise. So it is not at all accurate to say that Bon equates to shamanism alone.

According to Tibetan legends its Bon kings had the power to transport themselves instantaneously to any realm using the so-called 'Cord of Mu' (Tibetan: 'dmu thag' or Bon Zhang-Zhung: 'mu tsug'). As to whether the myth suggests a movement rather like teleportation or that of actual aviation, remains an unsettled point of conjecture. This cord was said to represent Earth and heaven and when kings ascended to heaven they did so by using the Mu Cord. There is also a version of this called the mu ladder which again ascends to connect to heaven and allowed mankind's first ancestor to ascend to Earth, as featured in the legend of an ancient king called Gri Gum. It all begins to sound like Churchward revisited over again – flying transport, the origin of the human race and the name Mu.

Tibetan history states that the first seven kings were direct descendants of beings from heaven and that they retained a connection to their homeland by the dmu-thag, a cord that ran from the top of their heads to the sky. The thread has a very complex nature ascribed to it by Bon practitioners. When the kings died, they left no corpse but simply ascended to heaven via this cord. According to legend Gri Gum became first mortal king in Tibetan history, who unlike his royal forebears, chose to sever the Mu Cord and in so doing forfeited his connection with heaven above. In the tale of King Gri Gum the ruler's mind is seized by a demon which causes him to prophesy that he will die by the sword. In due course, Gri Gum challenges a lowly horse groom by the name of Lo-gnam to a dual to be held at the time of the constellation of Arcturus and Alpha Librae. Prior to the death-match, the wily horse groom confided in a royal aide, telling him that the king's victory would be assured if he followed certain magical instructions. On the day of the dual the king was to wear a black turban and hang a mirror on his brow. He must also drape a fox corpse over one shoulder and a dog corpse on the other and avail himself of 100 red oxen and cows carrying dust. Should these instructions be carried out to the letter, the horse groom said, then he would be no match for the monarch. Upon hearing this from his spy, King Gri Gum is persuaded to follow these outlandish plans. Dressed accordingly and with a retinue of dusty cattle in tow, the monarch went into combat with his foe. As the dual commenced, Lo-gnam let out a whistle causing the oxen and cows follow him, and a wind whipped up scattering the dust everywhere, blinding the king. The king's protector spirits resting on his head and shoulders were rendered useless by the animal corpses and the black turban, and as he swung his sword in combat King Gri Gum unwittingly sliced through the Mu Cord that connected him to heaven.

Thus the king became mortal in one fell swoop. An arrow from Lo-gnam's bow dispatched the king, whose lifeless body plunged into a river. The victorious horse groom claimed the king's throne as his own and in a final indignity to the slain monarch, Lo-gnam married his opponent's widow and appointed her as his own horse groom. However the Tibetan Naga spirits called 'Klu' who resided in the river had other ideas and carried the body of the deceased king to a mountain top. Eventually the scheming horse groom Lo-gnam was killed by poisoning with the hair of a white dog. In time, the widow's son, Ngar-la-skyes, who was also begat by a mountain god, went in search of his step-brothers and the deposed heirs to the throne, whereupon he recovered the king's body.

This folk tale is one of the better-known Tibetan myths and is subject to variation according to where it is told. Oddly it echoes a lot of what Churchward might have said and we should note that the king's son bears the name Ngar or Naga. The name is researched in an academic paper by one Mr Dotson who takes note of the different spelling of Ngar-la-skyes and how the meaning is rendered in various ways in doing so. In one rendition of the name Ngar sos po – the meaning is given as 'self-nourished' and is important in the lexical understanding of Tibetan myths, as this suggests a magical child.

Returning to the Mu Cord once again the term is used mundanely inside houses and tents today, it refers to the hole through which smoke from the central fire exits skyward. It is also name given to the line that holds the ubiquitous prayer flags of Tibet. 'Dmu thag' as a word means 'heavenly rope' but in its earlier form Mu, the etymology changes to a 'heavenly god'. Because the words 'thag' and 'vjav', meaning 'rainbow' have been linked, it begins to explain the Tibetan Buddhist reverence towards the rainbow and the efforts made to obtain a 'rainbow body' as a sign of enlightenment.

Many spiritual traditions mention the 'body of light' – the Diamond Vehicle or Body of Vajrayana, the 'body of bliss' in Yoga and so on. Dzogchen practices in Buddhism see the attainment of the rainbow body to be the 'Jalu' – a body of pure light as was accomplished by Trungpa, whom we encountered in Chapter 3. What differs in Bon practice to the above is the historical perceptions of the Mu Cord and its spiritual implications. Within the modern Buddhist Kingdom of Bhutan the practitioners of Bon engage in a ritual technique called 'Phywa' or 'Srid-pa'i'. It is little known, as the kingdom is so isolated to foreign travel and documentation that few outsiders have experienced it, but essentially it is used to build a spiritual connection to heaven using cords of light.

These practices are exclusively clustered in the Eastern Himalayas of Bhutan. Bon priests employing these techniques believe in the deities often classified as Phywa who reside in heaven and while they are connected to the Earth by the Cord of Mu, but it is important to understand that they may never dwell there. Those priests assigned to make contact with heaven are usually hereditary initiates who follow strict lifestyles and certain taboos. Part of this knowledge involves holding the 'rabs', or rites, concerning communion with the ancestral spirits that involve ritual chanting made in unison with specific gestures.

In these rites, the priest ascends through as many as thirteen different levels of heaven so that they may accompany the spirit deity and bring it down to Earth, whereupon secrets are learned, powers bestowed and general benefits gained before the spirit is sent back to heaven at the ritual's conclusion. What makes this practice different from the spirit journeys of shamans who perform similar feats in other cultures is that this involves a verbal journey, not soul travel or an ecstatic trance state, or under the influence of hallucinogens. Another unusual aspect of the Phywa or Srid-pa'i is the connection between the mythological figures mentioned in the rabs and their ancestral connection with the contemporary priest performing the ritual, ascending and descending the cords of light.

Perhaps if the much-maligned Churchward had encountered the example above instead of relying on Paul Schliemann's discredited *Lhasa Record* then his academic reputation may have been quite different. It is recorded that in the Bon tradition one of the royal tribes is the Mu-Shen or dmu-gshen from which Tonpa Shenrab – the Bon equivalent of Buddha – is descended. Dmu-geshen is the name of the clan, but it also translates as Zhang Zang: Mu-Shen: soul of Mu or in Tibetan: priest of Mu. Therefore the name of the Chinese immortal goddess Wang-Mu, might just be the tenuous link some have been looking for?

Yangdrung – The Eternal Bon

The tribe of Mu settled in the Tibetan plateau thousands of years ago with a view to bringing with them the teachings of their spiritual teacher Tonpa Shenrab – note the title 'Shen' or gshen. The type of Bon they practiced was the older Tibetan worship and not the more organised Bon practices we know today. According to tradition the Mu tribe, like their spiritual leader, come from a Shambhala-like paradise called Olmolungring. Here in this utopia, godlike beings resided practicing the teachings of Tonpa Shenrab who ascended the throne in 16,027BC. He took his teachings into Tibet, colonising and establishing an important Bon centre at Mount Kailash. It was here that the famous teaching of the Dzogchen purportedly originated.

Other elements of the Mu tribe also reached high spiritual status such as the Guribs. They produced several historic saints and holy figures and had the sense to preserve the manuscripts of the teachings of the monk Ozer, which have recently resurfaced. The text contains a curious reference to the origins of the clan; "We are the clan of Gurib, are not like others, we are emanated from the god of effulgence thus we are radically distinguished from others."

Their own folk tales recount that the Gurib descend from Mu Yangje who descended from heaven to marry a mortal. The Mu tribe were also on hand to assist the rites of other tribes who requested access to their deities. At this early period direct communion with the spirits through the use of mirrors would have been a likely service provided. It is clear that the tribe of Mu held a special status in these royal bloodlines of the clans. According to the Bon lineages Tonpa Shenrab descended five generations from Mes-po dMu-phyug sKyer-zhon who spawned the Royal Mu lineage.

Tonpa Shenrab was born in Olmolungring and he became the teacher of Bon. He enjoyed various incarnations in different places emanating as Dzam-bu-gling in India, Bal-po in Nepal, Kha-che in Kashmir, Li-yul in Khotan, Mi-nyag in China and in various guises in now defunct kingdoms of the region too many to list here, or in the modern world better known as Shenrab Miwoche (Tonpa Shenrab). The etymology of Olmolungring is instructive: 'ol' means unborn, 'mo' undetermined, 'lung' belongs to the prophecies of Shenrab and 'ring' denotes compassion. It would have been easy to write about Olmolungring in the section explaining Shambhala as the two concepts are almost interchangeable, both are mythic far-off lands out of time and space populated by indestructible, enlightened practitioners working for the benefit of mankind. Yet, it is important to separate the two, as Olmolungring needs its own explanation as it belongs to the Bon tradition.

Let us simplify things. As Olmolungring means 'the long valley of Olmo', it has both an ethereal existence and an actual existence being located in its latter form in the land of Tazig, located to the north and the west of Tibet. Some have posited that this fabled land occupied modern-day Tajikistan. Practitioners of Bon say that even the physical aspect of the sanctuary is invisible to the ordinary man, even though it occupies a third of our known world.

The concept is not an easy one for the Western mind to grasp. The other aspect of Olmolungring in its otherworldly, ethereal aspect is that like Shambhala it is only accessible to those who are enlightened or favoured by pious virtue or blessed karma. It is populated by those who command the secrets of all esoteric teachings and knowledge, especially the Eternal Bon called Yangdrung. In Bon lore representations of its mythical landscape show this holy sanctuary as being composed of a sacred mountain which is the centre of all things in the universe, from the foot of which flow four special rivers. Each river contains a rock representing the shape of a specific animal, these being the lion, horse, peacock and elephant.

Painted mandalas of the magical kingdom share a common theme, but the design differs in the Buddhist and Bon versions. Buddhist mandalas show an inner and outer kingdom but Bon has three concentric worlds: the outer, middle and inner. The Buddhist mandalas are generally round with the king and his entourage featuring heavily, obscuring the sacred mountain to some degree, while in the square Bon paintings the sacred mountain is alone and majestic. These are significant numerological differences that may not be noticeable upon first inspection, but certainly are not lost on those practicing. One of the names for the king of Shambhala is the 'King of Three Worlds', which makes the Bon version closer to describing that condition than its Buddhist counterpart.

Another curious feature is the focus on the number eight in Buddhism, whereas the older religion Bon focused on the number with a central space, totalling nine. These are the nine ways of Bon and are closely associated with the swastika symbol which is stacked nine times to form a crystal mountain in the shape of a pyramid called Yungdrung Gutsen. The four rivers coming off this mountain also equate with the four cardinal directions of the swastika's arms. In Bon the swastika symbol is associated with the diamond, a stone with indestructible or everlasting attributes, which in turn also equates with the word 'Yangdrung' – meaning 'eternal'.

The location of the holy mountain in the centre of the universe has been the subject of debate for some time now, with scholars in various camps offering their favoured potential sites. Mount Kailash is often mentioned, as four rivers emanate from its foot and it has been depicted as the most likely site for Olmolungring. Kailash is also identified with the sacred symbol of the swastika. Bonpos however seem to disagree on this explanation for theological considerations although they still revere the spot, albeit for entirely different reasons – the worship of a deity called Me Ri. Bon texts are specific that the Olmolungring sacred mountain was found at the middle of an ancient kingdom, now defunct, called Zhang-Zhung. Yet again we are drawn one step closer to the fabled places frequented by the masters. Gurdjieff scattered some clues where one of the ancient founts of esoteric knowledge is found and it was a physical place anyone could find.

Chapter 5

Beating Hearts
of the Masters

"Without questioning a wise person,
One cannot measure their depth.
Without striking a drum with a stick,
One cannot distinguish it from other drums."
Sakaya Pandita

Padmasambhava: The Lotus Born, Guru Rinpoche
Gurdjieff mentions a 'Saint Lama' in his writings and there is no doubt at all he is referring to a real historical figure. The lama in question hailed from what we now know as Pakistan and is credited with founding Tibetan Buddhism. His entry into Tibet via India during the 8th Century brought with him a mission to transform men through enlightenment and it is a further clue to the origins of Gurdjieff's own teachings that he points towards this great teacher, who was himself a representative of the inner circle of masters sent on a mission to deliver a new teaching. This great lama crossed the mighty Himalayas headed for Zhang-Zhung. His name, Padmasambhava, literally 'the Lotus Born', was undoubtedly a mystic of gargantuan proportions. Gurdjieff said there were five major religious doctrines but in the case of Buddhism he made a distinction, referencing normal Buddhism and Tibetan Buddhism, the latter he called Lamaism.

Before we discuss the ancient kingdom of Zhang-Zhung, a place imbued with mystical history, perhaps we should look at four of the main spiritual teachers and their roles during the final stages of Zhang-Zhang, with its ultimate bearing on the struggle for dominance between Tibetan Buddhism and the Bon lineage. Padmasambhava, also known as Guru Rinpoche (Precious Guru), travelled to Tibet at the invitation of the Tibetan King Detsen, who provided a retinue of 108 translators for the task of translating the Dharma from Sanskrit to Tibetan. Padmasambhava was, and still is, revered as the saint who seeded Buddhism in Tibet, but there is another more unorthodox history regarding the great saint, which is both heretical and esoteric. Gurdjieff may have touched upon this in his writings, in a style redolent of his tales of the masters and their secret methods of transmission, where teachers go to great length to obscure, or even hide, their doctrines.

That Padmasambhava was a Tantric master is generally agreed. Where the story starts to deviate from the 'official' account is that Padmasambhava may have been involved in the Bon religion. There can be no doubt that Tibetan Buddhism is radically different from the types of Buddhism practised in Thailand or Southern India, for example. Lamaism, to use Gurdjieff's term, combines aspects of Tantra with the worship of nature spirits, shamanistic deities, mountain sprites and so on, to the point where it certainly does cross over into what one might consider to be Bon. According to some traditions, the Buddhism that Padmasambhava brought to Tibet was actually a carefully disguised version of Bon. This subterfuge allowed for the preservation of the esoteric teachings of Tibet, countering the possible resistance that would likely have arisen among certain Bon clans and nobility. The introduction of Lamaism therefore presented a more palatable form of Buddhism – one which was, at the very least, partially familiar to the Tibetans of the time. To this day in Tibet, Bon and orthodox Buddhist histories disagree on many points surrounding Padmasambhava's mission. The first attempt at establishing Buddhism in Tibet failed after King Detsen died and his people returned to practicing Bon once more. The period is described by Buddhists as a dark age in the country's history. This religious vacuum and uncertainty left a power struggle for the hearts and minds of the Tibetan court.

Most hagiographies assert that Padmasambhava, regarded as a second Buddha, came from the Swat Valley in modern-day Pakistan (in antiquity called Oddiyana), born of noble birth. His standing inside the semi-mythical histories of the region cannot be underestimated, as illustrated in this quote from the Muktinath Foundation:

"In order to propagate and spread the teachings of the Dharma in general, and particularly the secret mantra and Dzogchen teachings, he appears to every being of the three thousand billion world systems in a form to benefit them according to their personal karmic vision. In this way Guru Padmasambhava has countless unimaginable biographies, one biography for each being."

We shall attempt another somewhat more straightforward hagiography here, based on compilations of his life story dating from the 14th Century. In these writings it is said that a beautiful red lotus appeared one day on Lake Danashokar and that upon one petal the syllable 'HRI' appeared before dissolving into pure light, whereafter a fully developed eight-year-old child appeared. Padmasambhava self-manifested from this lotus flower, hence his later title 'Lotus Born'. It should be noted that Lake Danashokar is refreshed from its source, the holy Mount Kailash.

Having been immediately installed as a Prince of the court by his royal adoptees, Padmasambhava began to yearn for a return to the ways of enlightenment. He requested to be relieved of his royal duties but his pleas met with refusal. It is told that one day while dancing on a rooftop, he dropped the trident he was carrying, which fell and killed a child below. This unfortunate incident led to his banishment from the royal court in shame. Freed from his responsibilities, he went on to marry a Dakini of great renown by the name of Prabhavati, but later in his Tantric story other consorts are mentioned.

He was also attached to Yeshi and most prominently and frequently to an Indian Princess called Mandavrava, who hailed from Zohar (Himachal Pradesh). She, like Padmasambhava, had renounced her privileged life in order to follow a spiritual calling. Her father the king, being incensed by the behaviour of his daughter and the antics of Padmasambhava, had the pair burnt on a pyre. Expecting to find nothing but ashes the king discovered, to his surprise, that his daughter and her new lover had survived destruction by fire and were subsequently found on a lotus floating on a lake. The lovers continued to practice Tantra in a cave located in Nepal and both attained the Vajra body of enlightenment as a result. The standard biography reiterates that Padmasambhava was an accomplished Tantric master living in India who upon invitation of the Tibetan Emperor Detsen, came to the country as a translator of Buddhist texts, bringing with him the first direct knowledge of the Dharma, including the Secret Mantra. He is said to have expelled demons from every corner of Tibet and founded the first monasteries in the country. His biography however does have certain aspects that are disputed or questioned.

Scholars such as Herbert Guenther have called into question Padmasambhava's origin in the place known as Oddiyana. Written records describe him simply as a 'foreigner'. Another location for the birthplace of Padmasambhava is Balkh in modern-day Afghanistan. Such was the secrecy observed by the Tibetan authorities of the time with regard to Padmasambhava and his esoteric knowledge, that it might almost appear similar to the way in which modern intelligence communities guard their own information. There have even been suggestions that the Padmasambhava legend is a kind of compendium of different personages, with a view to personify his divinity. Padmasambhava remains deified to this day for his contribution to Tibetan Buddhism and is one of the only examples among the exalted masters of the country who employed Indian Tantric practices, yet there is confusion surrounding how some of his teachings were disseminated. Here may be found vital clues to the activities of the Masters of wisdom, the so-called hidden directorate, and possibly a greater perspective may be gained as to the methods employed in the transmission of such teachings.

As first suggested in Chapter 1 with Gurdjieff's tale of Lama G, Padmasambhava founded his own order called the Nyingma or 'red hat' lamas, and it is believed Gurdjieff himself may have had contact with the same Vajrayana school. As for the Dzogchen teachings, these were taken from Oddiyana, the supposed place of Padmasambhava's birth. The Dzogchen Tantra teachings are known as 'The Ancient Ones' and what is significant here is that these mystical tenets are found in the other major religion of the region in the 'Nine Ways' of Bon. Therefore, we may conclude that Padmasambhava was not only a Buddhist teacher but a learned master, well-versed in a hybrid of different mystical systems. Depending on which history one reads, his alleged opposite number at the time within Bon was a great sage and greatly feared magician. If one looks closely at events unfolding around him, one suspects that the official history is expedient but there is a feeling of the hidden hand of the masters who secretly sought to advance the Bon cause in the midst of a wave of enforced religious conversion.

Drenpa Namkha – the Great Gyerpung of Bon

Tibetan history is deeply divided on the role of the man known as Drenpa Namkha. To the practising Bonpo he is considered a great sage, while the Buddhist perception of his legacy perhaps seems slightly tainted. What is important is to look between the lines and understand the importance of his legacy in preserving the world's oldest religion inside Tibet.

'Gyerpung' is a Bon honorific, which in Tibetan is 'Lachen', meaning 'Great Lama'. In Bon history there exists a mighty figure, the Bon magician Drenpa Namkha, who became known as the 'Great Guru' and is considered a major figure in the tradition. Gyerpung Namkha is one of the first Bon luminaries who is not a mythical figure but is actually known to have existed, who played a key role during a pivotal moment in both Tibetan Buddhist and Bon history and development. Greatly respected or feared, depending on which side one is on, Gyerpung Namkha was the greatest Bon magical practitioner of his day and may have acted in several ways to preserve his tradition from extinction, including his conversion to Buddhism. It is this last aspect that makes his name so controversial, forcing a clear historical distinction between the two paths.

Born near Mount Kailash, the great Namkha obtained valuable education while still young, gaining knowledge of the teachings via eight different Bon masters. He quickly became fully realised, going onto understand Dzogchen, Sutra and Tantric practices. His iconography shows him holding the symbol of Eternal Bon, the Yundrung Chakshing, a double-headed wand with the swastika at either end. His name means 'Recollection-Sky' and in murals he is often depicted as a blue-skinned, god-like figure. Drenpa Namkha married Oden Barma ('od ldan 'bar ma), a lady born of high-cast Indian parentage who produced twins, both remarkable in their own right; Pema Tongdrol who went onto become a notorious magician and his brother Tsewang Rigdzin, who led an unusually long life. Both are canonised by the Bon religion. It was said that Namkha and his wife split, each taking a son with them. Namkha took Rigdzin who grew up in a magical retreat whereas his mother and brother Pema Tongdrol lived with a royal couple who could not produce babies. Here Pema spent his time practicing magic and was greatly feared during his lifetime.

The Bonpo equate Pema alongside Padmasambhava in their religious pantheon, in fact there are some schools of thought within Bon who suggest that the two personages are one and the same individual.

Gyerpung Namkha enjoys three portmanteau identities and they are: Tazig Drenpa Namkha, Zhang-Zhung Drenpa Namkha and the third is the Tibetan Bökyi Drenpa Namkha. As Tazig Drenpa Namkha he is born of a lotus, rather like Padmasambhava, but his birthplace in this case is given as Zhang-Zhung. The word Namkha is a form of the Hindu Siddhe (or Siddhi), meaning 'attainment' which implies his attainment and possession of mystical powers. Lastly he is the Namkha of historical repute who is considered the saviour of Bon and preserver of many important religious treasures whose unearthing centuries later is considered the result of the action of a great teacher.

Despite attempts to place Bon at the heart of the Buddhism of Padmasambhava, there were many in the Tibetan royal court who were less than impressed by the annexation of Bon by the incoming foreign religion. One such was the chief wife of the slain Bon King Lig-mi-rhya, who sought deadly revenge upon King Detsen for inviting Buddhism into the country. She summoned the great Bon magician Gyerpung Namkha who arrived to find the enraged wife of the murdered king had prepared much finery and feasting for his reception.

A special tent of white cloth embellished with paintings of deer was erected upon an island on a lake in honour of the Bon priest. A lavish throne laden with nine heavy silk quilts was set inside and offerings of chang (rice beer) and nine savoury dishes were prepared. The grieving wife lamented over the kingdom of Zhang-Zhung's destruction at the hands of the treacherous Detsen and the withering away of the religion of the Eternal Bon. In response Namkha suggested the remedy to avenge the murder of King Li-mi-rhya was to perform the 'bTso', a Bon curse which literally translates as 'bomb'. To this end, the magician Namkha set to work, undertaking a ritual from inside the tent over the course of one week. The resultant bomb spell was placed on a piece of gold that was then divided into three pieces. At sunset he hurled the first piece into a lake, which immediately dried up, causing the serpent spirits (Klu) that dwelled there to flee. During the night he hurled the second piece of the gold at a mountain, killing three deer and paralysing another five. The final piece he flung at the castle 'Tiger Peak' belonging to King Detsen, causing him great sickness.

The ailing Tibetan king immediately suspected a Bon plot involving the infamous bomb curse. In his desperation, King Detsen sent out one hundred horsemen carrying a yak's horn of gold dust to find the Gyerpung responsible. Coming across a shepherd the king's party asked for news of the Great Gyperpung and were told that he was ensconced in a white tent surrounded by a lake. The horseman were advised that the Gyerpung could change shape and there was no guaranteeing what form he would assume on their arrival.

With that the horsemen went in search of Gyerpung Namkha. Upon finding him at the tent, negotiations for his surrender began, starting with the offer of gold. The Bon magus Namkha struck a bargain, stipulating that four demands be met in return for reversing his curse on the king. These were: firstly, that the Bon religion would not be suppressed; second that a golden shrine be erected in memory of the dead King Li-mi-rhya which would house the holy symbol of Bon – the swastika; third, that the Guirib family (an off-shoot of the Mu tribe) would sit at King Detsen's right hand and be exempt from state taxes. His fourth and final condition was that a form of restitution for the loss of King Li-mi-rhya would be settled. An agreement was struck and Namkha, true to his word, reversed the curse and Detsen was restored to good health. In return the four wishes of the Bon priest were honoured.

The Bon/Buddhist spat did not end there however, with King Detsen going on to sponsor a two-year debate between Buddhist and Bon scholars as to whether the country should adopt one or the other as its state religion. King Detsen, despite his obvious grab for power was something of a Renaissance man in some respects, having commissioned the translation of the Sanskrit Buddhist texts into Tibetan with the aid of Padmasambhava and the 108 translators.

Also, during his reign he encouraged a Buddhist scholar called Shantarakshita to introduce the monastic system into Tibet and dispatched a deputation to investigate the Korean teachings of Kim Hwasang in Chan Buddhism. Detsen seemed to have left no stone unturned in his search for the true teachings that would benefit his subjects, yet Tibetan history remains sharply divided on his legacy. To Buddhists, Detsen is one of the three Dharma-kings who brought Buddhism to Tibet; while the Bonpo regard King Detsen as a villainous and immoral character who destroyed the Bon lineage of Zhang-Zhung.

Tibet had swallowed up the kingdom of Zhang-Zhung under Detsen and now the king had to decide what religion the state should endorse – would it be the old ways of Bon or the newer teachings of Buddhism? A lot was at stake here, as the losers would be banished from the land or expected to commit suicide so that they might reincarnate under more favourable circumstances, while those who did not comply could expect even worse. Buddhism as the new state religion required allegiance from the Tibetan population in something approaching Europe's Holy Inquisition. The debate had found in Buddhism's favour and conversion was now a requirement, with non-compliance punishable by death or exile. It seemed that at least one of the demands made by Namkha had been rescinded by King Detsen – the ways of Bon would be suppressed after all.

In 761AD, Detsen and his Tibetan court converted to Buddhism. What followed was a decision on the type of Buddhism that would be adopted as the state religion. The two-year-long state debate called the 'Council of Lhasa', which took place far away from the capital inside Samye, the first Buddhist monastery in Tibet, reached a crescendo as religious heavyweights such as the celebrated Vairocana appeared before Detsen to put forward their case. The decision based on these arguments was to follow a gradual patient journey to enlightenment through Buddhist Dharma, as opposed to the sudden realisation school akin to Japanese Zen teachings. Korean Chan Buddhism, from which Zen derives, was rejected in favour of the teachings of Indian masters such as Shantarakshita and Padmasambhava.

It would seem rather obvious that what happened back in Zhang-Zhung and the sudden, violent unfolding of events affecting teachers such as Padmasambhava and Namkha required equally swift political manoeuvres in order to survive the times. Looking at the actions of the Bon and Buddhist spiritual masters, we can see that these were not made purely in the light of tradition or faith but as strategic chess moves made by high initiates with a long-term mission in view. While they may well have worn the outward mantle of dogma, in this case Tibetan Buddhism falling in line with the despotic ruler Detsen, there was another entirely different raison d'être, one carefully concealed from the profane. It is clear to see if one looks deeply into the affair that Bon, Tantra and Buddhism were prepared to exchange teachings, bending to the winds of change so that they may continue to spread enlightenment, regardless of the external conditions brought to bear around them. King Detsen made his choice of Buddhism but had he not done so, would it have made any difference if Padmasmbhava and Namkha had changed their outward or exoteric roles of converter to converted?

Like true agents of the mythical Shambhala, the hidden directorate were not overly concerned with the transient wishes of King Detsen, but had their own agenda it seems, a long-term plan to further the cause of enlightenment and to promote the esoteric teachings of Dzogchen, Sutra and Tantra, regardless of who sponsored their transmission. If Buddhism was to be the 'official' chosen vehicle to bring the teachings, they adopted it to fit their mission. The actions of Namkha at his conversion from Bon to Buddhism are pregnant with meaning. He shaved his head of long hair with a blade of gold, refusing the help of the Buddhist lamas about him and then much to their apparent disgust he self-initiated himself into to their religion. The words of the Great Lama Namkha leave us in no doubt as to his true thoughts on the conversion, for he stated that there was no difference between Buddhism and Bon, save only on the level of relative truths. It could be interpreted that Namkha saw only one universal truth, beyond the mantle of all religious dogma.

The Mysterious Kingdom of Zhang-Zhung

Zhang-Zhung was a pre-Buddhist civilisation that existed in Western and Northern Tibet approximately 4,000 years ago. Although relatively unknown to most Westerners, this kingdom is a cornerstone in the mystical legacy of the Roof of the World due to its great antiquity, power and influence. It is recognised as the cradle of one of its main religions – Bon. Covering approximately 6,000 square miles, it is home to a great many temple complexes, forts and other archaeological and historical sites of interest. Zhang-Zhung had its own language by the same name and it is here that the Bon religion first flourished. Due to its obscure origins the history of Zhang-Zhung lies in four tribes (in some accounts there were six), including the Mu tribe that we have already mentioned. The founding of the illustrious kingdom was said to be by non-humans. These primordial rulers were semi-divine in nature or even at times the powerful spirits found in nature, such as the Klu who rescued the body of the deceased Gri-Gum in the last chapter, ruled Zhang-Zhung, according to the mythical histories. This leadership of the Klu then fell into the hands of the so-called Ma-sangs, a race described as almost, or nearly, human. Tibetan historian Chogyal Norbu says of them, "…it is therefore that their appearance coincided with the advent of humankind."

Norbu identifies the point at which Zhang-Zhung came to be ruled by humans as when the rulers begin to use the term Mi, meaning 'human' in their names.

Zhang-Zhung sprang up west of Kailash, with its capital city being Khyung-lung. Tibetan conquerors overcame the Land of Zhang-Zhung in 645AD according to historian R.A. Stein. Zhang-Zhung was a vast region and at the height of its powers ruled at least 18 kingdoms, so it was a good prize by any standards. Without the presence of precise records its history remains disputed, including key events. Not aiding this is the fact that Bon and Buddhist histories often depict the same events but draw different conclusions from them. Any character can be celebrated as a hero in one religion and yet vilified in another. Some sources suggest that Zhang-Zhung was not made up of 18 kingdoms but was in actual fact a confederation of 18 chieftains ruled by one leader. With such paucity of written records we are largely reliant on Bon material to fill in the gaps of what is known. But it is here in the Kingdom of Zhang-Zhung that Tonpa Shenrab instructed others in his path and Bon blossomed. Oral traditions taken from the Bon religion tell us of one of the monarchs that ruled the kingdom was Lig-mi-rhya. From this account it showed that the military strength of the mysterious land was far superior to its neighbours such as Tibet, with Zhang-Zhung possessing nearly four times the troop numbers, standing at close to 100,000 men. This did not save the people of Zhang-Zhung from Tibetan political ambitions and through acts of subterfuge the reigning Tibetan King Detsen and his ministers managed to lure the mighty Li-mi-rhya to his death and to seize his throne.

The treacherous plot was first hatched by inveigling the youngest of Lig-mi-rhya's three wives, an 18 year-old called Nan-dron-lek-ma, to accept a Tibetan proposal to waylay the king in an unguarded moment. She agreed to the plot in return for a yak horn of gold dust and the promise of a large portion of land after the murder of her husband took place. The Tibetan assassins placed themselves inside a cave on the top of a narrow mountain pass and lay in wait for the king of Zhang-Zhung. Seizing their moment, the Tibetans pounced on Lig-mi-rhya and his personal guard who had thinned out on the icy narrow pass and a swift arrow felled the king. After the regicide Zhang-Zhung was leaderless and the Tibetans lay hold of his throne and his lands. So fell the mighty Zhang-Zhung.

Vairocana

Once the new Buddhist Tibet was underway, Padmasambhava transmitted the secret mantra to Namkha, who in return passed on some of his secrets, but essentially we understand that the former was master to the latter. Surrounding himself with 25 pupils (26 if you include Pamasambhava) he passed on the teachings of the Dzogchen, whose spiritual homeland was Oddiyana. Having said this Dzogchen or the 'Great Perfection' was composed of three elements – the Tantra of Primal Spontaneity, the Tantra of Primeval Purity and the Great Tantra. The last section of practices was banned under Detsen. Because of this unusual situation Padmasambhava buried some of these texts (better known in Tibet as treasures) in order to preserve the teaching in its whole form. The Bon and Buddhist histories vary at this juncture, which brings us to a Tantric student of Padmasambhava, a translator named Vairocana, who was to play a pivotal role in the spread of the teachings.

Identified at the court as an exceptionally gifted young man, Vairocana was sent to study at the first monastery Samye, where he is said to have reached enlightenment after years of study. Later in life he was dispatched to Oddiyana by King Detsen to retrieve certain Tantric secrets. He returned with various Tantric teachings which is why today Buddhists regard the Dzogchen as an intrinsic part of their own tradition. The Bonpo however, point out that according to their records, a twelfth-generation member of the Tonpa Shenrab lineage by the name of Garab was a Tantric practitioner and since he could lay claim to a direct link the founder of Bon himself, it is they who were the true guardians of these esoteric teachings, and who were responsible for bringing Dzogchen teachings to Tibet.

It is clear during this period of great uncertainty that despite his apparent conversation, Namkha and his Bon cohorts were busy burying their own treasures. We are told in the Bon version of the story that on his return, Vairocana collaborated with Namkha to preserve the Bon heritage from destruction. According to Bon sources, Namkha modified the Bon teachings to bring them in line with Buddhist thought and then passed these onto his acolyte Vairocana.

Vairocana translated Bon texts and passed them onto the king and managed to gain influence in royal circles at a time when Bon and Tantra were not overly popular. He was not without enemies, however, and some ministers pressed the king for his exit. Their entreaties met with refusal until the great translator spurned the advances of the wife of Detsen, Queen Margyen, who in her frustration saw to it that Vairocana was sent into exile. Detsen sent his own son to Bhutan because he had too many connections with Bon and Vairocana was the son's tutor. The implosion of Zhang-Zhung had left pockets of esoteric Bon teachings inside Tibet, Nepal, Bhutan and elsewhere, with questions hanging over allegiances and provenances. What or whose side these masters were actually on has become somewhat muddied by time, exacerbated by petty squabbles over which version of history is correct. It is quite possible that this dichotomy in histories came to pass as a result of the masters working for both sides – Buddhist and Bon.

The conversion of Namkha is highly suspect, and then again Padmasambhava's acceptance of the suppression of the Great Tantra is another troubling question; we cannot know whether he agreed with this, but we do know his student Vairocana was rumoured to be concealing Bon treasures with in collusion with Namkha. Vairocana was a most esoteric translator and an erudite scholar who had travelled widely, studying under some Masters of great renown; in China alone he visited at least 19 different teachers to learn all he could. His work in translating the esoteric teachings was second to none concerning itself with dissolving the body into light. Upon his passing it was said Vairocana left no physical body but simply dissolved into rainbow light.

Tonpa Shenrab

Born in Zhang-Zhung, some say the mystical sanctuary of Olmolungring itself, was the enlightened father of Bon – Tonpa Shenrab, a towering figure in the Roof of the World histories. A direct descendent of the Mu tribe, Tonpa Shenrab taught the path of Bon and is regarded to this day as commensurate in status to the Buddha among the adherents of the Bon tradition. The teachings of Shenrab diverged from the traditional 'Old Bon', which was shamanistic in its approach and often revolved around blood sacrifices to appease negative spirits or demons, with practitioners calling upon the aid of the gods. With the arrival of Tonpa Shenrab the old practices were reformed and blood sacrifices were condemned. Tonpa Shenrab's 'Eternal Bon' focused on a nine-stage path with an emphasis on remembering the impermanence of life and the everlasting qualities of the soul. These practices separated Lha-Chos (divine) and Mi-Chos (human) conventions.

The Yandrung or Eternal Bon is in its Sanskrit rendering the Swastika Dharma, the ancient symbol of the solar cross, which corresponds due to its indestructible nature, to the diamond Vajra path.

Two biographies remain of Tonpa Shenrab, *Dho Zermig* and *Dho Due*. He married and had children but the age of 31 he shaved his hair and became an ascetic, abandoning his former life as a royal family member and giving away his wealth to the poor. As a result of his renunciation of materialism he pleased the Enlightened Ones who blessed him with robes and objects of faith that fell from the sky. At one point during his life a demon stole his horses and made off to Tibet with the stolen booty. Tonpa followed in pursuit and caught up with the demon at the Kongpo valley, where he defeated and converted his adversary using the teachings of Bon.

Today Mount Kongpo is revered by Bon pilgrims who circumambulate around it counterclockwise to receive supplication. Mount Kongpo has several caves dedicated to Tonpa Shenrab and a special stone at its centre called 'The Heart of Kuntu Zangpo'. While there, Shenrab also reformed local shamanistic practices and introduced a placebo offering in the form of ritualised ransom which replaced blood sacrifices used to ward off bad luck, illness, pestilence and the like. He stayed here for three years teaching the people of Tibet astrology, medicine and methods of psychic defence against negative influences through spiritual practice. Throughout his life Shenrab instructed the people in new practices to help perfect themselves in this life towards liberation. Shenrab returned to Olmolungring at the age of 82, after proclaiming his wish to demonstrate the nature of impermanence. His teachings were continued by his siblings, who continued to spread the Eternal Bon throughout Zhang-Zhung.

Some essential differences between Bon and Tibetan Buddhism are not always apparent as they appear to overlap in so many areas. However, to the trained eye the two religions are quite separate in their respective outlooks. For instance, the circumambulation of mountains – the Bon go counterclockwise, while the Buddhists go clockwise, and this also follows with the use of the swastika symbol – with the Bon version the arms going to the left while the Buddhist variant turns to the right. Tibetan Buddhism tends to be more monastic in focus than Bon, whereas feminine deities are more prominent in the Bon cosmology. However, the biggest difference between the religions is the notion of karma, which is a large part of the Buddhist philosophy, but not so important to the Bon, who ascribe ones actions to deities and spirits of place or circumstance. The two, as said in an earlier chapter, have compared notes and swapped ideas over the millennia in the melting pot of ideas that is the Roof of the world. Tantra, Sutra, Dharma, Yoga, Shamanism, Animism, Buddhism, and more besides – all have been examined and, it may be argued, assimilated into the Bon tradition. Tibetan Buddhism is no different. Tonpa Shenrab is also Buddha Shenrab, being a highly respected figure across the region and thanks to Padmasambhava these sacred Bon teachings were assimilated into Lamaism. And so it is that the world's oldest religion and its 18,000 years of wisdom have reached us today.

Gurdjieff understood Padmasambhava the Lotus born was pivotal to understanding the transmission of the oldest teachings. By introducing him in his writings in a codified form, he was releasing important information which would be necessary to transform the planet.

Chapter 6

Children of the Magi

"All roads lead back to Balkh."
G.I. Gurdjieff

Secrets of the Bon – the Persian Connection

In his mind-boggling magnum opus, *Beelzebub's Tales to his Grandson*, Gurdjieff introduces his readers to 'Saint Lama', who we now know as Padmasambhava. Also namechecked are 'Saint Buddha' and 'Saint Jesus', both fairly obvious, but there is yet another great teacher whom he calls 'Ashieta Shiemash'. But who is this enlightened master and for what reason is he brought to our attention? Gurdjieff said he liked to 'bury the bone' when discussing esoteric knowledge, so once again we must dig.

The task of unpicking the lineage of the saintly Padamasambhava as outlined in the last chapter can be highly confusing. Padmasambhava carried with him the Dzogchen or 'diamond vehicle' – a semi-heretical teaching considered the most esoteric of Tantras and the ninth, or highest, aspect of Bon. The Dzogchen school is said to have received its original transmission by means of a deity that possessed a young boy named Gharab Dorje, who passed the lineage onto a disciple called Manjisrimtra. Some centuries later the aspiring pupil Padmasambhava was inducted into the same Dzogchen school. Yet confusingly we are told that Padmasambhava received his teaching directly from the first lineage holder Gharab Dorje, who at that point had been dead for hundreds of years. Whether Gharab appeared to Padmasambhava as a reincarnated tulku or as a deity is impossible to say. Being keen to preserve the Dzogchen teachings for future generations, Padmasambhava and his twenty-five pupils buried them upon Mount Gomposhar and it was these writings that were eventually unearthed by the red hat lamas centuries later. Note the similarity of the name Gharab Dorje to that of the Gharib family, who are among the descendants of the original Mu tribe.

Naturally, the claims of Bon to great antiquity are hotly contested. Detractors point to the paucity of evidence relating to an unbroken chain of command stretching 18,000 years into the distant past. This is partly due to the manner in which Tibetan spiritual lineages develop over time; rarely is it as straightforward as merely handing the baton of tradition from one generation to the next. Certain tulkus or masters are said to reincarnate – the Dalai Lama and Bogd Khan of Mongolia are two such examples – and these time-hopping individuals do not always elect to be reborn within their own sect of Buddhism or Bon.

Such a reliance on the reincarnation of previous spiritual masters who return to continue their work on earth can make lineages notoriously hard to trace. This, when coupled with the idea that certain tulkus choose to reincarnate in faraway countries, or wait several centuries before returning, can make it difficult in the extreme to work out who is who. To outsiders who may grapple with such esoteric notions, this state of affairs can be baffling at best and at worst, stretching the bounds of credulity to the limit. On top of all this, there are certain additional considerations, such as when a tulku splits his consciousness into several different individuals, imbuing a number of separate holy men with a facet or facets of the reborn teacher. All this has made the Bon lineage especially problematic because there are no written records to accompany the claims to back up the supposed 18,000 year-old tradition. Nevertheless, Bon history insists that Tonpa Shenrab, the founder of the religion, hailed from Central Asia in the region of Tagzig (modern day Tajikistan) in around 16,000BC. According to conventional histories this is a complete impossibility.

Linguistic experts point to the fact that the name Tonpa Shenrab bears more relation to the Persian language than the Tibetan, fuelling the debate as to whether Bon originated on the fringes of Western Tibet and beyond into Persia (modern day Iran). One theory, that puts forward the proposition that Tonpa was originally a priest at the court of King Cyrus of Persia, is widely acknowledged, with evidence cited of similarities between Persian and Bon funerary rites and beliefs. The religion of Parsi (variously spelt as Parsee or Farsi) means 'Persian' in Sanskrit. The Parsi bury their dead in open gardens to be picked apart by birds and scavengers. This practice is echoed in the open 'sky-garden' funerals of Tibet, in which the corpse is ritually hacked apart by special funerary officers as a demonstration of the fleeting impermanence of the physical vehicle on Earth.

In the Tibetan rite, remnants of the dismembered corpse are left as carrion in a fashion almost identical to the Parsi. A morbid and grisly tradition to Western minds, perhaps, but the Buddhist looks beyond the physical towards the development of the mind, which is believed to survive the body after death. The Tibetan-Iranian connection does not end there, with theorists promoting the line that Tonpa was actually Persian, seizing upon a clear connection between the Bon religion and the Zoroasatrian Magi. Tagzig, name of the supposed birthplace of Tonpa Shenrab, is indeed Persian and refers to both Persia and Arabia, so the inference is immediately drawn that Tonpa emerged from that part of the world. By way of reinforcing the Tibetan link to Persian traditions, some writers have noted the Bon custom of finding special 'heaven stones' in fields, nine being the luckiest of number of stones to discover as nine is sacred to Bon. The heaven stones have been examined and found to be very similar to Persian 'Luristan' stones that are discovered and revered in like fashion. The Bonpo, however, do not accept the Persia theory and instead place Tagzig firmly in Central Asia upon the Roof of the World. The writer Charles Allen has made a career of studying the region and is convinced of the links between Bon and Zoroastrianism. Allen compares the religions' respective myths regarding the primordial light and the cosmic egg, going further still to assert that the word Bon itself is derived from the Persian word 'bwn' meaning 'to construct'.

It is certainly true that people did migrate from Persia to settle in the north-west of Tibet many years ago in a place formerly known as Khotan, a very important staging post on the Silk Road and a major centre of Central Asian Buddhism. It is also true that Bon ideas on the formation of the universe are closer to the Persian than the Buddhist and that these beliefs follow the ancient dualistic hallmarks of the Persian Zoroastrian religion.

The Tibetan-Iranian connection was again resurrected with long-lasting implications in 1908 by Indian intellectual Professor Satis Chandra Vidyabhusana, whose work on the origin of the royal houses of Nepal and Tibet claims they were in fact descended from the Licchavis – a 4th Century clan of Nepal. The professor made the controversial assertion that the Licchavis were part of a Persian dynasty responsible for, among other things, founding the Jain religion of India. Once more there appears to be a suggestion that Iran, particularly at the time of Zoroaster (also known as Zarathustra), was a major centre of initiation and perhaps even a hub for the hidden directorate themselves.

The prophet Zoroaster was born within the borders of the Persian empire and to many historians he is regarded as the blueprint for all other wandering soothsayers who came after him. J.G Bennett quotes Gurdjieff in his work *The Masters of Wisdom*, who tells of a great conference of masters which took place in Babylon, where the great and the good of the ancient world convened in a gathering of the most enlightened individuals of their age. Bennett tells us that among the illustrious attendees were Egyptian high priests, Zoroastrian Magi and perhaps even the great Pythagoras himself, who may have been a long-time student of Zoroaster. Bennett surmises – and it is pure conjecture on his part – that the Babylonian conference coincided with the withdrawal of Prince Siddhartha from the outer world. In so doing, Bennett tacitly suggests that the man who would go on to achieve immortality as Gautama Buddha was also possibly drawn to this great meeting of sages and that he may have been influenced in his decisions by what he heard discussed there. It is entirely possible that Gurdjieff meant that the conference was a meeting of systems and ideas, rather than the actual personages that Bennett puts forward, but either way, he strongly suggests that the central protagonists were Persian.

If the key players in the school of masters were indeed Persian, then it seems natural that we should turn our scrutiny at this point to the elite esotericists of Persian society, namely, the Magi. This priestly caste were considered a race apart and enjoyed such elevated status that even the kings of Persia were careful to heed their counsel concerning matters of state. They were drawn from the Medes (the Kurds of the modern day), but the Magi were far from united and within their edifice were several sects, each guarding the secrets held by their respective orders. Much of these teachings went on to be preserved by the Parsi religion which was displaced eastwards towards India to avoid the Arab invasion of Persia. With the invasion and emergence of Islam the Zoroastrian religion of elite Magi disappeared, although the Parsi who had fled continued their tradition in safety from Muslim persecution. At the height of its influence, Persian Zoroastrian philosophy permeated deep into neighbouring states: from Asia Minor, Egypt and Central Asia including Turkestan, to places like Khotan.

Both the Parsi and Bon religions therefore, carry fragments of the Zoroastrian faith where the teachings of the elite Magi priesthood still persist. That being the case, some elements of Bon can be traced back to the time of Zoroaster, approximately 6,000BC, but other facets are definitely drawn from local shamanistic practices related to the worship of mountain deities and the Klu spirits that resided in lakes, rivers and other bodies of water.

These were not the only two religions to be affected by the Magi. One will recall in the Bible that several witnesses made their presence felt at the Nativity of Jesus. As named by the disciple Matthew in his Gospel, the wise men who followed a star and travelled to Bethlehem were none other than three Magi of the very same esoteric school of high esteem.

The Star of Bethlehem

We have already mentioned the magician advisors known as the mag who were based in the ancient Chinese court. Sporting golden-coloured conical hats adorned with symbols of the sun and moon, these astronomer priests dispensed arcane wisdom to the Chinese Emperor and his ministers. There are those who suspect that these men represented the remnants of the Magi – the secret Persian esoteric school that possessed knowledge above and beyond our ken even now. In their country of origin, the Magi had become king makers, predicting the arrival of Christ hundreds of years before the event itself and taking steps through the centuries that preceded the birth of Jesus to ensure the safe passage of his teachings.

In fact, one of the key pieces of historical evidence in favour of the existence of the hidden directorate comes to us from the Biblical nativity. At the birth of Christ a group of men appear who are described in the Bible as being 'from the East', but without further explanation we are reliant on various ancient folklore myths to fill in the gaps. There is no conclusive answer to who they were, but we know from the Gospel of Matthew that the trio are certainly identified as being Magi. The word 'magician' is derived from the Magi, who, while inextricably linked to the Zoroastrian tradition are also quite separate in identity. In fact, the Magi pre-date the Zoroastrian tradition, as it was they who vetted and ultimately promoted Zoroaster himself. The Magi brotherhood were divided into three distinct castes; the first who oversaw religious duties in Zoroastrian practice, while the second were preservers of the archives and were privy to secret teachings – the 'magicians' of ancient record who possessed the 'maga' power. The third and ultimate caste, who in the words of J.G. Bennett were, "… the true esoteric society who were aware of the significance of the great event that was being prepared."

Their appearance in the Bible is perhaps not overly surprising as the Magi were gifted astrologers and diviners whose presence was expected at any major rite or ceremony of the time. If a Middle Eastern tulku-like god-king and future Messiah of the Jews was to be properly prepared, then it was only natural for the Magi to be present at his birth.

This candid revelation from Matthew about the Magi attending the birth of Jesus allows us to cross-reference the Gospel with that of local folklore pertaining to the sect to gain insight into who these mysterious visitors at the scene of the nativity might have been. It appears we have strayed far from the Roof of the World into the Middle East but have we? Indications are that the Christian story may have umbilical cords stretching back to Asia and the hidden directorate.

The Gospel of Matthew tells of the Magi being drawn by the appearance of a star that pointed the way to the scene of the nativity. Matthew does use the word Magi to describe these notable visitors but does not give their number. In Christian lore there are three presents delivered in respect of the birth of the Messiah which were: gold, frankincense and myrrh. The inference is that these three gifts were offered by three individual men of the orient. In actual fact, the Bible accounts are unspecific on how many Magi were on hand. There may well have been three gifts given to Christ at his birth, but the actual number of benefactors is unknown – the trio of Magi remains a folkloric aspect. In the Bible, *Matthew 2:2*, we read:

"Where is He who has been born King of the Jews? For we saw His star in the east and have come to worship Him." When Herod the king heard this, he was troubled, and all Jerusalem with him. Gathering together all the chief priests and scribes of the people, he inquired of them where the Messiah was to be born…"

This is strangely redolent of the situation of the Mongolian tulku the Bogd Khan, born in Tibet during 1932, whose existence as successor to the Buddhist throne was kept secret from the Soviet authorities until the fall of Communism in the early 1990s. In this case, if we were to substitute the Communist state for the despotic King Herod then the parallels between the Bogd Khan – 9th Jebtsundamba Khutughtu – and the infant Jesus become clear. Both may be considered as tulkus representing the ambitions of an oppressed people seeking leadership, autonomy and freedom to worship at their own altar, with the authorities in both cases being greatly fearful of the popular response to the appearance of such a religious figurehead. There may also be another parallel here too. The birth of the Bogd Khan affected the politics of not just the Mongolian people but the whole Lamaist Tibetan Buddhist world and so therefore deeply involved Tibetans, Bhutanese, Ladakhis and other peoples of the same faith (See Chapter 3 – the Shambhala War).

The arrival of the Magi in folklore may also signal interest from peoples other than the Jews. The three alleged Magi have been given names in certain folkloric traditions: Balthazar, Gaspar and Melchior. Rather than representing three individuals it is understood that these names are indicative of three separate races. In one adaptation of the Magi story they are described thus: Melchior is King of Arabia, Balthazar, King of Ethiopia and Gaspar, King of Tarsus (a city in Southern Turkey). The first king being eldest bore gold; Balthazar in his middle-age, bore frankincense and the last king, Gaspar of Tarsus was a man in his twenties who bore myrrh. The King James Bible does not describe the Magi as kings, but folklore does have them as royal personages, as do the churches of both East and West who have conferred sainthood on the three kings of the orient. In an Armenian Gospel the Magi kings have different labels: Melchior is King of Persia, Balthazar, King of Arabia and Gaspar, King of India as before. Other Christian traditions have entirely different names for the Magi based on their own Persian language: Larvadad, Gushasaph and Hormisdas.

Saint Gaspar may not be tied to the city of Tarsus alone, as other sources including the *Encyclopaedia Britannica* quote other traditions referring to

Gaspar, sometimes spelt Caspar, being an 'initiate of the East'. In one such role he is cast as an astrologer possibly hailing from Northern India. King Gaspar is an interesting ruler who leaves much of an imprint in both Middle Eastern and Asian folklore, but none of these stories are mentioned in the standard versions of the Bible.

To find out more about Gaspar we must look at those Biblical tracts excised from the accepted version, a collection known as the Apocrypha. In the Acts of St Thomas, written in the Syriac language once spoken in much of Arabia the Middle East at the time, a man is introduced called King Gudnaphar, a ruler in Northern India. St Thomas travels to India by sea and encounters the Indo-Parthian peoples, or in simple terms, those of Indo-Iranian heritage. This region also just so happens to be a place of Buddhist tradition. Some Biblical scholars have identified King Gaspar and King Gudnaphar being one and the same person. The timings are right to point to these rulers as the two co-existed during the same period, pointing to the fact that the name Gudnaphar translates through various local neighbouring languages as Gaspar, to take other forms such as: Gastaphar (Armenian) and Gondaphares (in its Parthian form). History records that that Gondaphares I was the first ruler of Balochistan, an area encompassing parts of the Persian coast (today Iran) and areas of what are today Pakistan and Afghanistan. He was part of the House of Suren and the founder of the great Parthian Dynasty. The Parthian ruler established the capital of his empire in a place called Taxila. Coincidentally, Christian lore tells us that the capital city of Taxila was the last resting place of St Thomas.

Another rendition of the name Gudnaphar is taken from the Pashtun peoples of the Pakistan/Afghan lands as Gandapur – which is a tribal surname of a nomadic people who have their own localised lineage. Their forebear was the Tairi Khan; the tribe later held the title Afghanpur and were highly esteemed by other Pashtun tribes. The Afghan city Khandahar is almost certainly founded on the back of the Gandapur name. Returning to King Gaspar of the Magi myth and St Thomas who by his own account travelled to India, we are left with several intriguing lines of enquiry. Melchior the Magi king who came from Arabia or Persia, portrayed as the oldest of the trio, may have held the title rab-mag (Chief Magi). Notice how similar this word is to the rab (rites of Bon) or gshen-rab (priest of Bon). Melchior bore gold, which it is said was given to Christ to symbolically denote his kingship. According to legend the three Magi prostrated themselves before the infant Christ, another custom indicating their Asian origin. They appear in the Bible when Daniel speaks of them as master astrologers and magicians (*Daniel 5:11*). Daniel himself was said by some to be a rab-mag or master Magi.

As astrologers, the Magi passed on their teachings to other non-Zoroastrian religions and there is evidence this included working with the Essenes, a religious group mentioned in the Dead Sea scrolls, which were discovered in 1947. There is a strong link between the Essene brotherhood and Jesus, who is said to have been an initiate. It would certainly appear there is a convincing correlation between the life of Jesus and the Magi, taking the figure of Christ ever closer to the kernel of Asian mysticism.

Scrolls of St Issa

Nicholas Notovitch was a Russian traveller who trod lightly on the Roof of the World in 1894. His sojourn took him to a place known as Ladakh, a former Kingdom which is today part of Northern India. Ladakh is a mountainous region formed in the wake of the dissolution of Zhang-Zhung and like many hinterlands of the Indian subcontinent in the North, its people are aligned to Tibetan Buddhism. Notovitch recounts a strange tale which is often dismissed as delirious fantasy, or worse, as outright fraud. The Russian traveller came to be welcomed as a guest at a remote monastery called Hemis, which lies 30 miles from the capital of Ladakh. The Hemis Monastery is both idyllic and historic in equal measure, and is host to the festival of Padmasambhava each June. Hemis is also associated with the famous yogi Naropa whose exploits are celebrated in Tibetan Buddhism in which he is revered as one of the great teachers, sometimes called 'Guardian of the Northern Gate'.

Notovitch gained access to the monastery due to a broken leg sustained during his travels in the area; hospitality was duly granted by the inhabitants which was no small honour for a non-Tibetan back in 1894. His hosts extended their injured guest an even greater courtesy when they showed him a set of old scrolls containing texts concerning one Saint Issa, a wandering prophet. The Russian had the texts translated by a local lama and became convinced that they were both a previously unknown gospel and an account of Jesus' life during his 'missing years' which told of the Messiah's travels in India before his return to the Holy Land to begin his mission. It seems that Saint Issa was considered a great Buddha, 'the son of Buddha' and therefore highly revered. It is also worth noting that Isa is a classical Arabic name, which translates as 'Jesus'. Veneration of Saint Issa was closeted to the highest lamas in the land, so the name remained unknown among normal worshippers.

According to Notovitch, Saint Issa was regarded as dwelling at the heights of the pantheon of divinities. He maintained that the scrolls the monks had shown him were not originals but copies made around 200AD, with the originals residing in the archives in Lhasa.

Since neither photographic nor actual evidence have been presented since, his account has been placed firmly in the best tradition of great historical hoaxes. In his defence, several witnesses are also alleged to have been made privy to the secret documents of Saint Issa. These include characters such as two swamis – Trigunatitananda and Abhedananda; a Mr Caspari and Mrs Gaspe, who claimed they were shown them by a lama called Zangpo; a husband and wife, Mr and Mrs Noack and a Henrietta Merrick, who wrote about the scrolls in the '20s. Nicholas Roerich (featured earlier in this book) and his son attempted to locate the texts but failed, it is said. The legend of Jesus in Asia failed to gain much traction and so the scrolls of Saint Issa will have to stay where they are until the texts see daylight once again or fresh eyewitness reports appear.

The snowcapped, mountainous terrain of Ladakh has some unusual landmarks to share with the curious traveller. In the Alchi Monastery, which contains some of the oldest paintings in the region, are frescoes featuring crosses. These Christian symbols were left by the Nestorians who brought Christianity to Tibet at approximately the same time as Padmasambhava came up from India with his message of love through Tantric Buddhism. When one looks at history this way it is easy to sense the comparative, and significant, antiquity of Bon.

In 1907 the British/Hungarian explorer Sir Auriel Stein, while carrying out excavations in China at a place wonderfully named 'The Cave of the Thousand Buddhas', unearthed a number of important Buddhist scriptures, but his Chinese find was significant for Christianity too. Among the mass of texts discovered was a picture clearly showing a man with Caucasian features holding his hand in a mudra – a meditative gesture belonging to Eastern religions. How a Caucasian came to be pictured in this pose remains a mystery. The man is pictured with a halo gracing his head, a symbol used in both Buddhism and Christianity. Whether this scroll was of Nestorian origin is not proven, but probable. But even so, this discovery found by Sir Auriel Stein only dates the Christian material at around the 8th Century, the same time that Buddhism came to Tibet, but it does not prove that Christ walked in Asia centuries earlier. Quite why the Nestorians chose to come this way is perhaps pregnant with musings; did the Nestorian Christians who came to Asia from the Middle East believe they were literally following in the footsteps of their master?

While it would be easy to dismiss tales of Christ's time in Asia as pure conjecture, the fact remains that much of what we know about Jesus from Christian sources is also equally unreliable. The image of a simple man earning his living as a carpenter is no more certain than the scrolls of St Issa, if the truth be known. The Western Church has traditionally fostered such images of Christ but what basis these actually have in fact is flimsy to say the least.

Evangelists have glazed over the details of the historical Christ to carry the message of love while the more traditional elements of the Church have fused a number of images of the Messiah into an overall mythos. When one thinks that conventional Christianity only accepts four main Gospels, or accounts written about the life of Christ, while another forty-odd have been rejected as unreliable or in some way dubious, we can see that the accepted idea of the Saviour is incomplete by any measure. Even the foundational beliefs of the modern Western Church such as the resurrection are known to have been added to the Bible some two hundred years after the supposed crucifixion. The Christian faith is therefore clearly underpinned by faith, not cohesive histories.

Even biographies of modern figures, say a politician or famous artist, often disagree about minor details of the person's life, but after 2,000 years the standard versions of the Bible present a very selective view. With so much editing and revision of the life of Christ, is the idea we have of Jesus today real in any sense? The Jesus we know of in the Western portrayal is one crafted by men of the Church in around 500AD and built upon since. Are we prepared to believe that Jesus between the ages of 13 and 30 lived in relative obscurity in Nazareth working as a carpenter? Or did he, like many of the other masters featured in this book, work continually towards a specific aim with the aid of a school of illuminated scholars? Could it be possible that Jesus was an initiate whose travels took him away from Palestine in his lost years into Asia?

It has not gone unnoticed among Eastern commentators that the way of Jesus is very similar to that of Buddha. Both preach a simplicity of being, non-violence, the protection of the vulnerable or the downtrodden, to love all beings and be merciful without judgement; these and other teachings are almost identical. It is hard in our age of globalisation to appreciate similarities as everything now is melded, homogenised and compromised, but imagine for one moment two religions completely separate in their geographical location and cultural identity both sharing near-identical spiritual values. Some might say that these values expressed by both Jesus and Buddha are intrinsic human virtues and therefore natural conclusions to the condition of humanity. Let us hope that they are, but as for the Jesus-Buddha connection it could just be a case of the common currency of ideas. Then again, as we saw with Trungpa and Gurdjieff, the esoteric schools produce definite ideas for specific times. The two spiritual masters, Christ and Buddha, both appear to have been spreading the same message to humanity albeit in different regions and among different cultures, but we must ask the question, is this just a case of coincidence, or were Jesus and Buddha both part of a greater mission such as that engendered by an esoteric school? Put simply, are we prepared to believe they were acting alone?

Another fascinating fragment of the story belongs to Kashmir, which enjoys a strong connection with the Biblical mythos. It is here our that firm, yet brittle preconceptions of Jesus may find their undoing.

Khanyar Srinagar is a place that for approximately 1,900 years held a secret, for it contains the Rozabal Shrine, the last resting place of the great prophet Youza Asouph. Some believe this to be Jesus himself and cite the spelling of the name, giving various renditions of Jesus: Issa (Sanskrit), Yusa (Persian), Azuz (Arabic), Lesus (Greek). A nearby relic reputedly showing the footprints of Youza Asouph are said to also bear the marks of the crucifixion wounds. One man who was wholly convinced of the argument was a Muslim by the name of Mirza Ahmad who lived in the mid-19th Century and wrote a book about Jesus' life in Asia post-crucifixion, which involved the Rozabal Shrine and local customs of the area. Ahmad proposed that Jesus settled in Kashmir having survived the crucifixion in a somewhat more prosaic manner than the story of the resurrection would have us believe and that, rather than being God incarnate, he simply died a natural death and was buried in the Rozabal Shrine. An Islamic sect grew up around these ideas of Jesus in India which followers believed were interpretations of the Quran. It would seem that the folk memory of the local people had retained the Jewish Messiah's visit to their homeland. Local customs are often vivid interpretations of events but also hold vital clues to what actually happened at key points in history. One has to ask why such a Muslim sect sprang up around Jesus living and ultimately dying in India? Christians tend to deify Christ to make him, among other things, unmarried, celibate, even against carnal passion. Recent discoveries about Christ suggest that he was indeed married and if he did travel to India is it not possible he was a Tantric scholar too?

At the time of Christ, it would have been inconceivable for a Jewish leader, not least the Messiah himself, to have been unmarried. Many have suggested that the chaste figure beloved of the western Church is just another useful construct, not least as a model for a celibate priesthood to emulate, and that Jesus was indeed married to no less a figure than Mary Magdalene, a sinful woman who was, according special teachings by Christ, causing jealousy in St Peter.

The Gospel of Philip, which was discovered in 1945 among a collection of 4th Century Gnostic texts known as the Nag Hammadi library, describes Magdalene as 'koinônos', a Greek word meaning companion or partner. After the resurrection of Christ, Mary is questioned by the bereaved disciples and replies that she has known Christ in a different fashion to the men who followed him. So controversial and inflammatory to the disciples' ears was this comment from a woman, especially one of Mary's repute, we are told that a man named Levi had to spring to her defence. The apocryphal Gospel of Philip does seem to give credence to the fact that Jesus and Mary Magdalene had a more intimate relationship which one another. In the Bible she is described as having been a demon-infested adulteress, a former prostitute who was rescued by Christ from death by stoning. This account is taken from the Gospel of Luke and was later revised by the Catholic Church to exemplify the submissive and penitent model of a once sinful woman. It was this same special bond between Jesus and Mary that caused the bereaved disciplines to question Mary as to the exact nature of the relationship between the Messiah and his female friend. The Gnostic tradition of Western mysticism focuses on these ideas to elevate Mary to superior status within their perception of the Christian teachings. Mary Magdalene, as so-called partner of the Messiah, was privy to higher 'secret' teachings and this comes across in the Gospel of Matthew and the teachings of the Gnostics. Were these teachings only possible between a man and woman? If so, it begs the question were these secret teachings possibly Tantric in nature?

The Pashtun Inheritance

The theory regarding Jesus' time in Asia is controversial as it suggests that he survived crucifixion, recovered and escaped his persecutors to live in Asia. It is connected with the 'lost tribes' of the Israelites which surprisingly crop up in Afghanistan and Pakistan in the Pashtun tribal lands. This idea emerged in 1908 and was popularised by Hadhrat Ahmad, founder of the Ahmadiyya Movement of Islam. Ahmad published his thoughts in the book *Jesus in India*, only a few years after the supposed discovery of the Saint Issa scrolls. Curiously, Ahmad advances the histories of the Khawaja Nimatullah circulated in 1018 in Herat in the reign of Moghul Emperor Jahangir. The very same Jahangir whose liberal-minded court entertained Jesuit missionary Andrade who first encountered strange tales of a Christian community in Tibet mentioned earlier.

Ahmad seriously proposed that the histories of the region stated that the Afghan race was descended from the lost tribes of Israel and more specifically a man named as Malek Thalut who is identified as the Biblical Saul. The evidence put forward is a taken from the work of Khwaja Niamatullah, in a piece called *Makhazan-i-Afghan*. It states that Nebuchadnezzar, an initiate of the Magi, conquered the Israelites and banished them from the land. During the Israelite exodus these refugees became divided into three constituent parts known as Beni Israel, Beni Asif and Beni Afghan. The latter settled and gave their name to the lands of present-day Afghanistan. In some subsequent histories exploring this theme there is some evidence to suggest that the Arabs referred to the Afghanis as 'Sulaimanis', a title reserved for descendants of King Solomon. By tradition the Afghan Royal family itself claims its descent from the tribe of Benjamin.

Ahmad and others have made a study and comparison of Israeli and Pashtun tribal names which it must be said do bear remarkable similarities. The Pashtuns, a tribal nation that span the borders of both Pakistan and Afghanistan, are now avid Muslims who follow their own tribal Pashtun lore and customs called Pastunwali whose duties are above and beyond Shariah lore. It is a duty of every Pashtun not only to live by the Pashtunwali but to explore the essence of this code of honour.

Some have compared this tribal code to that of the Jewish Torah. We see Taliban fighters on the news without realising that most of these warriors are drawn from the Pashtun tribal lands. They are not, strictly speaking, Afghanis as they do not recognise the artificial borders created by politicians. The Pashtun fighting prowess, fearlessness and indomitable warrior spirit has been the stuff of legend since the British Raj and Rudyard Kipling first brought back tales about them to the West. Both the Russian and US forces have also been forced to concede to the Pashtun tribesmen as a formidable enemy on the battlefield. Yet, they will bestow magnanimous largesse upon any friend or visitor who is a guest in their homelands and defend until death any guest who is dishonoured during their stay.

Pashtun tribal customs which invite speculation that they originate from the Jews include:
- Following a Saturday Sabbath day called Shanbay
- Displaying the Star of David in their homes
- Use of a now-defunct Jewish custom found in Deuteronomy, whereby a brother-in-law is required to marry the widow of childless husband
- During times of pestilence the Pashtuns sprinkle sheep's blood on their doorsteps, which the Jews did in times of the Biblical plagues
- Use of scapegoats to alleviate blame on the nation.

The similarities have not been lost on modern Israelis who have funded a genetic study to determine if the Pashtuns are related to the Jews. In 2010 the *Guardian* newspaper reported that Israeli anthropologists were conducting a study taking blood samples from the Afridi Tribe of Pashtuns located in Northern India. Shava Weil of the Hebrew University of Jerusalem said of the Pashtun-Jewish heritage, "Of all the groups, there is more convincing evidence about the Pashtuns than anybody else, but the Pashtuns are the ones who would reject Israel most ferociously. That is the sweet irony."

Many other striking similarities exist for one to suspect that this must be more than mere coincidence. The Jewish tribe of Asher is near identical to the Pashtun tribe of Ashuri; likewise, Isaachar to Ishaqzal, Reuben to Rabbani and so on. With so many of the tribes holding the belief that they are descendants of King Saul, there is every reason to suspect a Jewish lineage, even inside the Royal Houses of Afghanistan. Inscriptions found in Afghan caves provide evidence that Jews had settled there at least a thousand years ago and many of the great chroniclers of the time reference the existence of a Jewish community in the region.

Ahmad cites that Jesus, like the Israelite people before him, had to flee persecution and did so by settling in Eastern lands. If Jesus had known about the final destination of the Beni Afghan would it not make perfect sense to seek refuge in these parts? In our modern minds we view the world in terms of maps, consisting of artificial borders created by government politicians, aided in many cases by natural geographical features. The British divided up the Indian Raj after the exit from its Jewel in the Crown colony. Similarly, the Durand line demarks the border between Afghanistan and Pakistan, another British political legacy of the Great Game.

To the Pashtun tribesman these divisions are not precise, as they divide tribesmen of the same ethnic group, rather similar to the way in which Germans were carved up into East and West after the Second World War. When the US-British led incursion took place many Pashtuns merely relocated away from Afghan soil to Pakistan as they felt legitimately entitled to do so as the land across the border had belonged to their tribe for thousands of years. The Durand line is a mere century or so old dating from 1893, having been imposed by foreigners without tribal consent. Due to present-day politics the border is less porous than it has been but in the mind of the tribesman it is artificial. If there was a referendum undoubtably the Pashtuns would plump for full independence from either Pakistan or Afghanistan.

Their peoples can be found in the mountainous districts of what we today call Northern India – Jammu and Kashmir. Their conversion to Islam came when a Pashtun called Quais befriended the Prophet and converted to spread the faith to his people. But there are strange anomalies that are thrown up again here which underscore a distinctly unsettling feeling that we do not fully understand the region outside of the British constructs of borders and political geography. Speaking of Kashmir a travelling Arab historian called El Bironi in the 12th Century wrote, "In the past, permission to enter Kashmir was given only to Jews."

Messages of Love
In his book *Jesus in India*, Ahmad recounts the apparent flight of Jesus, who travelled continually from country to country, fearful of discovery. We are told that he took cover in the jungle at night so that he might eat as he fled certain persecution following the failed crucifixion. Eventually, so the story goes, the

Messiah arrived at Kashmir via Punjab, but although Ahmad and other authors supporting this theory tend to use the words 'Jesus in Kashmir', using the modern name of the Indian state concerned, could we not equally say 'Jesus in Ladakh'?

The ancient land of Ladakh is today positioned across both the Jammu and Kashmir Indian departments. If we think in terms of Jesus being in Ladakh during the 1st Century could we not then be talking about Christ living inside a long-dead empire ruled the Kushan dynasty? Ladakh itself did not come into being in the 8th Century. At the time of alleged flight of the Messiah the area of Kashmir-Ladakh was ruled by King Shalivahana of the Kushan Empire. This king is recorded in a work known as the *Bhavishya Purana* which translates in Sanskrit contradictorily as 'Tales of Old and Prophecies'. In the work, one of the major Purana scriptures in Hinduism, there is also mention of the 'Son of God' Isha Putra. It is believed via this scripture that the two men met when Shalivahana was on a hunting trip in part of this empire in Ladakh. Shalivahana encountered a light-skinned man dressed in white, a veritable Holy Man whose serenity impressed him greatly. The travelling Holy Man informed the ruler that he was the Son of God and born of a virgin (*Bhavishya Purana 19.23*). The mystic, when asked his creed replied: "Love is my faith."

It seems that the Hindu scripture had prophesied the coming of a Messiah. The story above is seen very much by Ahmad and others as proof of the veracity of the promised master. We should not be surprised, as the Magi had already predicted the same Messianic arrival, albeit in the Middle East. If people did believe, like King Shalivahana, that this holy man was the son of God then it is almost certain that the same person could rely on the help of the esoteric orders in the area. We have seen Jesus being firmly connected to the Magi, the Essenes and possibly to the Pashtun tribes through their connection with Solomon and the House of David. Being a guest of the Pashtun he would have enjoyed the Pashtunwali hospitality and protection in his travels through this land. If the Hindus also recognised Jesus through their scriptures, his passage into India would have been made even more secure. It looks from the outside that Jesus was a person welcomed by several spiritual paths, suggesting an interconnectedness only possible with the aid of the hidden directorate or inner circle of humanity.

The empire of King Shalivahana (Ladakh/Kashmir) was and still is a sparsely populated, mountainous retreat far away from the political strife of the Middle East, a perfect spot for the fugitive Jesus to escape his Roman-sponsored tormentors. Ladakh is a Persian-language version of the Tibetan word meaning 'Land of High Passes', an excellent hiding place both politically and physically. Here a kingdom firmly under the control of those loyal to the prophesied Son of God who preached love. A question here might be, did Jesus continue roaming or did he simply settle down to live the remainder of his life in peace? Some believe Jesus crossed the Himalayas into Tibet. If he did so he would have encountered the Bon religion and the animistic beliefs then prevalent. The Arabs provide some tantalising clues to possible connections here.

In an Arabic text known as *The Treasure of the Doers of Good Deeds* we find a passage of great import, as it appears to lead Jesus ever closer to the Roof of the World.

> *"The Holy Prophet said 'The people most favoured in the sight of God*
> *are the Ghareeb'. When asked, what was meant by the term Ghareeb,*
> *he replied "They are the people who, like Jesus, the Messiah, have to flee*
> *from their country to save their faith?"*

For years the Quranic scholars have interpreted the word Gharib to mean 'stranger' in its masculine form or 'poor' or 'innocent'. In Tibetan, Gharib is the Lhasa dialect word for 'pauper'. It is true that Jesus Christ identified with the poor and down-trodden but it does not explain the reference to Ghareeb fleeing to save their faith. Could the word Ghareeb be referring to an altogether different connection? Could this passage possibly refer to the remnant of the tribe of Mu found in Zhang-Zhung that we examined earlier in Chapter 4?

> *"We are the clan of Gurib, are not like others,*
> *We are emanated from the god of effulgence*
> *Thus we are radically distinguished from others"*

The Gurib clan as a contingent of the ancient Mu tribe held a special position within the Eternal Bon tradition due to giving birth to the founder of the religion Tonpa Shenrab, which led them to becoming highly placed in the kingdom of Zhang-Zhung and other lands too. Their royal lineage was traced back to the mythical Mu Yangje, a non-human who descended to Earth to reside in Zhang-Zhung, where he took a bride and started the Gurib line. The ancestral bloodline often bears the Mu name such as Mu Berkya, one of the early figures in the history. Inside the Bon version of Shambhala – Olmolungring – the Gurib are one of the six semi-legendary royal races from that exulted Bon mystical haven. As stated earlier in this book the language of Zhang-Zhung went by the same name, but the ancient name for this tongue was dmu-ra with a silent 'd'. In other words the language of the Mu.

All of this still does not explain why the Gurib would want to flee to save their faith. The Gurib clan, descendants of Mu tribe, were not persecuted in the time of the Prophet Muhammed (570 – 632AD), nor were they at the implosion of Zhang-Zhung three hundred years later; in fact one of their high-ranking members assisted the assassination intrigues launched by Tibetan King Detsen. Could the Prophet Muhammed be talking about the Ghareeb fleeing their country for an altogether reason, such as a national calamity or global cataclysm?

Much of the ancient scriptures refer to such an event – the Great Flood? We assume the Prophet Muhammed to be among those whose information and authority was privy only to the highest masters. Was this quote an oblique reference to the origin of human civilisation and the people who preserved the ancient wisdom? Could the Prophet Muhammed have been referring to refugees who survived a disaster that befell the antediluvian land of the Atlantis legends? Was it not the Mu clan (Guribs) who had steadfastly preserved their spiritual teachings even after the Great Flood. The Mu and the Gurib held the keys to the world's oldest continuous religion – Bon, which if we calculate the timing of the deluge, generally believed to be around 12,000BC, then it existed before that time, as did Tonpa Shenrab. A spiritual teaching so esoteric in nature that when Tonpa Shenrab taught the Bon way, he was forced to hold back five of the Nine Ways of Bon as people were not sufficiently developed to receive them. Could the Bon of Zhung-Zhung have been preserved by the Mu clan be part of a greater esoteric centre as the legends of Shambhala and Olmolungring suggest?

Churchward, Ahmad and Notovitch have all been denounced as cranks or worst still as fakers and it is true that their theories are largely circumstantial, but is the jury still out? Could it be possible that Jesus returned to a place close to the court of the Magi having completed his undertaking to spread the message of love, forgiveness and charity which transformed the spiritual landscape to a higher plane which we now know as Christianity?

Court of the Magi

Christianity as it is known today has two original major traditions – Catholic, and Coptic, who parted company in the 5th Century. The Bible is different in each schism, with books added or subtracted as thought fit by Church leaders. Essentially in the West, Christianity came out of Judaism; Jesus himself was a Jew and was brought up in that tradition but reformed it with his own unique teachings based around love, forgiveness, healing and reconciling oneself with God. The main problem with this is that Jesus disappeared in his youth but no one knows where to. This lost period equates to about 18 years.

Much like Gurdjieff in his search for the Sarmoung, did Jesus return to the House of the Magi, the supporters of his celebrated birth? Recent accounts suggest he may have encountered the mystic sect of the Essenes, also placed in the region of his upbringing. So when Jesus reappeared about age 29 what was his belief system and what was he teaching? It was not Judaism.

The Oriental Orthodox Church has always kept close to the teachings of Enoch (Noah's grandson) as central to the teachings of Christianity. It was only after a chance discovery in 1947 that it become apparent some Western Christians would have to reassess their beliefs.

The story of the discovery of the Dead Sea Scrolls is largely apocryphal. The tale is a romantic one treasured by the Bedouin who discovered this extremely valuable archaeological find, which was to become a major boon to Christianity. A group of shepherd boys were throwing stones near some caves in 1947 when they accidentally stumbled across seven ancient scrolls. Taking these artefacts back to their Bedouin community the scrolls were inspected by a Syrian Christian and sent to an Arab antique dealer under the advice of a local man. It was not until the scrolls reached an American archaeologist Dr. John C. Trever of the American School of Oriental Research, did their true historical importance become apparent.

Dr Trever, also a Biblical scholar, compared the scrolls that had been found with an old papyrus and became convinced that they were original documents of great antiquity. Another academic named Albright rightly said that in terms of manuscripts this was the greatest discovery of modern times. He was not wrong. The texts revealed among other things the writings of the Essenes and became known as the Dead Sea Scrolls. Further professionally funded excavations were carried out in the area during subsequent years to make fresh discoveries. revealing over 900 documents including a copper scroll containing information on buried treasures. Up until this momentous discovery much of Western Christianity, whether Catholic or Protestant, or Eastern Orthodox, had to some degree been ignorant of the writings of early Christianity. The discovery of the Dead Sea Scrolls meant that subsequent translations of Biblical scripture could become closer to the original wording, which in some cases had been completely mistranslated and therefore misunderstood.

With the discovery of the Dead Sea Scrolls a number of texts called Jubilees were unearthed. These included the Epistle of Enoch and certain information on the strata of angelic forces i.e. angels in nature, personal angels, angels of the day etc. and there is no doubt that this teaching was taken directly from Essene thought. The discovery of the Epistle of Enoch surprised many Christians who were certainly not expecting fresh information about Enoch to come to light. The discovery re-ignited debate on Enoch, grandfather of Noah and his role within Christianity. The teachings of Christ are so radically different to Judaism one must ask where did it come from? Was Jesus Christ, as the Magi insist, sent on a divine mission delivering a transcendent new message for humanity? If that is the case then who prepared the mission?

The historical evidence clearly links the mystical brotherhood of the Essenes with the Biblical Prophet Enoch, whose name in Hebrew cannot fail to inspire curiosity, as it means in its root form – 'mouth' or to 'dedicate' or 'train'. In other words, an initiator. According to legends found in the Biblical lands, Enoch is said to have been the founder of the Essenes due to his knowledge and communion with the Angels. Enoch is featured in the book of Genesis, and it is said that he 'walked with God' and when his time came to depart from Earth, like his Tibetan Buddhist counterparts, he simply vanished into thin air. He is considered one of the seven pre-flood patriarchs, who in comparison with his fellows was fairly short-lived; by all accounts he only managed to reach a mere 365 years!

Three surviving works are attributed to Enoch: The First book of Enoch, which is part of the canon of the Ethiopian Church discovered by maverick Scottish explorer James Bruce in 1773. This it did not see translation into English for a few decades due to complete disinterest, largely due to Bruce's reception in London. The Second book of Enoch is preserved by the Eastern Orthodox Church called 'The Book of Secrets' and a Third book of Enoch translated in 1928 which is found in Hebrew dated to the 5th Century, which is a magical document related to the Kabbalah. The book of Enoch remains controversial for it suggests angels deliberately and sinfully copulated with mankind to produce a hybrid race. One Biblical researcher who has ressearched the Dead Sea Scrolls and the Essenes has made some astonishing claims that depart radically from the normal ecclesiastical view of the Messiah. Lawrence Shiffman states:

"Scholars have devoted considerable attention to this section of Enoch, focusing on the parallel use of the term 'son of man' in the New Testament to describe Jesus. But this section of the text, not found in any of the Qumran manuscripts of Enoch, is believed not to have been part of the original book. Yet these beliefs will be ascribed to Jesus by the Essenes following his crucifixion as they made comparisons between Jesus and their Angel-Messiah. Therefore theology was created around Jesus which finds it origin not in Divine revelation but in sun-myths held sacred by the Indo-European nations of the world... like India, Egypt, Iran, Babylon, Assyria, etc."

This observation made by Shiffman points to the Essenes' connection with Central Asia, as suggested in the writings of the time via Pliny, the Roman naturalist who said of the Essene Brotherhood:

"...the oldest of the initiates, receiving their teaching from Central Asia,"

It is this constant turning to Asia that is most recurrent in the commentaries on the Bible, which number far too many to dismiss without reflection. The Patriarch Enoch is no exception. The book of Enoch was greatly respected by the Essenes as the Dead Sea Scrolls discoveries and archaeological researches at Qumran have revealed. Oddly, within this work we find stories of the Angels holding cords which are redolent of the 'Cord of Mu' allowing travel to other parts. In the book of Enoch, the angels take their cords and fly north to carry out measurements which would 'reveal all the secrets of the depths of the Earth'. This sounds distinctly like a geological survey. This theme is a worldwide one in myths and legends from all lands, strongly suggesting an actual survey after the Great Flood.

Naturally the discovery concerning Enoch was not welcomed by those who still wish to cling the fixed notions of who Biblical characters were and what they were actually teaching. Bonding Moses and Jesus with the Essenes may have been an upset to the Biblical applecart but then adding in the Essenes-Enoch-Magi connection may have been too much for some Christians, as it strongly suggests the hand of secret mystical schools working in tandem behind the main events in the Bible. What is more thought-provoking is that the Magi held the rank of kingmakers in Persia and explains why Herod greatly feared their appearance at the nativity, as it was effectively a challenge to his rule. The Magi committee called the Megistanes selected the kings of Persia, who were then crowned by the Magi priesthood who later instructed them in their ways.

Jesus it seems was no different, although he may have passed through the initiatory framework of the Essenes at some point. From his birth the Magi had ordained him as King of the Jews driven by certain astrological prophesies. The scene of the nativity is very unlikely to have involved three men but a large contingent of Persian cavalry supporting the visiting Magi. Herod entertained the Magi to try and inveigle them into a plot to report back the location of the new-born child but they were wise enough to agree to this but then ignore it when safely away. The Magi were there to fulfil their secret mission, not the wishes of King Herod.

In the 1947 discoveries of the Dead Sea Scrolls came the book of Daniel. In the standard Bible is most certainly tied into the Magi although the term 'wise men' is applied in the texts which can interpreted as wise-man, astrologer even Chaldean, a euphemism for Magi in any case. In the book of Daniel this is clarified beyond all doubt as Daniel is described as Rab-Mag (Chief Magi). He was of course according to Biblical stories the man elevated in society to a very high rank, a ruler, by King Nebuchadnezzar. It was Daniel who transmitted the coming of Jesus to the Magi with complete accuracy several centuries before the arrival of the Messiah. Daniel's agreed resting place is Susa or Shush in Iran. His tomb stands under a pointed conical tower and is revered by Jews and Muslims alike, but legend has it his remains were disinterred long ago to the middle of a river amid a dispute between the peoples on other side of the waterway. Author Paul Kriwaczek has noted it is odd that a Jewish spiritual figure with no real place inside Islam is revered in his tomb by those worshipping in Shia circles. His thoughts are as follows, "…could it be explained by Daniel's significance as the one who first united the prophetic traditions of Moses and Zarathrustra?'

Daniel as Rab-Mag, ruler and Jewish visionary, set in motion the whole chain of events leading to Jesus being received as King of the Jews some thirteen centuries later. This account can only underscore the true nature of the time scales and complexity of the workings of the inner circle or hidden directorate in human affairs, to assist spiritual evolution on a global scale, acting rather like the effects of radiation to produce waves of consciousness in the world. Jesus' overall mission may or may not have been successful – it seems to have elevated consciousness among men and so we see a chain of initiatory preparation predicted by Rab-Mag Daniel, kept for centuries by the Magi, honed by the Essenes and then taught by Jesus to his Tantric bride Mary Magdalene along with his disciples, with Jesus' final retirement to Asia to retreat to the school of the masters.

Gurdjieff himself constantly referred to esoteric Christianity as his teaching – was he trying to convey that this ancient lineage of Zoroaster was very much alive? His enigmatic comment was "All roads lead back to Balkh", an ancient city very much connected to both the Magi and Buddhism.

Chapter 7

The Maps of Pre-Sand Egypt

"We attract forces according to our being."
G.I.Gurdjieff

Gurdjieff said cryptically "All roads lead to Balkh." This time-worn place once dubbed the 'Mother of Cities' is a mystical melting pot – the Magi, the Sufis and the Tantric teaching of Kalachakra are indelibly marked by its locality and so too the name of Shambhala. Now in our modern age it finds itself placed within a relatively new country we call Afghanistan, but it in its heyday it was an empire boasting much advancement and learning. It was the birthplace of Zoroaster, the Sufi poet Rumi and the first Aryan leader Bakdhi, who founded the original settlement according to Persian traditions. In some accounts Padmasambhava was himself from this hallowed place.

Alexander the Great, who married Roxanna, the Balkh Princess of great renown, may have conquered the celebrated settlement but paid dearly with his life; legend has it the inhabitants poisoned him and he perished there. Balkh saw many conquerors with the merciless Mongol leader Genghis Khan laying the place to waste in 1221AD. It was the end of its halcyon days, alas.

Gurdjieff referenced the city but no one can be certain why. He wrote about the source of his teaching in the Sarmoung brotherhood as being taken not from Tibet but a people know as Aisors, an ancient people from Assyria who had fled and taken their knowledge with them. Gurdjieff composed a song with Thomas De Hartman about the Aisors, again giving a vital clue to some of his knowledge.

The Maps of Pre-Sand Egypt

Gurdjieff spoke of his astonishment on discovering that the childhood tales his Ashokh father told him were word-for-word identical with the ancient cuneiform text of the Mesopotamian epic poem *Gilgamesh*. It is likely he is referring to the twelve clay tablets discovered at Ninevah in 1852 at the library of the

Assyrian ruler, King Ashurbanipal. This shocking realisation caused Gurdjieff to immediately re-evaluate the authenticity and accuracy of the ancient myths. He deeply regretted not seeing their great historical importance earlier. Another source of the Gilgamesh story, which may or may not have been read by Gurdjieff, was in the book of Enoch found by Bruce in Ethiopia, as we saw in Chapter 6.

Gurdjieff hinted that fragments of his teachings were taken from the Aisors, an ancient people whose civilisation flourished between the 25th and 1st Centuries BC in the region now known as Kurdistan. Together with Thomas De Hartman, Gurdjieff composed a musical score dedicated to the Aisors, giving a vital clue to some of his knowledge, as it was believed that the score was based on sacred or 'objective' music. The piece is a lamentation – a musical form that plays a large role in esoteric and religious traditions – so much so that there is even a book of Lamentations in the Bible following this bygone Middle Eastern tradition.

It was through his search for the Aisors/Sarmoung that Gurdjieff encountered an Armenian priest whereby he took possession of a map of pre-sand Egypt. All of this is pregnant with meaning. The map had to be dated 7,500BC or older, hailing from the period when Egypt was still a lush and fertile land. This was an era long before the Sahara desert had come to dominate Northern Africa and according to Gurdjieff, a time when man lived in complete harmony with his environment. This chance discovery led him to reconsider the true origins of the Sphinx. We know from the De Hartmans in Chapter 2 that Gurdjieff had the ability to decode dolmens and standing stones as if he were reading a compass. He was also given to the reading and dating of prehistoric cave art. It seems clear that Gurdjieff possessed a key to reading such monolithic byways and if so, what was the significance of pre-sand Egypt? Gurdjieff told the journalist Solita Solano, one of the Parisian 'Ladies of the Rope', that he had been initiated into the Egyptian mysteries a total of four times, but where and by whom?

The Guardians of the Sphinx, right up until their suppression, were a highly respected people rarely credited in the byways of esoteric thought, yet their important preservation of the most advanced sciences of the ancients and subsequent contribution to humanity is unrivalled. It is almost certain that the Arab and European Renaissances would never have happened without their vital input. We are talking here about the people known as the Sabeans (sometimes spelled Sabians). The origins of the Sabeans are disputed but there are three branches; two in the Arabian peninsula and another in Ethiopia. We must remember that Ethiopia as mentioned by the ancients used to take in other lands whose caravans traversed areas including modern-day Armenia, Eritrea, Yemen, even Syria.

Controversy rages around the widely held belief that the 'Sabians' settled in Harran were a later people (possibly a blanket term for assorted pagans) who adopted this name Sabian to protect themselves from Muslim persecution, knowing as they did, that the Quaranic and Biblical references partially protected them. It would appear if we accept the notion of the pre-sand maps theory, i.e. stone worship and navigation using dolmens, that the Sabian star worshippers were already ensconced here as far back as Chaldea and beyond to the time of the Patriarchs. Evidence attested by their pilgrimage from Harran to the Sphinx; no other explanation for this last reverence can be explained.

The Sabeans placed great importance on making pilgrimage to both the Sphinx and the pyramids, a tradition they upheld right up until their suppression. By this can infer the Sabaeans were a stellar cult and part of a hidden tradition now largely ignored by historians.

Their ritual encampment was built to receive pilgrims who had made the journey to the Sphinx whose original name, 'Hwl', they preserved. The names Sinai, Sahara and Sheba are also of Sabean origin; all being named after deities from their pantheon of gods. Many well-known historical figures are said to have stemmed from Sabean stock, not least the Queen of Sheba, who famously met and possibly eloped with King Solomon. Likewise the Prophet Muhammed originated from Sabean heritage and it is from this tradition that the familiar Islamic practices of praying five times a day, ablutions and fasting in line with lunar movements, are derived. Indeed, the Prophet spoke highly of the Sabean people in the Quran. Gurdjieff may have recognised the origins of Sufism here in these Sabean practices and sought to understand the origins of an esoteric germination of such import; one key example being that Allah is believed to be a name for God which may have come from the Patriarchs who existed before the Great Flood.

Sabean gods included Sin (pronounced Sheen) who was a Moon goddess from whom Sinai takes its name. Her temple complex was found in Harran (known as the Blessed City) among the Taurus mountains, being dominated by a tall, highly-famed astronomical observatory known in the Akkadian tongue as E-Hul Hul (House of Rejoicing). Here the priests observed the complex celestial movements from their mighty tower.

As a race of celebrated astrologers possessing a profound knowledge of the heavens, the Sabaeans became known as the 'people of the stars'. Some consider them to have been worshippers of the Pole Star, a celestial body of great significance in all accounts of the masters and the hidden directorate. While the Sabaeans hailed from what we now call Turkey, their great affinity with the Sphinx caused them to observe the pilgrimage to Egypt and the monument of such crucial import to their religious beliefs. An ancient people whose tongue was purportedly derived from that spoken by the patriarch Enoch, they were tolerated in the region and allowed to practice their religion in peace through the paying of tribute. In later times they were even referred to by both Christians and Muslims as the 'Subbos' or 'the ancients'. By repute they were also highly skilled silver and goldsmiths and some believe that the sacred square and compass emblem used in Freemasonry is almost certainly derived from the Sabaeans. It is certain that they had a strong connection to the Pole Star and therefore the swastika mythos.

Accounts of their great knowledge speak of their now lost skill in the irrigation of arid places and their mastery of language which made them renowned among all peoples of the region who encountered them. Their holy books included: The Book of the Sun, the Book of the Hidden One and the Emerald Tablets of Thoth. Some called them the 'People of the Book'. It is understood that they later retreated to Harran where the fabled astronomical tower dedicated to their moon goddess Sin became home to their priesthood. From what is known of them their writing and modes of worship were adopted by the Babylonians and Chaldeans. The Babylonian and Hebrew word for Sun is 'Shamash', also identical in the Sabean language pronounced 'Samas'. This word corrupted across lands as Sama, Semon, Simon, and of course Saman, another name for the Sufi 'Dhikr', or remembrance. It is no accident that the sacred word Dhikr was given to Muhammed in the caves on his flight – Muhammed the Sabean, who worshipped a crescent moon and revered the Hidden One who later became Quidir. Sufism itself comes from Sabean worship. The Kaaba in Mecca around which the faithful circumambulate during the Hajj pilgrimage, is believed to be the site of a former statue of Hubal, the Sabean God of divination, which was reconsecrated by the Prophet and thereby cleansed for Muslim worship. It must be noted most mosque minarets bear the crescent moon at their summit.

The name Hubal is taken from the word Hwl, which we have seen is an ancient name of the Sphinx. This word was later corrupted to 'hu' as in 'Allah-hu', the traditional Sufi chant used during the recitations of the Sufi Dhikr. The Sufis adopted the Sabean Hidden One, who they reappropriated as the Prophet Quidir, along with the sacred number 30 and the words of the Dhikr. The font from which Sufi mysticism drinks is therefore Sabean. One strongly suspects that Gurdjieff might have known this, given his strong connection with both the Middle East and Turkey and his affinity with the Egyptian Sphinx.

The exalted priesthood of the Sabaeans were known as the Mu Karib (meaning 'close to God'); the sacred guardians of ancient knowledge who founded the Arabian port of Muza (based on the root word Mu) and for years the Sabaeans dominated trade in the region. Later the term Mu Karib became the Syrian surname Malik. Out of four kings in ancient Arabia only two bore the elevated title Mukarib. These priest kings soon found their way to rule in Ethiopia which helped to preserve the sublime teachings and mysteries only marvelled at by other peoples in the region.

Reverence of their superior knowledge and power reached the Arab court of Baghdad and the centre of learning called the House of Wisdom, wherein sat a Sabean scholar, a polymath to rival Da Vinci, who translated most of the Greek writings for the Arabs, introducing them to many of the sciences taken from Sabean sources. One cannot underestimate the influence of the scholar Tabit who never renounced his faith and educated the Arab court. Without his work much of the modern knowledge which passed from Sabean to Arab then finally to Renaissance Europe, may never have reached us. Logic, medicine, trigonometry, chemistry, philosophy, all flourished under the influence of the Sabean polymath Tabit. One area of knowledge was astral magic, no doubt coming from Chaldean sources. It shows Harran as an immense powerhouse of learning.

The 17th Century non-conformist theologian Theophilus Gale, wrote in his book *Court of the Gentiles*, that: "Zabaism, so termed from the Zabii, a sect of Chaldean philosophers, was the first and more natural piece of idolatry, which consisted in a religious worship given unto the sun, moon, and stars." Gale also rightly identified that Afghanistan had instructed the Chaldeans in knowledge gained at Harran. Were the Zabii the Sabi-un of the Arabs? Almost certainly.

It is said the Sabaeans revered the Sphinx and the pyramids as the final resting places of both Seth and Enoch, which runs counter to the accepted story of Enoch being taken up to heaven at the end of his life on Earth. The Giza plateau was certainly seen as the burial place of prophets. The Sabaeans were custodians of the Emerald Tablets, and they practiced the Hermetic tradition along with its unique brand of magic. If they identified Hermes with Thoth, the alleged builder of the pyramids, then the Sabean cult might also have had a reason to make their sacred pilgrimages to the Giza monuments. These Sabaeans who were clearly masters of the stars, navigation, possessors of the earlier name of the Sphinx, worshippers of Enoch, keepers of rare holy books whose god was found in the names of the region – did these people belong to a time harking back to the lush climes of pre-sand Egypt as Gurdjieff and others understood? Why did the Sphinx, built in the likeness of a Pharoah, hold so much fascination for them?

Harran – City of Sin
In Chapter 2 we saw Gurdjieff taking J.G. Bennett to the caves of Lascaux. For some reason the latter thought he may have caused offence in doubting

Gurdjieff about the precise aging of the cave art. Bennett mused that the art the caves contained was around 20,000 years old, very much in line with theories of his day. Gurdjieff insisted otherwise, almost as though he could relate the etchings of bison, sphinx-like creatures and so on, to a particular historical phase, stating that the art was the work of a conscious school attempting to preserve their knowledge in the light of a great cataclysm. He firmly believed the art to be the work of an Atlantean brotherhood working some 7,000 to 8,000 years before. Gurdjieff's interpretation was so precise as to have caused Bennett to reconsider. As part of this revelation to his pupil, Gurdjieff spoke of the cave paintings' use of a stag motif – an emblem employed by the brotherhood in question. According to Gurdjieff, the number of branches on the antler headdresses depicted on human figures denoted the attainment level of the person concerned. Perhaps the most significant aspect of Gurdjieff's apparent knowledge, now lost, was that within a few miles of the cave paintings there would be several dolmens acting as compass markers by which the cult's initiatory centre could be located. Could there have been a worldwide system to aid navigation cleaved from stone?

In the book of Genesis, the Bible tells us of Jacob's vision on his way to Harran, "Taking one of the stones there, he put it under his head and lay down to sleep. He had a dream in which he saw a stairway resting on the earth, with its top reaching to heaven, and the angels of God were ascending and descending on it."

Jacob is commanded to erect a stone like a pillar (or dolmen) which he annoints with oil and names the 'Bethel Stone'. 'Beth' is the Hebrew word for house, and 'El' is indicative of divinity, or God, so it becomes the 'stone which is a house of God'. Both Jacob's ladder and the Bethel Stone are linked to Harran and this makes it remarkably similar to Gurdjieff's comments that certain stones mark the way to great centres of initiation.

Harran, stronghold of the stargazing Sabaeans who studied the cosmos, is situated but a few miles from Göbekli Tepe, the oldest known Neolithic stone temple. Harran is mentioned in the Bible as the place where Abraham and his wife set out to go to the land of Canaan and according to tradition it was founded by the grandson of Noah – Cainan, the son of Ham. Abraham had arrived there from his Chaldean birthplace, the city of Ur. The same Ur that was the cradle of the earliest civilisation of Sumer whose priests made the city the chief seat of the lunar worship of Sin[1]. As for Sabean Harran, its influential city dominated by its astronomical tower, is mentioned several times in Biblical stories and again we catch tales of Gurdjieff, as if by chance. But this is not a Sunday school class. Harran is the springboard of the Hermetic tradition. Hermes-Thoth-Enoch-Idris-

---

[1] In 1927 Leonard Wolley identified Ur Kasdom with the Sumerian city of Ur (founded c. 3,800 BC), in southern Mesopotamia, where the Chaldeans settled much later (around the 9th Century BC).

Quidir-Elijah. Harran is the crucible. Keen astronomers they may have been, but the Sabaeans also possessed a cult devoted to stellar mysteries indelibly linked with the pyramids and the Sphinx, as attested by their own lengthy pilgrimage to Giza. The name of the moon deity Sin is often said to have been taken from an earlier pronunciation Su-en, which itself when magically reversed became En-su. The sacred direction for the veneration of Sin was the North towards the Pole Star and the 'Lord in the Moon', similar to one title for the lunar deity Thoth. According to some theories, the goddess Sin may have been associated with the full moon, with Su-en representing the moon in its crescent phase. However, much evidence emerges that Su-en was a moon god from an even earlier time, that of the Sumerians – the earliest known Mesopotamian civilisation, which conventional historians believe to be the true cradle of all those that followed, including our own. Its ancient name is the 'Land of Shinar' – a name possibly linked to Sin worship. Harran, Göbekli Tepe, Babylon, Uruk and Ninevah, all are encompassed by the 'Land of Shinar' and therefore bound by the stellar cult. Cainan, the grandson of Noah learnt from rock carvings left behind by previous inhabitants that had perished in the Great Flood; this rather heretical knowledge, it is said, was left by those who had rebelled against God.

Gurdjieff claimed to have read the *Epic of Gilgamesh* directly from the Sumerian cuneiform tablets translated by archaeologists. He would have known then that the moon god had a select name – Su-en – and that En-su and Su-en were interchangeable names for the same lunar deity. The Gilgamesh tablets discovered at Ninevah, if these are the source Gurdjieff refers to, were written in Akkadian which had two dialects, Assyrian and Babylonian, but the series of myths belonged to the oldest culture, Sumeria.

Cuneiform, the earliest system of writing, was primarily developed to record ledgers for the purposes of trade. Over the course of time, the system became more complex and nuanced, which eventually allowed for the writing of epic tales and stories. Historians date the origins of cuneiform to around 3,500BC, describing it as a pictographic language, much like Egyptian hieroglyphics or Chinese Hanzi, where syllables or words are represented by certain pictograms. We are fortunate that most cuneiform was written on clay tablets, which has allowed examples of ancient writing to reach us today largely unscathed. What is rarely mentioned is the fact that much of the cuneiform language is actually allied to the sexagesimal mathematical system.

Put simply, it is based on a mathematical system which revolves around the number 60. Imagine a clock face, which we know represents one hour divided into 60 minutes. The unique numerical quality of the number 60 is that by being a composite number, it has more dividing possibilities than any other.

The number 60 can be divided by 1, 2, 3, 4, 5, 6, 10, 12, 15, 20 and 30, making it extremely useful when calculating fractions, angles, weights, measures and most importantly, time. One of the great advances that the Sumerians introduced was the number or value zero, without which the so-called Arabic number system could not have existed. That too is sexagesimal in origin. Clearly this civilisation was more evolved than some that came later, negating the idea that everything is constantly 'advancing' from age to age. Cuneiform is both a lexicon and numeric system. This language revolved around a system, from what is known, where each character is both a letter, a number and an entire word. This is our modern understanding of cuneiform but there may have been additional values attached to the characters which we are unaware of.

This system passed onto Old Babylonian and later to Arabic itself, where it is reflected in its magical systems. The Sabaeans may also have been recipients of the Chaldean/Babylonian magic too. As such all deities were assigned names but were also classified by their corresponding numerical values. For example, the goddess Sin was 30, whereas her daughter Ishta, being only half the 'worth' of her mother, was 15. Likewise, the number 20 was assigned to the deity Samas, who was worshipped on the 20th day of the month. Nanna is equated, like Sin, to the number 30. Another aspect of cuneiform rarely mentioned is its link to astronomy. A man named Ossendrijver recently observed from reading cuneiform that the Babylonians and possibly the Sumerians before them, had exact methods of calculating the orbit of Jupiter, something which up until recently historians only supposed was possible from the time of the European Renaissance onwards. Science historian Jens Høyrup at Roskilde University in Denmark also weighed in on the controversy by adding that it was not the first hint that the Babylonians were suspected of using geometric calculus to record the motion of the moon. What no one has really delivered here is that the very language they uesed to decode all of this was also its own cypher. The cuneiform is both numerical and pictorial, but also astronomical. Now if Gurdjieff is true to his word and had studied the cuneiform writings as he claimed, was this indeed the watershed of information that he purports to have found? Equally could the so-called map of pre-sand Egypt be written in the dolmens? Could Gurdjieff have literally unlocked the secrets of the very first civilisations?

We mentioned his musical score about the Aisors – a lamentation no less – that strikes a chord with an old tale of the region which tells of the last survivors of the flood, who wept when they committed their stories to stone. As their tears flowed over the tablets they knew in their hearts that after such a great cataclysm, mankind would never again rise to the heights of angelic civilisation he had once achieved. Again, this old tradition is bound up in mystery.

The Archaeoastronomer James Jacobs claims to have discovered a link between the layout of Harran and Ur, thereby linking their lineage within the secret stellar tradition of the Sabaeans/Chaldeans. This now gives rise to the suspicion that both the Biblical Jacob and Abraham were also both enmeshed in the celestial cult. Harran and Ur are, according to James Jacobs, connected by a geodetic latitude and this also links in, albeit tentatively, with the oldest stone temple, Göbekli Tepe, situated a mere 25 miles away. Could Gurdjieff, through his knowledge of cuneiform and the decoding of its numerical and astronomical features have rediscovered the geodetic knowledge of ancient man? Were these monuments, time-worn citadels and temple sites laid out by precise trigonometry literally taken from the stars?

James Jacobs certainly thinks so. It may explain the sacred compass and square and their original usage in esoteric circles adopted by the Freemasons.

The Sabaeans ceased to exist much beyond the 13th Century AD but we can rest assured that much of their knowledge of science, mathematics and astronomy has been bequeathed to us in the modern age via the work of the Sabean translator Tabit, based at the Baghdad Court. Sabean esoteric lore, even magic, passed via Islam to the Sufis and in a second transmission to the Yezidis, another faith that exerted a deep influence over Gurdjieff.

What the Egyptians Said of the Great Flood

The ancient Greek historian Herodotus, dubbed 'The Father of History', once recounted some very unusual chronicles concerning the Egyptians' superior engineering capabilities. He claims to have visited a vast underground city built beneath the Giza plateau and while there, he discoursed with the famed Egyptian Priests of Sais who made him privy to many of their mysteries. In wonderment Herodotus saw first-hand their immense understanding of history, telling of the existence of a labyrinthine library, the scale of which eclipsed anything the Ancient Greeks had constructed in their time. In February 2021, British newspapers reported the discovery of a mysterious doorway in a passage beneath one of the Giza pyramids, sparking fresh interest in Herodotus' claims. Yet the Greek was not alone in his assertions; a 10th Century Arab historian named Al-Masudi similarly claimed the same underground chambers located beneath Giza contained ancient wisdom not known to ordinary men. He tells us that the great library's records of art and science were left for the benefit of mankind and whosoever found it again could benefit according to their understanding.

Let us pause here. Al-Masudi stresses 'according to their understanding', which is echoed in what Gurdjieff said of objective art left behind by the masters; it can only be understood by consciousness, not intellect. One could only decode any message at one's own level of being, redolent of the old adage, 'beauty is in the eye of the beholder'. If the underground repository, the pyramids and the Sphinx are constructed in such a manner, then surely the discovery of the secrets they contain will only mirror the inner state of mankind as it finds them? Normal physical, emotional and intellectual responses could be a mere runway to inner space when looking at objective art – an artform created consciously for precise effect by people who have obtained higher consciousness, perhaps even enlightenment. Of course, all of this is mere conjecture, much like the legend of Shangri-La; these ideas are fictional approximations of old legends, or so we are taught.

Most photographers learning their craft will be made aware of the importance of the 'rule of thirds'. Each picture they compose must observe this law in order to make the subject beautiful, interesting and harmonious. Essentially, the law dictates that any composition, whether landscape or portrait, is divided into nine equal parts. The subject is placed in the left or right third of the image, with space dominating the rest of the area. All classical painters knew of this law, and if we go further still perhaps the sculptors of the classical period were aware of it too. Architects certainly make use of it, as did the builders of the pyramids. This is but one example of objective art in its most base form. Chimpanzees randomly pointing cameras cannot expect great results – one must plan a successful composition. The riddle of the Sphinx is as much sensoria as it is physical/ historical. It moves in eternity beyond the limitations of physical time itself.

The discovery of the Rosetta Stone by Napoleonic forces in 1799 paved the way for the decoding of many Pharaonic secrets of Egypt. Until that time, the modern understanding of Egyptian hieroglyphics was largely down to guesswork, but the passage engraved on the stone was repeated in three languages; Egyptian, Demotic and Greek, two of which were known. This provided a vital key to linguists when deciphering the meaning of the Egyptian script, but no such template has yet been found to explain the building of the pyramids and Sphinx. Historians who dare to speculate outside the confines of the academic mainstream posit that the Ancient Egyptians merely inherited these mighty infrastructures from an earlier, superior civilisation; a highly advanced race possessing great knowledge which was lost due to a great flood. Herodotus implied as much, citing the Egyptians as those who had inherited fragments of this advanced knowledge, including the true history of humanity itself. He specifically mentions the High Priest of Sais in this regard, an Egyptian called Sonchis, who related the story of the antediluvian kingdom to the Athenian statesman Solon. This curious tale was eventually recorded in writing by Plato a century later. Of all the Ancient Greek storytellers Plato perhaps stands above them all.

His dialogues entitled *Timaeus* and *Critias* give us the prospect of an age-old mystery which has defied scholars through the ages; an enigma Plato felt drawn to recount as he neared the end of his life, perhaps sensing its great import to humanity. The full account was never realised – the story ends in mid-flow, leaving his dissertation unfinished. These dialogues are presented as fiction, yet tantalisingly this may have acted as a convenient vehicle through which to convey an oral history that may otherwise have been lost to us. Choosing to present the tale as an imaginary dialogue between scholars about a long-forgotten civilisation, Plato would forever more be coupled with fabled Atlantis.

The first dialogue, *Timaeus* (written c.360BC), examines the nature of the physical world and the human condition by means of a discussion between four philosophers whose conversation soon turns to the idea of a perfect State. *Timeas* refers directly to the real-life journey of the elder statesman Solon, who travelled to Ancient Egypt as part of a trade mission. Among several other accomplishments Solon is credited with returning to Greece with the legend of Atlantis, although this is still a great bone of contention among historians. The general consensus has since prevailed that Plato gave vent to his artistic license, embellishing the account of Solon and therefore cultivating the myth of Atlantis. In light of recent discoveries about Ancient Egypt can we now be so sure?

Solon lived around 630BC and is noted as being one of the great lawgivers and social pillars in Athenian democracy. As a statesman, democrat, poet and social reformer who acted against the injustices of his time, particularly those tied to land and debt, his legacy survives to this day. In a broad sense he was a prototypical socialist who believed in freedom from serfdom. He opposed the oppressive land ownership laws that often left farmers bankrupt and beholden to a higher landlord class as little more than indentured slaves. Solon was partially successful in his social reforms and greatly celebrated among Athenian democrats for his efforts.

According to Plato's fictional account, Solon sojourned to Egypt as part of trade mission and became a guest in the city of Sais where he befriended the Egyptian priest Sonchis who lived on the Nile Delta. Berating his Greek guest, the Egyptian priest accused him of reciting child-like stories in his account of the Greek pantheon, saying that Greek history was far older and more noble than its people knew. Sonchis of Sais confided in his guest that the Greek, and indeed Egyptian, history stretched back far in time to a great global cataclysm. The priest told Solon that the Greeks had fought a war of global proportions but had been effectively wiped out, leaving the survivors with no idea of their own history. However, the priest said the opposite was the case in Egypt, where knowledge of the event was still preserved. Softening his stance towards his guest the Egyptian priest took Solon under his wing, sympathetically explaining that the Greeks were not in possession of any thought handed down by the ancients and therefore had no tradition by which to live.

Through his accounts of Solon's journey to Egypt, Plato bequeathed to us the central story of Atlantis, said to be an island state of harmonious development whose populace had attained a high degree of advancement in every known discipline. It must be said that the name Atlantis is a Greek invention – no such name was used by the priest Sonchis. The Egyptian narrative tells of a place dominated by a mighty citadel surrounded by three concentric rings of land and encircled by canals. In the centre of the citadel stood the pillar of Poseidon. In the account entitled *Critias*, Plato explains that the pillar was central to a religion dominated by the bull, whose sacrifice was a central focus of the cult. Ten priest-kings oversaw the rites dedicated to Poseidon, the principal god of Atlantis. The harmony of the Atlantean state was shattered, however, when a global war erupted. Caused in part by the arrogance of the Atlantean leaders and the indolence of its populace, the conflict led to its ultimate destruction. Atlantis was swallowed up by the Atlantic ocean and its people decimated by flooding.

Having recounted the tale of Atlantis to the Greeks during a festival, Solon's story was soon consigned to the fiction shelves by the Athenians who heard it. Even students of Plato were inclined to view it as no more than an interesting, though fanciful, tale in support of superior Greek origins. From that moment on to the present day, the matter of the historical existence of Atlantis has remained contentious, with opinion divided between those who consider it to be pure fiction and others who believe it to be documentary evidence taken directly from the Egyptian Priesthood. Subsequent considerations about Atlantis have nearly always been consigned to the realm of myth, but in light of recent discoveries in Egypt can we now be so sure that Plato's account of Solon is just fictitious drama? Of course, to conventional historians, any deviation from the accepted view that Atlantis is no more than a myth is seen as wishful thinking. Leaving Plato out of this for a moment, the Egyptian texts speak of seven sages who brought civilisation to the world, with the Egyptians carefully recording that the pyramids were built by Thoth during an earlier age than their own. All of this is identical to the seven sages found in Mesopotamian lore, written in cuneiform, called the Apkallu/Apgal, or teachers of all wisdom, knowledge and magical sciences.

The Sphinx Unmasked

In 1973 a quasi-military research group calling itself the Stanford Institute travelled from the United States to conduct a series of investigations on the

Sphinx. Headed up by a man named Dr Dolphin and making use of cutting-edge sonar equipment, the team drilled into the nearby bedrock. Their explorations uncovered a tunnel situated to the rear of the structure which led to the gap in between the front paws. Dr Dolphin subsequently announced that sonar readings indicated the existence of a rectangular room situated directly below the Sphinx's outstretched front legs. Fast-forward 17 years and the Sphinx Project once again confirmed the discovery of the room beneath the statue using their own equipment. Since these discoveries the Egyptian authorities have forbidden more research or excavations near the Sphinx. Other audacious researchers, perhaps rogue investigators, say this discovery is but the tip of the iceberg and that a metropolis lies beneath Giza, just as described by Herodotus. No evidence to support the findings of Dr Dolphin or his team has yet been conclusive in our own times, but older reports remain.

Other explorers, such as Arab explorer Al-Masudi, have added their own accounts that appear to confirm the pyramids and the Sphinx are not what they seem. Such chronicles echo alternative views that Giza as we know it has not been fully explored and many mysteries await discovery in the rock below. The Turin Papyrus records several kings before Menes (also known as Min, Mena, Meni), the so-called originator of a unified Ancient Egypt. Another record, 'The Palermo Stone', goes further still by listing scores of dynasties before Menes.

Another fascinating account reaches us from two hundred years ago in that of Henry Salt, a British diplomat and his companion the Italian explorer Ginovanni Caviglia, who in 1817 entered a number of underground passages leading to a huge chamber. They described these as 'catacombs' reporting paintings of birds and animals on the walls and even a zodiac of sorts there too. They could not continue onwards, describing the cave passages as 'uninviting'; perhaps they were driven back by the spiders and bats that reside there. These discoveries were made only a few hundred feet from the pyramids. It was Caviglia who dug out the sands around the Sphinx in later adventures whereupon he discovered a series of steps leading to the paws, as if created for effect and to add a sense of marvel at the sandstone creature. The merciless desert winds put paid to his heroic efforts and the trench his Arab labourers had created was soon backfilled once more.

Another learned man who had heard of the hidden chambers containing rare maps of remote antiquity beneath the pyramids was Ma'mun, whose father was Caliph Harun al-Raschid, author of the greatly fabled *The Thousand and One Nights*. Ma'mun wasted no time in visiting the Sabaeans in Harran in 830AD to discuss these mysteries. His name will ever be remembered for excavating the Great Pyramid to look for this stash but he came away empty handed. In 1992 a French engineer by the name of Jean Kerisal went drilling in Giza and his radar equipment uncovered evidence of a previously unknown shaft inside the pyramid pointing toward the Sphinx. It appears that people are ready to believe that there may have been a civilisation that belonged to the fertile, lush planes of pre-sand Egypt. To those who say it is an invention or construction of the Ancient Egyptians, let them consider that the Egyptians themselves placed likenesses of the Sphinx at the entrance of great mystery sites as a guardian of sorts, to remind the curious enquirer that the guarded sanctuary was accessible only to the initiated. Given the size of the Sphinx at Giza, could the secret it conceals be of equally momentous scale and stature? As a motif, the figure of the chimerical Sphinx predates Khafre and all other Pharoahs, which could speak volumes to most modern historians, but not so unfortunately. Circumstantial evidence supports the theory that the Sphinx's facial features were reconfigured at a much later date than the original construction, with possible causes including erosion or damage by water, rather than sand and wind, as one might expect.

Then there is the curious fact that the monument's proportions do not appear to match the current face, leading to the theory that the builders accepted it would be obscured by sand once constructed. Common sense tells us the Sphinx could never have been built with the intention that it be mostly concealed beneath dunes of sand and that it must have been constructed with observation of its mighty form in mind: ergo it must have been built in pre-sand Egypt. As a monument, the Sphinx presents many uncomfortable questions for conventional historians, with the ever-present spectre lurking of a much older unknown civilisation that possessed the technology to allow them to build the pyramids way earlier than is currently thought.

Advancing a theory of a pre-sand Sphinx, several researchers have noted that the face of the statue must have been altered by the dynastic authorities seeking to aggrandise their own ruler Khafre. Major figures in the controversy such as Graham Hancock have advanced the idea of the face being that of the astrological lion Leo, while Robert Temple posits it is a representation of the jackal-headed god Anubis. There may be a host of other projections onto the face of the Sphinx, such as the Egyptian god Horus.

Rarely mentioned however is Thoth, supposed architect of the entire site, which would partly explain why the Sabaeans thought the Sphinx so important. Thoth is portrayed as ibis-headed by the Egyptians and since the elongated beak would have caused structural problems at such a scale, it seems improbable. But if we render Thoth in his earlier Sabean form, the progenitor of Thoth, if you will, the Sphinx could have borne the features of Enoch. This would make sense as Enoch was a pre-flood patriarch of great antiquity revered throughout the region, especially by the Sabaeans. Sin/Enoch/Thoth and the Islamic Idris/Quidir, the latter being identical with prophet Elijah – all these figures are one and the same personage. It would at least explain the pilgrimages made by the Sabean people to the sandstone creature. Yet, the Sphinx will always be a mirror of the internal state of the onlooker. Some have reflected that Gurdjieff used the pre-sand map as an allegory to signify wisdom untainted by distortion. A teaching not untainted by distortions, or misrepresented by dogmas or religion.

Keepers of the Ark

Enigmatically, Gurdjieff's writings on Egypt talk of a man named Professor Skridlov, whom he befriended following their joint exploration of the ruins of Thebes. The pair decided to travel together up the Nile towards Abyssinia (modern day Eritrea and Ethiopia). Most histories of Africa pass Ethiopia off as a relatively unimportant backwater and therefore unworthy of further significant cultural enquiry. Their position, it would seem, is that nothing remarkable came from this place. However, if we leave the conventional histories behind and dig a little deeper we must accept that the region holds clues to an altogether more fascinating heritage. For seekers after antediluvian mysteries and forgotten teachings, Ethiopia and Eritrea present a veritable cornucopia of intrigue. In his final years, Gurdjieff confided to Solita Solano, of the Ladies of the Rope, his female entourage in Paris, that he once saw himself retiring to Ethiopia. It is known that in his dotage Gurdjieff also made similar remarks to others among his pupils.

His book *Meetings with Remarkable Men* talks of a living tradition and its importance in conveying the meaning of life, pointing toward the source of the Nile which is, in fact, Ethiopia – more precisely Lake Tana. It is here, he suggests, that the teachings regarding the inner meaning of life were preserved. Gurdjieff stated that, "Prehistoric Egypt was Christian many thousands of years before the birth of Christ, that is to say, that its religion was composed of the same principles and ideas that constitute true Christianity." Gurdjieff took the view that the blueprint for Christianity stemmed from prehistoric Egypt and that same tradition, he suspected, lay hidden in Abyssinia (Ethiopia).

The Ethiopians consider themselves to be the true custodians of many Christian traditions. Within their own religious writings there is a tract known as the Kebra Nagast (Glory of Kings) which details the life of the legendary Queen of Sheba and her fabled visit to King Solomon. It dates from the 14th Century and therefore carries no weight with conventional historians, while others maintain it is taken from much earlier sources – again another bone of contention. Some even believe that the grail legends of Europe were lifted wholesale from the Kebra Nagast by the German knight-poet Wolfram von Eschenbach, who penned the famous 13th Century epic *Parzival*.

Examining this celebrated meeting between the fabled potentates, Solomon and Sheba, we know the latter was greatly enamoured with Solomon. In the Western Bible we know she is identified as being from Saba, probably Arabia, although due to Sabean connections with another state called D'mt it is certainly possible she came from Ethiopia. The Quran also mentions the two rulers meeting, with similar accounts of what transpired between them. In recognition of his wisdom, which she prized greatly, the Queen of Sheba lavished Solomon with opulent gifts and bountiful praise. Later accounts embellished these stories further, but the Kebra Nagast is not one of these and it stands in contrast with the Biblical and Islamic texts.

In the Ethiopian version the Queen of Sheba was called Makida – she eloped with Solomon resulting in the birth of their son Menelik, who grew up in Sheba unaware of his father's identity. As he matured into adulthood, Menelik learned he was the son of the celebrated ruler and visited Jerusalem to study the Torah under his father. All went well until Menelik stole the Ark of the Covenant and replaced it with a fake. Menelik returned to Ethiopia and unbeknown to him he was pursued but made it back with the sacred artefact intact. To this day Ethiopia is associated with this holy relic, believed to be housed in the city of Axum (the second Jersualem) inside the Church of Our lady of Zion. For centuries, virgin monks have guarded the sacred Ark, never stepping foot outside its hallowed precincts until they shrug off this mortal coil.

Based on the Biblical descriptions, several modern scientists have attested that the Ark of the Covenant resembles a modern-day capacitor, which in layman's terms is an electrical storage device. It must be noted that gold, which Makida bestowed upon Solomon in great quantities during her stay in Jerusalem, is an excellent conductor of electricity. Did Solomon and Makida have a business deal going? A deal to produce electricity? If traditional accounts are to be believed, it is certain that the Ark was a repository of great, even destructive, power. It is said to have laid waste to armies, while Moses is said to have communicated directly with God with the aid of two cherubim mounted on the Ark's cover. It could prove fatal to those who touched it unexpectedly and it had to be supported and carried using wooden staves. Could this have been a precautionary measure to prevent death from electric shock? God also commanded that it be curtained off, which suggests a radiative element too.

The Bible tells us the Ark was the repository of the stone tablets of law as received by Moses. According to the book of Hebrews it also contained Aaron's rod, which caused so many miracles and pestilences to light upon humanity, alongside a container of the divine foodstuff, Manna, that supposedly fell from the skies as the Hebrews wandered the desert in exile. It is worth noting that the Ark was originally constructed by Moses under God's instruction while he was on Mount Sinai, the place named after the Sabean Moon Goddess Sin. According to one theory regarding the Ark's whereabouts following its disappearance from the Biblical narrative, the relic was transported up the Nile to its source, Lake Tana, where it rested for four centuries before being moved once more under great secrecy to Axum, where it resides to this day. Patriarch Abune Paulos, who was head of the Ethiopian Orthodox Tewahedo Church until his death in 2012, made statements partially confirming this position in the year of his enthronement. Several conventional historians have poured scorn on such theories with great venom. During the same year of 1992, a Professor named Edward Ullendorf, a specialist in Ethiopian studies in London, issued a claim that he had personally inspected the artefact in Axum during the Second World War. Ullendorf tells of an empty wooden casket dating from the late Medieval period; a revelation that seriously undermined the claims of Biblical treasures held by the Ethiopian Priesthood. While such commentaries appear to debunk the Ethiopian theory, there are many potential resting places for the Ark of the Covenant and every reason for those holding plundered relics to conceal their looted treasures, if such things ever existed. Some have suggested that the Priests guarding the object at Axum do not use the word Ark at all but refer to their treasure as a tablet. Could this be in reference to the tablets given by God to Moses? It will be remembered that he received these after 40 nights on top of Mount Sinai – yet more stories of sacred stones from the Bible.

In Chapter 6 we touched briefly on Bruce's discovery of the book of Enoch, which displayed remarkable similarities with texts subsequently found among the Dead Sea Scrolls. The Jews also preserved fragments of the book of Enoch and, as we have seen, the Sabaeans identified themselves as being the offspring of Enoch and therefore the bearers of his teachings. The account we have of the Patriarch Enoch places him historically before the Great Flood. One of Enoch's sons, Sabi, reputedly founded the Sabean (or w) religion which bore his name. A keen worshipper of the planets, Sabi saw the influences of the heavenly bodies at work on the Earth, and a priesthood arose centred on his starry creed. Early accounts including the Bible point towards the Sabaeans' adoration of the Pole Star in particular, in whose direction they were said to offer their prayers.

Several later sects have their histories closely entwined with the Sabean mysteries; one such being the Baptisers, who some sources say later retreated to Harran, the city of the tower of the Sabean Moon goddess Sin. Leaving this aside for a moment Enoch and Ethiopia come ever closer in the Mashafa Henok, the Ethiopian book of Enoch, the manuscript penned in a script called Geez discovered by explorer Bruce. Enoch is a cornerstone of Ethiopian belief whereas in the West he is largely a pre-flood Old Testament figure. The rediscovery of the book of Enoch with its strange tales of Angelic intelligences called 'Watchers' has not been ascribed proper significance but it does reinforce Ethiopia as the preserver of forgotten knowledge and perhaps as a valued custodian of the pre-flood histories of humanity. Gurdjieff knew that at the source of the Nile lay Lake Tana, the largest lake in Ethiopia, and it was here he felt sure the knowledge of Egypt had been transmitted to Abyssinia in the horn of Africa (Ethiopia, Eritrea). He focused on a place where the Lake Tana community commemorated the Ethiopian Christian festival of Timkat – a rite of Baptism.

Mages in Ethiopia

According to Jewish lore, Moses spent 40 years living in Ethiopia. Some traditions maintain that Zipporah, his wife and mother of his two sons, was a black Ethiopian Kushite. It is highly likely she came from a small ethnic group based in the north-west of the country called the Qemant, who are said to have descended from Noah. As a people, the Qemant are curious, since their religion follows an ancient Hebraic form, untouched by any developments in mainstream Judaism over the last two millennia. The Prophet Muhammed had similar connections in Ethiopia through his marriage to Umm Habiba with the Negus, or Abbyssinian King, paying a sizable dowry. Both wife Hibaba and her father the Negus were descended of the Quraysh tribe. Her father was its leader. As a tribe they were invested with much importance in both the Islamic and pre-Islamic world as the people who controlled the sacred site of the Kaaba (shrine of the Sabaeans and later centre of the Hajj pilgrimage in Mecca). It explains perhaps how Muhammad was able to reconsecrate the revered stone there to Allah through his alliance with the Quraysh to assure their conversion to Islam.

The Prophet's own family took refuge in Abyssinia alongside other early Muslims during a period of religious persecution, much like Moses before him. Many of the later kings who sat on the Abyssinian throne were of Sabean lineages. The books of Enoch and Job were preserved here. Suddenly Ethiopia doesn't seem such a boring backwater after all. What was it that drew these mystical heavyweights to the area?

The writer William Patterson theorised that Gurdjieff had discovered the ancient source of Christianity in Egypt and then later Ethiopia, but found that some core elements of the keys to inner development were missing. In other words, Gurdjieff recognised this proto-Christianity as a fragment of the bigger picture of mankind's spiritual development. This element in the Gurdjieff story has been overlooked. There is no doubt, however, that Gurdjieff drew his wisdom from many sources both traditional and unorthodox; there is no single source or esoteric teaching we can point to as the wellspring of the Fourth Way. As Gurdjieff made his way upstream of the Nile he had to pass through Sudan. Given his great interest in stone circles, dolmens and menhirs it is not recorded whether he happened upon, or even knew of, the world's earliest stone circle, Nabta Playa, thought to be the oldest astronomical observatory. The 7,000 year-old circle situated about 100 kilometres west of Abu Simbel in Egypt, was discovered by accident in 1973 when a member of a team working on the major Nile dam project stopped to answer a 'call of nature' in the Sahara desert. Subsequent investigations by a leading astroarchaeologist questioned historians' basic analysis of the site. Professor Emeritus of Colorado University, a man named Malville, said of the discovery: "I discovered that these stones were part of an alignment that radiated out from a major tumulus [burial mound]," Malville says. "A pile of these megaliths formed the covering of a tomb, and it turned out that every one of the megaliths that we found buried in sediment formed a line, like spokes in a wheel radiating out."

Kim Malville has spent decades studying solar and astroarchaeology – his background in physics is very problematic for those who wish to dismiss the stone circle as a throwback to primitive times. It appears the circle is very complex indeed, measuring certain astronomical movements with great precision.

A person in possession of a map of pre-sand Egypt could perhaps have been aware of this Neolithic site. Gurdjieff himself said of the pre-sand map that he came to an altogether different understanding, not only of the Sphinx, but other monuments too. He even abandoned his search for the Sarmoung brotherhood following the discovery of the map; it completely reframed his understanding of these ancient schools and their antiquity, leading to a complete realignment of his own quest for enlightenment.

Was Nabta Playa on map of pre-sand Egypt too? If Nabta Playa of Sudan was a destination along the way, did its sacred stones illuminate the way forth to Ethiopia and ultimately places such as Axum and Lake Tana? Gurdjieff insisted that all such stone monuments were built by an ancient, advanced civilisation and contain objective features. Could they be serving an energetic function whereby the seeker can gain access to otherwise hidden initiation centres run by the mystery schools of the masters?

Joseph Gandy, an early writer on Freemasonry said of Ethiopia, "The Ethiopians had a table of the sun, with twelve signs or gods. It was an immense altar, four cubits high, situated in a great plain. For twelve days in each year it was filled with all kinds of meats and fruits, a sanctuary where any person might go and satisfy his hunger. To this origin we may ascribe feasts and festivals, the Saturnalia, Druid, and Christian holidays. The zodiac, or golden circle of Osymandes (one of the earliest kings of Egypt), divided into 365 parts, with the engraved aspects of the stars, was an imitation of the Ethiopian altar."

It appears the area of modern-day Sudan, Ethiopia and Eritrea is something of an originator of ideas, a far cry from the unremarkable backwater historians might have us believe it to be. A haven for ancient artefacts, books and traditions, it is even home to the 1974 discovery of the remains of an early protohuman, dubbed 'Lucy', that proved our ancestors walked upright here around three million years ago. In Gurdjieff's book *Beelzebub's Tales to His Grandson*, he recounts a vital clue to his innate beliefs on Ethiopia's importance in the scheme of history. In a fictional account, he describes an ancient society that survived the Great Flood which he called the Akhalden and without any obfuscation he tells us that they settled at the source of Nile, which we know to be Lake Tana in Ethiopia. That he travelled in the area is undoubted, but why was he so enamoured of the locality? It has been suggested by former pupils that he was drawn to the Ethiopian church ceremonies which employed dance, both inside and out in the open. Remember that Christ himself, the 'Lord of the Dance' also used dance in ceremonies he performed. Gurdjieff studied these motions; some such as the Timkat Baptismal rite can be quite ecstatic and wild.

There can be no doubt that Gurdjieff may have given serious consideration to Lake Tana as the site of Eden, the post-diluvian agricultural project to re-establish mankind as described in the Bible. Hence the reason for weaving the Akhalden story into his fiction and firmly anchoring it to Lake Tana. Perhaps he came across this information while in Egypt as some texts talk of an exalted King Sopdu whose presence is at the seat of gods – he too is found at the source of the Nile. This equates to the star Sirius, another masonic symbol and one closely entwined with Egyptology. Infact one ancient name for the river was Sopdu. New year falls in the Ethiopian religious calendar on or around June 24th, which aligns it closely with masonic feast of St John (midsummer's day).

A rural town in northern Ethiopia called Lalibela is home to a number of curious cross-shaped churches hewn directly from the rock in the surrounding hills. Modern historians claim they date from around the 7th to the 14th Centuries but their supposed Medieval origin is disputed. Their equal-armed cross layouts are certainly not that of the traditional crucifix on which European churches and cathedrals from that era are based. At Axum there is wonderful granite obelisk weighing 160 tonnes and standing some 79 feet high. For many years it stood in Rome, having been looted by the Italian army in 1937 but was repatriated in 2005, nearly fifty years after a UN agreement to return it was struck in 1947.

The monolith stands as testament to the old Axum Empire, an important strategic power in the region, yet its exact age and builder are unknown, although its official creation date is around the 4th Century AD. An impressively carved stone stele featuring false doors and flanked by window reliefs, it is hard to understand how such precision was possible without the use of diamond cutting technology. One possible purpose of such towers was for the marking of underground burial sites, again echoing the Bethel stone of Job and Gurdjieff's own use of stones as navigation points.

Monolithic sites abound in Ethiopia, perhaps the most remarkable being Tiya, a UNESCO world heritage site many miles south of Tana. Strange carvings on the stones include what appears to be a jet aircraft – whether this is a representation of the sky chariot used by Solomon in Ethiopian legends is unknown. Unbroken Solomonic rule ended in 1974 due to Soviet intrigues supporting an armed insurrection against the last Emperor Haile Selassie, who could trace his direct descendancy from that of Solomon and Sheba's son Menelik, the man who inherited the pillaged Ark. To write Ethiopia off as uninteresting historical aside or a far-flung backwood is sheer ignorance, forgetful of the great cultural longevity of the peoples who live there. Clearly it is an heirloom to prehistory, perhaps one of great import, as Gurdjieff made clear in both his fiction and in off-the-record comments to his pupils such Solano, Nott and Bennett.

Colonel Arthur E. Powell, Theosophist and writer, lived between 1882 and 1969. His literary output was impressive, but one volume in particular, entitled *The Solar System* published in 1930, detailed much of what Gurdjieff had held to himself. He described what are called 'root races' connected with Aryan tribes. In his account Colonel Powell clarifies where the Atlanteans settled after the flood waters receded, he says, "About 200,000 years ago Egypt was submerged and remained so for a considerable period. When it emerged again it was once more peopled by the descendants of its old inhabitants, who had taken refuge in the Abyssinian mountains, and by fresh bands of Atlantean colonists from various parts of the world. A considerable immigration of the sixth sub-race (the Akkadian) helped to modify the Egyptian type. This was the era of the second Divine Dynasty of Egypt, the rulers again being Initiated Adepts."

Whether one accepts his account or not, it is certainly redolent of the information passed on by Gurdjieff on the subject. Even the name Akkadian is similar to Akhaden, as if drawn from a similar source. Inside the *Secret Doctrine* written by Madame Blavatsky she explains and reminds us of Herodotus. He was apparently shown by the Egyptian Priesthood the statues of kings that had ruled back in the mists of time, his guides explained clearly that it was pointless to relate these histories unless one understood the previous root races that preceded the modern human. As we have touched upon, there are many skeleton remains that don't add up to our neatly calculated history of Darwinian evolution. Ethiopia is one such crucible where history is smelted.

A common thread in all these accounts taken from the peoples of yesteryear, is that they did not claim to have built the monuments, nor written the scriptures, nor even mapped the stars. In all cases they refer us to the gods, or the servants of the gods, like Enoch. None of them profess to have had the necessary knowledge.

Gurdjieff took this literally and may have really taken onboard that although he may have found Eden he had not found the missing fragment of wisdom that eluded him.

Chapter 8

A New Kind of Man

"... the Greek philosopher merged the history of Atlantis,
which conveyed several million years into one event which
he located on one comparatively small island [...] about the size
of Ireland, whereas the priests spoke of Atlantis as a continent
vast as "all Asia and Libya" put together."
Madame Blavatsky

Soundscapes of the Enlightened

Gurdjieff could floor a man with just one chord. During a piano recital before a group of his pupils, he struck a particular combination of notes and the audience watched aghast as the man went down; apparently the sound had hit his 'emotional centre', or solar plexus, in such a way as to cause him to lose bodily control. Was this a simple parlour trick or something more – a demonstration of a lost science of music known only to Gurdjieff?

The pianist Thomas De Hartmann, a long-standing student and friend of both Gurdjieff and J.G Bennett, often made mention of his teacher's absolute mastery of music and movement. Much of the Fourth Way teaching espoused by Gurdjieff concerns the importance of octaves and music more generally. Parts of the body called 'centres', equated to the chakras of Eastern philosophies, are seen as 'brains' attuned to certain types of experience, with music and sound playing a large role in emotional understanding and awareness – areas not easily understood from a purely intellectual standpoint.

Gurdjieff often said that the emotions moved more quickly than thought, with unconscious physical movement being swifter still. Anyone will know that when an object is accidentally dropped, the hand will often move to catch the mishandled item without the need for 'thought'. Movement and the 'brain' behind it have their own set of rules of engagement deep inside the being of a person. Emotions, although not as fast as such movement, are deeper still and perhaps perform some other important functions. For Gurdjieff, music could free a person to accelerate their state, shake-free their ordinary considerations and elevate other parts of their being, creating pathways to much higher functions within consciousness.

While in Ethiopia, Gurdjieff became intensely interested in what he saw as the area's esoteric 'Christianity', which was later transmitted to Ancient Egypt through the dances and music of the priests of the Ark.

Wild, ecstatic dancing is a universal element of religious worship, with the crowds flocking before the many replica Arks displayed in Ethiopia during religious festivals being no exception. Yet inside the elect precincts of the ordained, these rites are more precise and controlled; structured postures with inner meanings, coupled with timing and precision, coincide with meditations and recitations within the dancer. These rites and their postures are similar to those depicted on the wall reliefs of Thebes (modern-day Luxor). Clearly the ritual dances performed in Ethiopia and Thebes are connected. Just outside Thebes is the temple complex of Karnak, which Gurdjieff uses as the name for his spaceship in *Beelzebub's Tales to His Grandson*, thereby ascribing further significance to its importance in human history. Again, just like the Sphinx, Karnak is highlighted as an example of objective art with a deeper significance to be harnessed by the trained observer.

This observer cannot be passive and must maintain what might be called a 'tri-divided' attention. Observation of the outward is the passive process of 'looking', yet observation of the inner state as it unfolds in relation to what is outwardly observed involves great effort. Perhaps this is a recognition of the reconciling inner forces – a psychological birds-eye view of the entire struggle within, where the left and right hemispheres of the brain work in unison. Knowledge combined with being leads to understanding.

In *Beelzebub's Tales to His Grandson*, Gurdjieff introduces the reader to the concept of 'Shat Chai-Mernis', which is alluded to as an ancient Chinese science. Of course, all of this is part of the allegorical technique Gurdjieff described as 'burying the bone'. It is believed the Chinese science he was referring to relates to the layout of the notes on a piano keyboard. The chromatic scale plays each note and the semitones besides them. In the key of C, that would be: C C# D D# E F F# G G# A A# B. Twelve notes which align to the months, but not as one would imagine. The white keys represent: F (January); G (March); A (May); B (July); C (August); D (October); E (December). The black semitones represent: G# (April); A# (June); C# (September); D# (November), while the tritone is F# (February). The intervals are 31st July/1st August and 30th Dec/1st Jan. Now consider an octave: the two intervals are basically the pitch distance between two notes. Most notes have a semitone between them, except for E which goes straight to F and B which goes straight to C. Gurdjieff applied this example to every real-life situation, meaning that there could be an octave applied to cooking a meal for instance, or driving a car, even something as complex as performing open-heart surgery.

The Enneagram symbol used to symbolise the Fourth Way was essentially an octave-based system. *Do*, *re*, *mi*, *fa*, *sol*, *la*, *ti*, and then *do*. The two intervals became 'shocks' in the Gurdjieffian octaves; these, he said, were intentional, intense efforts needed to get from the low *do* to the higher corresponding *do*. One could not complete an octave, or any corresponding activity, without conscious attention and effort. Everything Gurdjieff taught came back to working with octaves. Gurdjieff said himself that all beings have vibrations proper to them and these vibrations varied in subtlety, so a person might say that the finer vibrations were related to their soul, while the grosser vibrations corresponded to his or her animal nature. Again, by studying the mathematical principles behind the musical octave, Gurdjieff was aware that objective effects, i.e. properties that acted in exactly the same way on every listener, could be achieved.

Colin Wilson quotes Michael Hayes when discussing the *I-Ching* and its relation to the number 64. I found the curious diagram overleaf in Hayes' book *The Infinite Harmony: Musical Structures in Science and Theology*. The diagram shows how the *I-Ching* links to the Gurdjieffian octaves. In the *I-Ching* there are two basic forms: a straight line and a line comprised of two dashes. Male and female energy no less. These two basic shapes when placed over themselves or against one another form four separate Hsiang symbols.

Then by placing the original two male and female lines over these Hsiang give the eight fundamental Kwa symbols, which are the building blocks of the Hexagrams in the *I-Ching* divination system. The complete system is comprised of 64 Hexagram symbols.

What Hayes has suggested in his research is that the four Kwa are octaves (eight notes) which are then squared to make 64. In essence he has demonstrated that one could continue this breakdown arriving at 128, then 256 and 512, ad infinitum. *The I-Ching* is therefore one complete and continuous harmonious octave. The inventors of the *I-Ching* did not labour the point and stopped at 64.

Did Michael Hayes unwittingly rediscover the mysterious Shat-Chai-Mernis of Gurdjieff?

In the West, art and music were produced for pleasure, but in the East these could be deciphered like a script. Once more we are in the territory of the cuneiform writing, where language, numbers and astrology all whirl together. Eastern music is famous for its microtones, that is to say, the notes inbetween the notes. Microtonal notes create further intervals and nano soundscapes that

The *I-Ching* Hexagrams and the octave

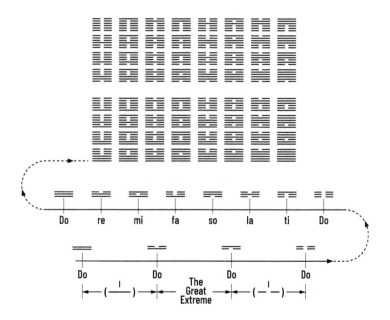

assail the senses. In layman's terms these microtones produce what might be described as 'inner' octaves. These build up the energy release inside the music and therefore unleash new intervals or 'shocks'.

Listen to the fretless bass or didgeridoo to hear microtonal sounds; endless textural nuances used by tribal peoples the world over in their music and song. States of transcendence are consciously used by musicians, perhaps even the folk singers like those Gurdjieff may have encountered in his childhood. The technique was certainly used by the Ashokh poets like his father. It is the delicate spectrum of sound vibrations caused by the inner octaves, which when framed by simple melodies, can be an extremely powerful tool for liberating higher forms of consciousness. One such story about Gurdjieff seems to confirm this idea of sound vibrations generating transformative energies. Whilst reciting the Lord's Prayer in a single long breath using a single note (according to the account given) Gurdjieff then placed the hand of the student on his breast. The student felt an electrical surge. From the scant details given it appears what the student described was subharmonic chanting.

During his travels in Ethiopia and Sudan, Gurdjieff may well have encountered the local musical tradition called *meleket*, that makes use of an original form of notation taken from the G'eez language – the same script used to record the book of Enoch stolen by the explorer Bruce.

Those who perform the Zema rites are trained male musicians who are part of a sacred tradition who use their own, sometimes improvised, modal melodies. It is a trance-like, mystical sound that they perform which can change rapidly in mood and tempo to control the religious ceremony it accompanies. Provenance for the musical tradition is ascribed to St Yared who, according to tradition, was instructed by angels.

The author Alan Jacobs in his 2010 novella *Eutopia: The Gnostic Land of Prester John*, seriously considered whether Gurdjieff was instructed in this old musical notation of Ethiopia and later used it in his own compositions. He certainly saw the religious dancing inside the churches and was deeply impressed by it, but then again Gurdjieff was a magpie, taking ideas that worked from a myriad of sources, traditions and lineages. His unique skill was allying them to the unknown, worldwide Atlantean culture of pre-sand Egypt or pre-Flood humanity. Gurdjieff believed, or was convinced, that the Atlantean roots of Egypt came from Ethiopia, acting as the fount of the great survival efforts after the Great Flood. While in Abyssinia/Ethiopia did he find the ancient custodians of an unbroken lineage leading back to Atlantis?

Almost all books on Gurdjieff reference his close affinity with the dances of the Sufis but few draw attention to his visit to Lake Tana with its Coptic rites.

There is every reason to suspect that Shat-Chai-Mernis is also a clue to Gurdjieff's apparent knowledge of dolmens as compasses. His mastery over the vibrations of the octaves may provide a vital clue to his understanding of locating the initiatory centres of the ancient mystery schools; a science innocently rediscovered by astroarchaeologists like Kim Malville and Jacobs, who through their specialist knowledge and academic discipline have put the spotlight on the sheer importance of this evolutionary discovery and its momentousness in unlocking our shared world heritage.

In Gurdjieff's writings the man who delivered the sacred science of Shat-Chai-Mernis was a Bokharan dervish by the name of Bogga Eddin. A whirling Sufi master, he invited the narrator to accompany him to a gorge in the remote mountains of Bokhara, whereupon he removed the cover of a small opening in the rock, from which protruded the sides of two iron bars. As they listened, a strange sound was emitted and the Sufi uttered a few words in an unknown tongue into the aperture. They returned the stone covering and continued on until they came to a standing stone. Upon their arrival the stone opened up to reveal a cave lit by means of both gas and electricity. The two ventured inside and came upon an elderly anchorite who gave them supper and the trio fell into conversation regrding musical vibrations. The anchorite had studied music all his life being an authority on Shat-Chai-Mernis.

Seeing the anchorite had many instruments in his cave, including a grand piano and monochord (a type of oblong single-string soundbox on a movable bridge to extract different notes), which is ascribed to being an invention of Pythagoras. Finding they had a common interest, the three men spoke at length about the esoteric art of music. One interesting aside is that the teacher of Pythagoras was of course Abaris the Druid, sometimes called Skywalker, who would have been familiar with the ritual harp, which is similar to the monochord in some respects.

Back to the story: Bogga Eddin and his dervish companion talked to the anchorite about his experiments in sound. It is through Bogga Eddin that Gurdjieff met the Sarmoung – the hidden directorate. His thoughts on soundscapes are real and tangible in every respect; music was, like the Sphinx, objective art – a science that was used to create finer vibrations to the benefit of mankind. Certain Middle Eastern languages have no letter or sound for 'G', which is rendered as 'H'. This being the case, Bogga Eddin becomes Bahauddin, none other than the founder of the Naqshbandi Sufis.

This takes us back to Chapter 2 and J.G Bennett's theories of the masters of wisdom. Yet let us think again. Music is a universal language, the megalithic system found over vast distances. This knowledge would seem to belong to a worldwide communication system much like the telegraph or the Internet, freed from the constrictions of mere localised cultures. The clues presented in the tale of Bogga Eddin are subtle but telling.

Sufism, music, standing stones and esoteric schools at the end. It is clear that a pre-sand map is not written on mere paper, or if it is, this is only a temporary medium for a superior navigational method underpinning the megalithic sites. Abaris the Druid would have been very familiar with traversing vast distances to initiate men like Pythagoras using stars, menhirs and dolmens. Megalithic sites stretch the length and breadth of the ancient world, evidently for this very purpose.

Songlines in Dream Time

Due to their isolation from Western cultural pollution and the corrosive effects of colonisation, the Aboriginal Australians were able to preserve their ancient way of life largely unhindered until the 19th and 20th Centuries. Since that time their ways have been eroded by the encroachment of outsiders and in many cases they have been subject to dire treatment similar to that meted out to the Tibetans, as we saw in Chapter 1. For the Aborigines this meant calamitous social disintegration. Yet once again, these people may hold vital clues contained in their oral traditions which reach us today in the form of so-called 'Songlines'. A person born in a particular place learns the songs of his birthright, with these oral histories recounting journeys, places, even geographical markers such as hills, rocks and waterholes – all highly valuable information when dealing with life in the intense and unforgiving Australian climate. Songlines were the method used to navigate the bush terrain: in some cases these were just local journeys, yet in others vast tracts of the countryside up to 2,000 miles, including walks across desert terrain, are detailed. What is remarkable is that each tribal group understood the universal identity and importance of the system.

While the transmission of Songlines was certainly a rite of passage, the system was more akin to a kind of cultural passport. Ancestor worship and spirit lore were integral to the belief system contained in the songs. Some of these journeys are so ancient – and this is controversial to say – that their routes pass over certain rocks that bear the fossilised footprints of those who went before. Modern historians and even many folklorists would sharply dispute all this, of course. They might argue that these so-called footprints are just geological scars on rock that resemble footprints, with folklorists calling 'ostention' – the making of a modern myth – on much of it.

Black histories and indigenous accounts are often dismissed, so we should not be surprised at this reaction, as attested by Western views on Ethiopia. What is clear, however, is that the dead-straight routes of the Songlines could not have been made without advanced surveys taking place, thereby begging the question how did technologically bereft tribesmen accomplish this task so accurately? Were these using techniques similar to those of the Biblical Jacob and Gurdjieff, who navigated terrain using megalithic markers?

A little-known Australian mound not unlike Uluru (Ayers Rock) called St Augustus Mound (Burringurrah) lies north of Perth in the deep reddish soils of the place. It too has a legend attached to it not unlike that of Jacob, for it contains identical themes once again – initiation, stones and dreams. Legend has it a young Aborigine male came to the mound for his initiation, it seems he was unfamiliar with the terrain and deciding to sleep on the mound, he had a spirit dream which unnerved him, so much so, he decided to flee. Passing through another tribal ground without permission or invitation was considered taboo. Local tribes, seeing he had crossed into their territory, killed him. At the spot of his burial he turned into a stone. The Aboriginal place name for the site is named after the young initiate – Burringurrah.

To dismiss the Aboriginal racial memory out-of-hand is to live in hubris. For a start, these Australian Songlines establish a firm continuity spanning thousands of years. The whole concept of the Songlines appears somewhat redolent of the Gurdjieff map of pre-sand Egypt. It immediately evokes standing stones, tribes, artwork, dreams, initiations and gods.

Magnetic Dowsing of Blood Memory

Gurdjieff himself did not realise the true import of his father as an Ashokh until his later studies in cuneiform proved the accuracy of the oral histories passed down through untold generations of storytellers. Likewise, the Songlines of the Aboriginal peoples were of much the same calibre, for here we find one more example of the Flood cataclysm story and its desperate consequences for humanity preserved in fine detail among the oral traditions of an age-old culture. Aboriginal standing stones and circles hold their own against any of European or African origin.

Murujuga on the Burrup Peninsula in Western Australia is home to a collection of standing stone formations and rock art of great ritual importance and equally grand scale. Typical of the dismissive attitude displayed by many Westerners to such places of unique cultural value, a significant proportion of these monuments and the art they contain has been destroyed to make way for industrial developments, with mining being the main culprit. What remains is fascinating, providing vital information about the Songline heritage. The Aborigines maintain the building of the standing stones and circles go back to prehistory or 'Dream-Time' – an era when gods walked with mankind. Up to 10,000 works of intricate cave art exist here at Murujuga State Park; just like Lascaux in France the artists of yesteryear were actively – and evidently – attempting to communicate something profound.

The British astrophysicist Professor Ray Norris has worked with both the Aboriginal peoples and NASA to present startling findings regarding a site called Wurdi Youang, a stone circle comprised of 100 waist-height, egg-shaped basalt stones that are perfectly aligned to the equinoxes. Already it has been dubbed an Australian Stonehenge, but since the site is estimated at being 11,000 years old, the fact that it predates its British cousin by several millennia has not been fully acknowledged. In a BBC report an Aboriginal adviser is quoted as saying of the site, 'It's truly special because a lot of people don't take account of Aboriginal science".

The 'quaint' Emu drawings found in nearby cave art have recently been discovered to be complex representations of the Milky Way. Just to correct a great misapprehension, we can now say with certainty that Aboriginal people can count beyond the number six – another disquieting notion fostered by previous Western researchers for many years. Of course, this type of misconception has spilled into observations about the intricate artworks found at Wurdi Youang.

There appears to be evidence of the usage of binary number systems found on many of the Aboriginal paintings which have unfortunately been interpreted as being no more than decorative 'dots'. Incidentally these are the same type of 'dots' found in Sumer, prehistoric Britain and more ancient sites besides. Gurdjieff himself claimed to be able read the art at Lascaux, telling his student Bennett he had ascertained both the number of letters in the alphabet used by the people who created it, and the heraldic symbol of the Atlantean society once based there.

One of the great difficulties for modern man is to realise that the 'spirit-language' of the Songlines and subsequent cave art may belong to an era, as stated in several ancient legends worldwide, before the time of multiple languages. Perhaps they are evidence of a universal mathematical language, a global navigation system and an objective experience, communicated at various centres for one and for all to understand at that level of being. If this is true, the evidence begins to suggest a single, worldwide, maritime culture, much as we might ascribe to something like Atlantis, one borne out of a cataclysm. People then would have belonged, it seems, to a common culture, as our shared landscape of dolmens and sacred alignments clearly shows.

Serpent's Gold

Gurdjieff may have hidden the greatest stone treasury in the Mediterranean to obscure uncomfortable truths. He wrote about the Pythoness who forewarned humanity of the Great Flood. This one is fairly easy to work out, being the Greek Temple of Apollo which had ensconced in its precincts the Oracle of Delphi – a certain visionary called the Pythoness. Her divine pronouncements are the stuff of legend. It was believed that by sleeping inside a holy site one might be lucky enough to have oracular dreams and portents (remember Jacob on the way to Harran?). This practice soon made Delphi a cultic centre of serpent worship. It is from this temple that the famous wise saying 'Know thyself' first originated. The Pythoness oracle was said to be a woman who would inhale volcanic fumes in order to see visions of the future.

Gurdjieff says in his work *Beelzebub's Tales to His Grandson* that the esteemed Pythoness warned the Akhaldans to flee to Africa (probably Lake Tana in Ethiopia) to escape the Great Flood. As we have said before, Gurdjieff enjoyed obfuscating his truths and never gave up his sources too easily. Could he have been directing us towards Malta, an ancient centre of serpent worship, bound inextricably with the myths of Atlantis?

Malta has long been inextricably associated with secret Chivalric orders and boasts a remarkable history of great esoteric import. The island is unique in that it is home to skeletal remains of a previously unknown race. Its flat terrain was not visible from Sicily and it was not large enough to support a hunter-gatherer society, instead attracting agricultural settlers, or so it was thought until an archaeological excavation threw some of these erroneous assumptions into the air once more.

During 1902 a dig in Malta unearthed what seemed to be a Christian catacomb in a place called Hal Saflieni. This discovery was not unlike many other underground Christian cemeteries left by early mystic brotherhoods in the Mediterranean, so the early conclusions were not that exciting for those excavating. It was a fairly predictable discovery the archaeologists felt at the time, until one of the underground chambers was subjected to closer scrutiny, when it became demonstrable to those investigating that something was amiss – the underground chambers belonged to a much earlier period in time.

They continued their excavations and by 1903 the magnitude of their discoveries became apparent. Due to the importance of the discoveries a new manager for the dig was found in the person of Maltese priest Manuel Magri. A Jesuit curator, he was a scholar of great renown, well-versed in several academic disciplines as well as the folklore of the islands. Events reached a crescendo when they came across a structure now known to tourists as the Hypogeum (Greek for 'underground chamber'); a mysterious underground complex, composed of three distinct levels.

By 1906 a plan was made of the three levels which were hugely impressive in their construction, being composed of huge trilithions and stone staircases hewn from rock leading to impressive chambers with ornate ritual areas richly decorated with wall painting and delicate carvings. Father Magri and his team came upon curved anterooms with corbelled ceilings that filled the main chamber. Behind this was cut the so called 'Holy of Holies' a temple room separated from the former space by a beautifully carved screen. One might say it is not what is normally expected of neolithic chambers, being vastly superior in construction.

Anthony Pace who wrote the pamphlet *The Hal Saflieni Hypogeum* published by Heritage Books in 2004 says of the Hypogeum, "The creation of Hypogeum interior is awe inspiring. The techniques employed by the prehistoric craftsman are not far removed from those employed by stonemasons and quarrymen before the advent of mechanised rock cutting. In the case of the Hypogeum, however, the rock cutting methods are even more remarkable considering that the temple-period craftsmen did not apparently possess metal tools".

While accepting the conventional wisdom that the site was constructed with flint and obsidian cutting tools, Pace's incredulity surrounding the fact that metal tools were not employed is somewhat betrayed by his use of the word 'apparently'. The construction of the Hypogeum is hard to fathom by any standards, regardless of whether you accept they used flint tools or not. If it were not for Malta's connection to the serpent cult we might well have left things there, but the mystery deepens further still.

Anyone who has used cheap alloy screwdrivers will understand the limitations of soft tools. It is a fact that people with Bronze Age tools could not have constructed something of that scale and certainly not when taking into account the hardness of the granite the Hypogeum is hewn from. History aside, it is plain common sense that metal or diamond-edged tools must have been used to create these gargantuan structures; how else could they have been made? The silence from historians is deafening. Add to this that the chambers are astronomically aligned and one is dealing with builders who had knowledge of surveying, astronomy and advanced stone masonry – none of which is explained away too easily. Now recognised by UNESCO, the Hypogeum is far older than either Stonehenge or the Giza pyramids. Historians say it could be as much as 5,000 to 6,000 years old. Graham Hancock commented that the underground site could be as old as the Ice Age, claiming that the wall art depicts a long-extinct species of cattle, a bison/cow hybrid jokingly dubbed 'Higgs Bison' by the team of scientists who first identified it. This is a species that first appeared 120,000 years ago. As one starts to investigate the Hypogeum, so many anomalies are presented that the official story becomes redolent of the communist 'apparatchik' thinking of sticking to a party line no matter what evidence is presented to the contrary.

The preservation of the conventional historical timeline, with the museum removing certain artefacts as they do not 'fit' with what is known in books, has led the sponsored academic narrative to supersede the actual discoveries made there to such a point that some observers have resorted to accusations of a cover-up. Even the ambient acoustic properties of the great chambers show that these were hewn from the stone with great care to institute sound engineering properties that even modern designers might envy. 110 Hz is a frequency found here which is associated with the temporal shifting of dominance in the two lobes of the brain, from the logical to the more inituative, artistic side of the brain. In this mode language, logical thinking and factual accounts are overridden to give way to an emotional state of mind, the type of behaviour one might expect at a festival or a concert. These acoustics could possibly have been used to enhance music or group chanting.

Perhaps the greatest issue in Maltese archaeological controversy are the curious skulls found at the same UNESCO site. In 1902, archaeologists made discovery of several skulls with elongated skullcaps that were found to be natural and not the result of any binding or other modification. The skulls were on display at the National Museum of Archaeology but were removed in 1985 and can now only be viewed by special permission. No small effort has been made on the part of the local historians to debunk any theory about their possible origins and there are suspicions that the skulls were removed from public view as they simply did not fit into the accepted historical narrative of Malta.

Two local archaeologists Anthony Buonanno and Mark Mifsud, who studied the remains, went on record to say of the skulls, "They are another race."

These skeletal remains were perhaps of the exalted priests of the serpent cult, a thaumaturgic priesthood using the underground Hypogeum in their rites. It appears that other skeletal remains show signs of enforced bondage of the skull, presumably to emulate these original skulls. Could it be that the exalted priesthood bred into its own – much like the pharaonic lines of Egypt – and eventually only had such a limited gene pool that they died out completely?

Similar skulls have been unearthed across the world, in places as far-flung as Peru, Africa, Crimea and Australia. Wherever these elongated skulls are found across the globe one is bound also to hear tales of pyramid structures and a rare metal, the very metal that Atlantis was famed for – orichalcum. In fact, Plato tells us that Atlantis was flashing in the copper tones of orichalcum. But what is orichalcum? Metallurgists know there are two types: the Greek-Roman orichalcum is an alloy of gold with copper, or perhaps zinc, but in the mythical accounts it has an altogether different composition, leading some to suppose it may have been an alloy of platinum, copper and gold.

Malta was known in the Bible as Melita – the word for honey. In esoteric terms, honey is an metaphor for knowledge. It was known from ancient times as a therapeutic centre famed for its curative disciplines, including snake-venom cures. According to Maltese folklore, St Paul found himself shipwrecked there and while kindling a fire he was bitten on the hand by a snake. To the locals' surprise the apostle was not poisoned and his survival of the ordeal was taken as a sign that he was a man close to God. This tale tells that Malta does not have any poisonous snakes because St Paul expelled them following this incident, however, Malta does in fact have snakes, including one venomous species.

One interpretation of the above Biblical story is that St Paul encountered the dying serpent cult of antiquity that had been centred on Malta from Neolithic times. The Saint supplanted the serpentine worship of the island with a new fledgling religion – Christianity?

There is evidence of python holes used by oracles dotted around Malta. Emblematic carvings of the serpent cult are found painted as well as carved on rocks across the island. After centuries of denying Atlantis as nothing more than a quaint myth some more enlightened historians are now reconsidering their stance after a chance discovery on a European seabed. During January 2015 an astounding underwater find was made which led to a new reappraisal of the Greek philosopher Plato and his work *Critias*, that features Atlantis.

Divers off the southern coast of Sicily at Gela, were searching an old shipwreck which sank 2,600 years ago when they recovered the ship's cargo of 39 metal ingots. The Italian marine archaeologist and expert in oriental antiquities Professor Sebastian Tusa brought samples of the metal to the surface and immediately began tests to ascertain its make up. He found it to be an alloy composed of copper and zinc with traces of nickel, lead and iron. The alloy was found to be orichalcum, the same metal thought to be a mythical substance as mentioned by Plato in connection with Atlantis. The excited Professor Tusa told the media, "The discovery is unique and exceptional because it is the first time that we find oricalcum ingots."

The source of the Greek legends about Atlantis came from Solon and Dropides who told the story to Critias who in turn told it to his grandson, also named Critias, who recounted the story to Socrates, who had never heard of the civilisation before then. Critias junior learnt from his grandfather, who in turn had been told about the Antediluvian kingdom when still in his childhood.

The story goes that the Egyptian Priesthood at Sais passed on the account to the Greeks where they described the destruction of Atlantis by a natural catastrophe. In Plato's account of the legends about Atlantis he describes the mythical kingdom 'flashing' as the highly-prized metal adorned the buildings including the temple dedicated to Poseidon. Orichalcum was valued second only to gold in Atlantis. Other academics have waded into the controversial discovery including Professor Enrico Mattievich, a Brazilian physics teacher who believes that the true orichalcum comes from South America and contains gold. Neither man publicly agreed with the dirty 'Atlantis' word but then again, rather unsurprisingly, neither offer a theory as to who may have made the precious cargo found off Sicily, only a short strait of nautical miles from Malta. Surely the Maltese islands, being home to one of the world's oldest pyramids plus the elongated skulls and their resting place inside the mysterious Hypogeum complex, must stimulate some small curiosity?

Chapter 9

Atlantean Gene Pool?

"Nasrudin, your donkey has been lost."
"Thank goodness I was not on the donkey at the time,
or I would be lost too."
Mullah Nasrudin

Discovery at The Cave of a Thousand Buddhas

Tall stories of the Gobi desert feature in Gurdjieff's work. While travelling with the Seekers of Truth, the party traversed the Mongolian deserts in search of an ancient city. During a raging sandstorm, blinded and harried by the merciless winds carrying tons of sand, the party decided to stand on stilts to find respite from the storm and view the terrain once again. The is clearly allegorical, signifying the role of higher conciousness in providing a unique perspective above the maelstrom of normal, everyday life. Yet, we must never forget that The Seekers of Truth did actually set foot in the Gobi in 1898 in search of an ancient city and came to the very region where it was subsequently discovered: only nine years later was it actually revealed by another excavation. The above allegory may again be a very subtle allusion to the pre-sand maps, a way of mastering terrain, of being able to see the Gobi from a pre-cataclysm perspective. Everything discovered shortly after the fruitless Seekers of Truth expedition suggests this may be the case. In Gurdjieff's own account the failed expedition linked to Professor Skridlov is replaced immediately by Bogga Eddin who we have established is linked to stones, music and initiation.

At the southern tip of the Gobi desert, a team of later archaeologists made an even more shocking find at the 'Cave of a Thousand Buddhas'. Gurdjieff and the 'Seekers of Truth' had been so close. This subsequent discovery located in Gansu Province, China, found caves approximately 15 miles to the south-east of Dunhuang, a crossroads on the once-busy busy Silk Road. While the artwork found in the caves is displayed on the British Museum website, much of the story has been left untold.

155

The Silk Road was a melting pot of races and cultures who carried their goods, services and messages up and down Asia by this time-honoured route, but by the advent of the Ming Dynasty in China (1368-1644) this section of the Silk Road had passed its zenith in importance and Dunhaung's fortunes had declined. Yet, as Dunhaung emptied of travellers and inhabitants, the nearby caves continued to be populated by Buddhist monks attending their religious duties with undiminished devotion. Unbeknown to its religious residents the caves contained a secret. During the 11th Century, literally thousands of documents, scripts, artefacts and artworks had been carefully concealed in a secret chamber.

In 1907 the British archaeologist Auriel Stein uncovered the treasures hidden behind a false wall. Stein was acting on information gleaned from a Hungarian national named Loczy, who had visited the site some years before and heard rumours of the secret horde. With the aid of a Chinese priest who directed him to the place, Stein discovered a large cache of papers piled teen feet high, in a near-perfect state of preservation thanks to the caves' dry climate. They had lain there undiscovered for approximately 900 years. Stein managed to purchase the collection and sent them on to the British Library in London. Among the collection were around 100 paintings of important Buddhist scenes. These included depictions of Bhaishajyaguru – the Buddha of Healing – who is seated in his incense-scented paradise upon Holy Mount Meru, and Avalokiteshvara – The Lord of Compassion and progenitor of the Tibetan race. There were also paintings of wandering monks that could not fail to arouse curiosity as they featured men with ginger or red hair with long noses and ears, who were clearly of a race other than Chinese.

Following a nuclear test carried out in 2005 by the Chinese Government, another discovery was made that supported the evidence found at the Cave of Thousand Buddhas for the existence of a long-forgotten ancient race. Here at Taklamakan Desert, several well-preserved corpses were disinterred, all of which displayed distinctly caucasian features. Due to the temperatures of the Tamrin Basin, the bodies were essentially mummified and as a result of their state of preservation much has been learned about these people from an examination of the bodies. It appears that they had a knowledge of surgery, as revealed by certain types of scar tissue, while their gold funerary masks exhibit a high degree of artistic skill. Once again, the mummy finds have not been given any rational explanation by the Chinese, or Western, academics for that matter, as they do not fit with the accepted history of the area. Clothing belonging to the mummies fits neither accepted histories nor oriental cultures of the time.

Local legends of the people of the Taklamakan desert inside the Tamrin Basin recall a white race who inhabited the region when the place was an inland sea.

The mythical white race were held in high esteem, being regarded as gods who possessed great prowess in metalworking, horsemanship and chariot building. The Taklamakan white men are credited with inventing the wheel and building tunnels leading to the sea. This was not a one-off discovery, as additional white mummy sites have also been found in China, proving that East and West have had contact since at least the Bronze Age.

Two American scholars have set their sights on unlocking the secrets of the mummies, which has led them to tentatively declare that they are European in origin, identifying cloth samples taken from the bodies as similar to those found in Austria. Dr. Victor Mair, a Professor of Chinese Studies at the University of Pennsylvania, asked a colleague Dr. Elizabeth W. Barber of Occidental College USA, to examine the corpses, particularly the weaving of their clothes. While the two academics are more open-minded than most, there is still the automatic reasoning that white men in the region at that time must have travelled from Europe, despite the incongruous nature of the discoveries.

Dr Mair proceeds along the logic that a nomadic culture spread from Ukraine into the Gobi using horses and chariots. His assertions follow the age-old myth of the descendants of Cain migrating to this region, as alluded to by the poet Coleridge in his classic poem Kubla Khan. Genghis Khan and the mythic Tubal-Cain are said to have sprung from these nomadic peoples, but is this actually the case? What if the white-skinned race sporting red and sometimes even blonde beards found mummified in the Gobi did not come from Europe? If the assertions of academia are wrong, where could they possibly have originated from?

In the modern world we like to suppose that global travel must have been impossible to our early ancestors, but recent discoveries unearthed in China and elsewhere have yielded examples of lenses that would have had astronomical uses, while extraordinarily advanced computational navigation tools such as the Antikythera mechanism, prove beyond doubt that people in the distant past possessed many sophisticated aids to assist them in their travels. Perhaps the traversing of such distances may not have presented such an insurmountable problem to the people of the past as we might like to think.

In our time the Gobi is an arid desert where life is precious, but once it was a lush and fertile place. Discoveries at the Cave of a Thousand Buddhas and finds by academics such as Stein have led us back to consider Chinese myths about white people and the ancient Uighur Empire. The Gobi must be mentioned when considering the last vestiges of Atlantis, Mu and Lemuria in Central Asia as it features in many of the theories surrounding the antediluvian survival.

It is believed by some that this is the exact location of the physical Shambhala. It is no accident that esoteric explorers like Gurdjieff and Roerich considered the Gobi to be among the fabled lands of antiquity that were great repositories of esoteric knowledge. The Uighur Khaganate at one time stretched from the Caspian Sea to the Asian steppes, with its peoples' ethnicity said to be of Turkic extraction. However, as the Tamrin mummies attest, they were clearly of another ethnic strain entirely. Throughout history, the Uighur have gone under many names: Chang-Di, Hu, Hun, Hsisung-Nu, Hui-Ho, Kashgari, Khitan-Liao, Minyag, Turki,Tangut and Tarhut, but most interestingly, they were known as the Mu. Today the Uighur are largely Islamic but they would once have embraced the nomadic traditions of shamanism practised across the steppes, much as it is in Siberia today.

Just prior to World War I, the St Petersburg-based Russian archaeologist Peter Koslov unearthed the remnants of a ruined city in Mongolia said to be 12,000 years old. Koslov and his team found a city of Uighur provenance containing a mysterious tomb in which rested the remains of the rulers of the ancient kingdom. The vault in which the married couple were interred was inscribed with a strange symbol – μ. This is generally regarded as the Greek letter 'Mu', which means water, and is also denoted the numerical value 40. Under the μ was an earlier inscription of a circle divided into four, essentially a swastika-like design similar to that of the Celtic cross. This discovery was almost certainly related to the pre-flood civilisation and provides further evidence for the existence of Mu. During 1898 Gurdjieff and the Seekers of Truth visited Taklamaka, the very spot where the mummies were later discovered. They too were looking for a lost city but their journey was brought to a halt by the death of one of the seekers, so the mission remained unfinished. This is interesting because Gurdjieff left Taklamaka disguised as a dervish to go to Baku the following year which is the centre of the Malamatiyya (or Malamati) Sufis, a mystic group that took its name from the Arabic word malamah, meaning blame.

It may point to him having accepted the path of the Malamati Sufis and adopting their signature 'Way of Blame' although there is no direct evidence for this assertion. As part of their spiritual practice, Malamatis shave their heads and grow moustaches, just as Gurdjieff did himself. Those Malamatis who do not shave their heads dye their hair with henna and become redheads and inside Sufism the group are considered to be the elect order.

Of course the possible links with the Malamati Sufis and Gurdjieff is pure conjecture, and it is a fact that Gurdjieff claimed to have continued his studies in Persian magic at that time. Certainly, if one were to adopt Tibetan Buddhism a shaven head might also be called for, although it must be said not many Tibetan

Buddhists are found to sport a moustache. It was on a second visit to Taklamaka in 1902 at a remote oasis that Gurdjieff renounced his practice of magical and hypnotic powers, vowing thereafter only to use such means for altruistic reasons. Perhaps harking back to this decision, Gurdjieff would later teach his pupils that renunciation of attachments was a sure method of attainment, yet once again, this teaching could equally be ascribed to either Sufism or Buddhism. One of the lost cities in this region was Subeshi, which would have certainly been of interest to Gurdjieff. Caucasoid mummies found here too. The mummies were laid to rest wearing conical hats two feet in height, instantly redolent of the Chinese mags, or court sages, mentioned in earlier chapters. According to their own histories these people were wiped out by a cataclysm, the cause of which is unknown.

Language of the Birds

Angelic encounters may be found in the holy books of many religions, including those of Islam and Judaism. Men on Earth are guided by spirits visiting from heaven who either appear either in dreams or, more rarely, in physical form. Such entities often manifest in some form of disguise when making their appearance on the gross physical plane. Much is said of angels as 'light beings' inhabiting a place where humans cannot exist. This relates to Blavatsky's theory, which identified the malaise of humanity in that things are becoming grosser and more materialistic, while our true nature is that of beings of light without need for the physical, which is an encumbrance to enlightenment. Naturally, Gurdjieff would have placed much of this on his step diagram, explaining it as an ascending and descending scale of octaves running through all aspects of creation. Energy passing from one level to the next, in its descent – Angel to man, man to Earth, Earth to Moon and so on like an ecosystem, each feeding the level above while the lower levels supply some service to the life force above them.

It must be remembered that the evidence of the Sumerian civilisation was only discovered in the 19th Century. Before that, no one even knew of its existence. Gurdjieff tells us of his shock on discovering that the very same myths his father told him as a child had been recorded millennia before on tablets of clay by the ancient people of Sumer.

Deep inside Kurdistan in modern Turkey, lie two of the oldest known temples known to humanity. Indeed they are so old that history had to be rewritten after 1962, when the second was discovered. They were not known while Gurdjieff was alive, at least not to archaeologists, who presume it was they who made the discoveries for the first time. But one in possession of a pre-sand map of yesteryear could potentially have known of their existence beneath successive layers of historical dust. Archeology may not be the only sphere of speciality in play here, if the pre-sand theory holds. Archaeology belonging to the past tense, astroarchaeology being aligned to the present.

The two sites are Nevali Cori (excavated in 1983) and Göbekli Tepe (excavated in 1962). Both temple complexes feature distinctive T-shaped stone pillars and it is believed that the ceremonial imagery found at both sites served important religious functions, now unknown. What is known is that a skull cult existed there, which venerated the dead by carving the craniums of the deceased. Again, just a few miles from Harran is another site of antiquity called Tell Sabi Adyad where pottery fragments depicting Shamen dressed in feathers with elongated skulls have been found. Clearly these deformed skulls must belong to a priest cult of some kind. It is almost a given that one might suspect that most cranial deformation is deliberate; certain tribes still practice it by tying planks and string to a newly born child's soft skull therefore deforming or elongating it in some way. A batch of skulls excavated in 1933 raised fresh doubts regarding this idea. Two anthropologists working in Britain, Molleson and Campbell, examined the find with startling conclusions. Their papers were published in the late 1960s.

Some of the skulls were indeed the result of artificial deformation but nearly half of the artefacts were genetically formed, with no evidence of artificially induced elongation. This suggested a new kind of skull not known to science and to add further alarm bells to our cherished notions, the skulls were found to have belonged to members of the same family. It was the Malta Hypogeum all over again. It would seem the family group wanted to distinguish themselves for some reason. Is it time to reconsider the occasional interbreeding between the Watchers (Igigi) so often mentioned in the Bible, the book of Enoch, Sumer legends etc?

Because of their bloodstock were these unique humans considered exalted beings? Many of the Egyptian depictions of the Pharaohs reference elongated skulls – albeit sometimes shown as crowns to elongate the shape of their heads – yet the inference remains. It will be remembered that Jesus himself was entombed in Golgotha (which means the place of the skull). The ancients likened them to birds, no doubt linked to the classical representation of the god Thoth being Ibis-headed. According to folklore anyone reading the Book of Thoth was granted the 'language of the birds', a subtle reference to higher knowledge, much like the Conference of the Birds tale we learned of earlier. It is a fact that the Sabians were accorded the language of the birds – people who had a birds-eye view of events in one sense, adherents of the Phoenix, seekers of the eternal in another. Portrayal of the mythos is found across the region with Yezidis, Zoroastrians, Sufis and Bon all using exotic birds such as peacocks, guruda and hoopoe to symbolically convey the inner meaning of the quest and its ultimate prize. The language is said to belong to the time of Enoch, an angelic tongue known to primeval man – Adam and his wife Eve. A primordial tongue known only to the initiated. David and Solomon were also blessed of its knowledge according to the Quran. Other ancient texts speak of significant birds, whether it is a dove appearing to Noah, the Angel Gabriel appearing before Mary in the guise of a dove at the Annunciation, or the Sphinx itself, clothed in wings.

Astral Weeks

In one sense birds are symbolic of angelic forces, higher transformative energies necessary for inner development or the psychological make-up inside a person. The birds are the many 'I's that lie behind the illusory mask of the supposed single 'self'. Using a Gurdjieffian model we could probably identify the hoopoe with his concept of creating a permanent 'I' – that aspect of the self that is eternal and not transitory. A level within us allied to the stars. *The Conference of the Birds*, which features the hoopoe, is a Sufi teaching story but the hoopoe makes an appearance elsewhere too, proving the antiquity of the teaching via Sabean magic.

Sheba travelled to visit Solomon but not until after he had sent her a hoopoe as his personal messenger. Solomon relates to other birds the perilous journey to Mount Qaf, a place containing the shining emerald and home of the Jinn is where all knowledge will be found. Birds are a recurring symbol in all myths relating to the paradise of the hidden masters. In Chinese mythology, nine ravens rest at the peach tree of immortality while the tenth bird assists the seeker.

Similarly, in the Conference of the Birds myth of the Sufis, the Mighty Simorgh is representative of an enlightened brotherhood or, in some psychological interpretations, the inner 'I' of man. Tales featuring birds are also used in both the Shambhala and Olmolungring mythos. The symbol of the bird is found in Ancient Egypt as a messenger of the soul and the afterlife. In the writings of Sumer, the oldest of civilisations, the word for bird was 'Zu'. The meaning of Zu is 'to know'. Sumerian myths talk of a mountain in a faraway land where Zu took the form of a winged, god-like, lion-headed creature. It is upon the Zu of Sumerian legend that the later Sphinxes of Egypt and Greece were ultimately based. We now see both the physical and etymological evidence that Zu-en, Su-en, Sin, Sheen, is none other than the Sphinx.

Anyone looking for the physical evidence of this paradise is going to have a very interesting journey, it seems. Gurdjieff certainly codified his restless quest in *Meetings With Remarkable Men* by relating in his own way that although there were physical places, ancient temples, dolmens, and bygone citadels where the earliest priesthoods resided, the end goal was certainly internal. He had intimated the two in tandem from the onset of his story about Lama G at the beginning of this book; enlightened schools exist physically but their aims are the psychological development of humanity. Gurdjieff relates that the death of the unfortunate Lama G led to a sacred teaching being lost, with devastating cosmic consequences for humanity, perhaps even perilous for our continued existence on Earth itself. What is unfathomable about it all is why one individual, Lama G, was tasked with carrying a sacred teaching belonging to the masters: why is it necessary to transmit a teaching through humans, tulkus, sages, sacred lineages, teachings and all the rest? It seems to suggest that esoteric knowledge is like gold – a valuable finite resource of limited supply. A pyramid of energy with the inbuilt assumption of natural hierarchy, or is it a case of natural selection of those who have made the necessary space to receive it?

Gurdjieff was one who believed that the Sphinx and other sites of objective art such as the Taj Mahal, were fashioned with the creators' intention to communicate a precise emotion within the onlooker. No ambiguity, no misunderstanding, no reinterpretation. If it is true, then objective art must have contained an electro-magnetic element – what we might call etheric, a presence within the shape or form, an emotional message even, that spoke directly to the onlooker. Even the mighty Mount Kailash, which is considered the physical embodiment of Mount Meru, is so symmetrical – seemingly emulating the swastika of the Buddhists, Bon, Hindus and Jain – that a 21st-Century Russian scientist, Dr Ernst Muldashev, advanced the theory that the mountain was man-made.

It certainly is a peculiar place. The mountain emits remarkable radioactivity levels above its peaks making it generally unassailable to most climbers. People who attempt the ascent report a rapid increase in the ageing process, with hair and nails growing noticeably faster. Mount Kailash emits energies that overcome pilgrims, leaving many to circumnavigate its girth in a perpetual high. It is regarded as the abode of the gods and as such has been a place of pilgrimage and initiation for several of the enlightened characters mentioned in this book: it is said that Milarpa is the only one to ever climb to its peak. Mount Meru is represented by the Sri Yantra symbol in Hinduism, whose mandala is regarded as a psychosocial map of spiritual evolution spiralling man into the physical, metaphysical and spiritual cosmos. One must ask why so many leading lights of Eastern mysticism from all traditions and religions have been linked to this place, so much so that the mountain is revered as a holy centre, not just of worship but of the universe itself.

Referring to its name in ancient Sanskrit, Mount Meru is prefixed to become Su'Meru. Su means excellent. This etymology opens up a vista, which although not instantly apparent, leads to an understanding of how the word ties in with many of the themes discussed herein.

In the Dravidian languages of South Asia, it is Mahameru, in the Indian sacred tongue Pali it is Sineru, while the Chinese call it Xūmíshān (pronounced 'shimmy shen'). There are other variants in the neighbouring languages of Korea, Japan, and Myanmar, and the many tongues of the Indian sub-continent contain similar words. Intrinsic to the design of all pagodas and stupas in the East is their representation of Mount Meru, which is perched symbolically at their peaks. It is clear that Mount Meru is recognised across, and central to, all eastern religions.

It has come to light that this etymology is found elsewhere, although the root language is entirely different, or are we having a James Churchward-style eureka moment? Are we tying together something deeper?

It transpires that the old Akkadian word for Sumer was Sumeru, identical to the Sanskrit name for Mount Meru when coupled with its honorific prefix. Curiously the general appearance of Meru is that of a ziggurat, and therefore redolent of the temple buildings of the first civilisation, Sumer. Co-incidental?

In the ancient Indian epic, the Mahabharata, the authors are described as gods who reside in a place called Mount Meru. It should be no surprise therefore that Mount Meru is also mentioned in the mythical paradise constructs of both Shambhala and Olmolungring. The Indians learnt of Mount Meru from sources in Central Asia who spoke of a paradise to the north in which all good things existed. Like the shamanic tree mentioned before, Mount Meru traversed all three worlds – body, soul and spirit. According to legend, seven great Rishis reigned there and who appeared to the world of humanity when new spiritual teachings were required. Their leader Manu was a Hindu version of Noah, which once again interlinks with the myth of the Great Flood, in fact the two stories share many striking similarities. The Hindus embraced this idea of flood survival which became integral to their own cosmology. Holy Meru is seen as the axis of the world, with the Pole Star always shining above it. Mention of the Pole Star in connection with Meru is striking, as it gives us a geographic fix on its supposed location, because the Pole Star can only be viewed as being directly overhead if one is standing at either the North or South Pole. Again we find ourselves in the territory of the swastika symbol, which is a clue to the solar rotation around the polar axis. It is no accident that the Bon call their sacred site 'swastika mountain'. The pillar, the axis and the cosmic tree are universal motifs and all religions seem to have something along these lines, the names may change but the concept remains the same. As we can see, the swastika is similarly found across the globe in all cultures in all places. Were the ancients trying to leave behind a vital clue about Mount Meru, and stressing its central importance to humanity's origins?

Su, Su-en, Zu-en, Shu-en, Sheen (remember moon god Sin?), could it be that Sineru is named after the lunar deity? Could it be just another coincidence that in Chinese Xūmíshān sounds so close to Sin? To add further startling thoughts, just across the border in Sudan lie the pyramids of Meroë, built at the height Kushite kingdom, this Nubian burial ground, where over forty kings and queens are interred, is now a protected UNESCO heritage site.

Hindu scholars sometimes trace the word to Sindhu. Two Indian writers Ranajit and Ranjit Pal published an academic paper in 1994 acknowledging that the word Sindhu (Mount Meru) may come from the Sumerian Moon god Sin. In Hindi, Sindhu actually refers to water over an expanse, although the two Pal researchers have their own interpretation, relating it back to the Akkadian language and therefore rendering it 'Sin-Zu'. The latter word in Akkadian meaning 'deep'. If you add the Akkadian word for water to this, one ends up with Abzu one of the Sumerian flood demi-gods. Apkallu/Apsu/Apzu, or back to Gurdjieff with his survivors of Atlantis who made it up to Lake Tana. Such etymology is easy to bandy around, however, and is far from conclusive.

The priest-hero of the flood mythos recorded in the Sumerian cuneiform tablets was a certain Gudu-Apzu. Gurdjieff may have known much of this but what had he made of it? His relentless search for enlightenment took all of this into account, as he was steeped in it from childhood. He codified the influences of ancient schools in 20th Century technical language referring to influences A, B and C. Or put simply mechanical life, mesoteric life with some esoteric message and then finally a fully conscious vibration that came directly from the school in question. He believed that by cultivating certain aspirations and aims inside oneself a person could at least reach the mesoteric life, which would lead them to become curious about things like astrology, reincarnation, tarot and religion.

However, when they had come across the school itself, the direct source or fount of knowledge, the laws affecting that interaction would change. A person would recognise it by an objective effect on their psyche. Perhaps best summed up by the old adage; 'When the student is ready the teacher appears'. Fate becomes destiny, the accidental becomes conscious. Pilgrimages to sacred sites were designed to engage the average man in contemplation of the esoteric

Suba, Saba or Subbos (meaning 'the ancient ones') was an appellation later ascribed to the stargazing Sabians. The prehistoric Mesopotamian Ubaid people gave their region the name Sabur, which later morphed into Subar, Subir, Šubur, which did indeed make them the eponymous 'the ancient ones', but were they perhaps the original humans from where all creation sprung? Conventional historians are at a loss to explain the sudden arrival of multiple sciences without the usual Darwinian theories of evolution over time etc. Or do we reevaluate Gurdjieff and his theories told to Bennett and others in the caves that a conscious school had survived the Great Flood? What can explain the rise of culture in Sumer?

Certain clues are out there which are derivative of the esoteric orders that practice them. In the 1960s the Beatles took up the Transcendental Meditation techniques of the Maharishi Mahesh Yogi. Like Gurdjieff, it is possible the Maharishi was releasing certain knowledge which may otherwise have been withheld from mass dissemination. Transcendental meditation, or 'TM' as it is known by its adherents, turns the idea of the mantra on its head due to its effortless nature. A unique and secret mantra is given to each student, who then uses it in meditation by repeating it silently and effortlessly in their head during practice. No concentration or robust effort is involved, in fact to do so would counteract the mantra's effectiveness. Distracting thoughts that arise during meditation are just left like clouds to float by; all the individual must do is return to the mantra and repeat again. Eventually over the time and with repeated use, the mantra loses its quality as a 'word' and becomes another vibrational quality or resonance inside the person.

This ritual performed twice a day with eyes closed, leads to a feeling of diving within, to a place where transcendence to pure being may occur. Advanced techniques of TM involving yoga and even levitation are given in private, intensive courses. These are said to lead the practitioner to acquire 'siddhis', the Indian term for magical powers. Some physicists operating on the fringes of their discipline claim to have evidence, from their experiments based on the Maharishi's claims, of the 'one percent theory', which posits that in areas where one percent of people are regular meditators, this has a positive effect on the remaining 99 percent who do not. This finding chimes closely with the 'hundredth monkey' hypothesis first popularised by the author Lyall Watson and expanded by Ken Keyes Jr, which found that mass behavioural change can occur in a population without overt communication once a critical minority of individuals within a certain group adopt a new habit, trait or type of knowledge.

The 'hundredth monkey' refers to a study made on a population of Japanese Macaques who were found to have adopted a method of washing food first exhibited by a small number of monkeys. This would not be so contentious were it not for the fact that the new behaviour was swiftly adopted by groups of monkeys on other islands, who had no communication with the instigators of the new technique. This phenomenon is also sometimes referred to as the Unified Field Theory; without too much explanation, this is the idea that at a subtle level, the place before thought, movement or desire, communication occurs between objects or minds, without there being any observable or physical means of transmission. Advanced meditators observed that their practice had remarkable effects on the surrounding environment. The Maharishi employed meditation in war zones or places needing peace, believing as he did, that the unified field that manifested as a result would have a tranquil, calming effect on others. His gentle technique was traced back to a secret school in the foothills of the Himalayas.

Among the other spiritual orders who are aware of the unified field in their spiritual mastery, and use it to great effect, are said to be the Sheikhs of the Suhrawadi Sufis who call this method the 'tincture technique'. It is so called because is it is likened to the way in which a single drop of rose oil when dropped into a large jar of water gradually permeates and intermingles with the whole. The Sheikhs teach meditations and recitations to a small group in the full expectation that it will be conveyed to the rest of their brethren by means other than physical meetings or instruction. Their messages are entirely etheric and accepted as genuine baraka (gifts) to a wider community. By use of this method, telepathic energies are utilised by a small minority as a benefit to the whole.

Interestingly enough, the tincture technique is a practice which originally stemmed from the Coptic Christians of Ethiopia, the very same church which holds the esoteric Christian teachings and identified as the antediluvian masters by Gurdjieff. Is this how the Tibetan Lama G conducted his own teachings and did he also give them in the expectation that they would radiate outwards by telepathic means? If so, could this be the method used by the hidden directorate throughout history to affect change in human civilisation as a whole?

Is this why Gurdjieff found the whole Younghusband invasion affair, engineered by the British, so repulsive? While he certainly wasn't alone in his opinions on the subject, Gurdjieff had additional reasons for considering the deleterious effect the Younghusband expedition had on the globe, for he understood very clearly the destruction and negativity that the death of Lama G would wreak upon humanity. The Russian mage sincerely believed this would happen. Ultimately it matters not whether Gurdjieff identified as a Tibetan Buddhist, Coptic Christian or Sufi, since all three systems are in agreement that such crass interference in spiritual matters equates to a degeneration in the unified field effects. Gurdjieff for once had spelt it out directly. A teaching had been lost.

If Lama G existed and did have a mission to spread a new teaching, it seems likely that its method would have been something akin to the unified field, operating in realms beyond the physical or even the gross levels of thought, to that of pure being. According to Gurdjieff, this was how all knowledge was disseminated by the schools of the masters. There is only a finite amount of knowledge to go round, so in times of mass hysteria, war and revolution, when people lose their heads and abandon their normal sense of dignity there is curiously more 'nectar' for those who seek it. Influence emanating directly from the masters is not to be digested by everyone, yet oddly, it benefits all – eventually as it permeates all facets of life. Christ gave mankind the concept of forgiveness and subsequently, 'turn the other cheek' superseded the older teaching of 'an eye-for an eye'. Buddha talked of compassion for others and people emulated this and grew as individuals. The tincture technique is doing its work, slowly and silently spreading through the ages.

The unified field theory could, in part, explain the sudden rise of the Sumerian civilisation, which still perplexes and amazes historians today. How did these hunter-gather communities rise up in a rampant ascent to acquire the skills of writing, farming, astronomy, advanced mathematical calculus and more sciences besides in such a short space of time? No one has ever come up with a satisfactory explanation unless, of course, one refers to the Igigi theories of the Sumerians themselves. A superior race of non-human entities taught humanity everything they know.

With few plausible explanations on the table at this time, the evolutionary rise of mankind was either a massive, spontaneous uplift in consciousness and intelligence, or the result of an external intervention by an unknown and highly advanced third party. What else could explain the fecund explosion of civilisation that was ancient Sumer?

Mention is made in the old Sumer legends of a sacred land called Dilman, a place where pain, suffering, old-age and disease were non-existent and predators did not kill. Dilman is found on the Arabian peninsula, another home of the Saba. Does such a fabled land give rise to the Garden of Eden myth? During the 1970s in Arabia archaeologists uncovered ancient earth markings dubbed mustatils, sandstone enclosures of enormous size and construction. Arabian mustatils are described as the earliest ritual landscape on Earth. So the Sumerian legends are accurate it would seem, as Gurdjieff knew himself. More recently in 2021/22 we see in Arabia more remarkable discoveries of a similar vein. Australian archaeologists from the University of Western Australia using satellite scans have found what they have described as funerary avenues – long corridors boarded by ritual motifs etched in the earth. Already it understood that these ancient highways extended thousands of miles. One Dr Dalton who is involved in this research said, "…populations living in the Arabian Peninsula 4,500 years ago were far more socially and economically connected to one another than we previously thought." The shift of understanding has led to a major rethink, albeit tentatively, linked to Bronze Age history. Perhaps it has not been said publicly but the petroglyphs found there are very similar to Tasmanian and Australian rock art, as if the same symbology is in use. Already Rebecca Foote, director of archaeology and cultural heritage research for the Royal Commission, has said the mustatils are much older, a finding supported by radiocarbon testing. Arabian explorers have long believed the lost city of Ubar, mentioned in the Quran and waxed lyrical into a *1001 Nights*, as the 'City of Brass'. Atlantis was said to be bathed in the copper light of Orichalcum.

Ubar, if it exists, is now hidden under Rub al Khali desert which once was verdant and lush long before the cataclysm of 10,000BC. Bedouin-influenced Lawrence of Arabia coined the term 'the Atlantis of the sands' – he sensed the import of Ubar in relation to the origins of civilisation. Lawrence suggested hiring an airship to find evidence of the lost city from the skies, a dream that was not realised. In 2001 that is exactly what Rebecca Foote did, calling it the museum of the skies, her efforts have already produced a wealth of results. Some say it is the largest archaeological survey currently being undertaken anywhere in the world.

Gurdjieff himself suggested that the energy of the West and wisdom of the East be combined to save the planet, but this view is now itself somewhat dated. East and West have now been co-opted into capitalism but the principle of uniting the two lobes of the brain, logic and intuition, to its sum result is the way forward.

With the future in our own hands, does it simply take one percent of humanity to decide to make it their business to actively access the unified field of their own volition to become enlightened beings? Rejecting exploitation of nature to our detriment is on everyone's lips nowadays but to consciously find our place among the beasts and indeed our proper relationship with Mother Earth is perhaps the greatest step change mankind has yet been presented with. So even in terms of pure self preservation, seeing the global perspective of man as a guardian of ecology if nothing else must be a priority.

Taking that model of living forwards non-violent living, resource equality and emotional awareness are the next level. Actualisation can no longer take place within the current industrial-military-political exploitation model whereby people, animals and the planet itself are seen as resources to own and exploit. Materialism alone is redundant. The right hand lobe of the brain knows this but cannot bring it about without utilising the logical intellect of the left lobe. Tribespeople knew this as they remained closer to nature. Nowadays colonialism and slavery are dirty words but so too will be capitalism, where one man hoards billions in currency while whole swathes of humanity left bereft to starve. If the current world model, as corrosive and divisive as it is, continues, then world extinction will follow as resources are finite. With its innate intelligence the planet may have mechanisms to rid itself of unwanted, harmful lifeforms. Humans call coronavirus a virus but equally it could be an antibody launched for survival of the host which in this case is the Earth. A warning shot perhaps?

Humanity occupies a unique place in the scheme of life on Earth, with self-awareness of personal health, wellbeing towards family, altruistic intentions fostered on a friendship circle and benevolence towards society at large, but also responsibility as a care-giver to the planet. Psychologist Maslow was one who recognised this in his pyramid of needs. Gurdjieff had refined this paradigm to a blueprint for humanity, both psychological and historical, even cosmological, his claims of spiritual hierarchy spanning from the cataclysm have never been more salient. One thing is abundantly clear: if we are to survive as species, our success will be brought to bear by the fruits of peaceable, hedonic beings like Lama G rather than violent exploiters such as Colonel Younghusband.

Gurdjieff lies buried at Avon, France. At either end of his grave are placed two roughly-hewn standing stones; perhaps a final clue to the font of his knowledge – the very means that enabled him to find those centres of initiation?

It is clear that materialism is bankrupt. The needs of the Earth are pressing; the key concept is for mankind to reconnect, not only with nature, but also with the demiurgic intelligence which requires people to attain inner freedom in order to manifest. Psychological evolution is a matter of survival.

Epilogue

After the death of George Gurdjieff, J.G. Bennett persisted in his quest to seek out other masters of wisdom in the hope receiving further instruction on the path toward enlightenment. Inevitably, his travels drew him back to the East. Perhaps the most remarkable of his recorded accounts is of a 1961 meeting with a Hindu 'saint' in the Himalayas, this time at Kathmandu, Nepal. So struck was Bennett with this character that he became his biographer, relating his experiences in a book called *Long Pilgrimage*, which features several photographs of the saint in question. The man went by the name of Shivapuri Baba and at the time of their meeting, the sage was said to have been in the region of 135 years of age. In the book he is pictured clothed in a simple white loincloth but the face looking out from the pages, it must be said, radiates kindness, his eyes windows of a soul basking in eternity.

Bennett visited the seven-foot-tall saint in his garden in Kathmandu to seek his teachings, but was taken aback in abject fear as wild tigers, snakes, other dangerous animals came and sat at the feet of the guru, who smiled and gently patted them as if stroking so many house pets. All wild creatures were completely placid in his presence; in fact they seemed almost drawn to him. Bennett later discovered certain facts about Shivapuri Baba's life, leading him to conclude that he had encountered a true living saint who experienced nirvana at every breath. At that time, his tale had not been told and it would never have reached the wider world had it not been for Bennett.

His story was in many respects parallel to Gurdjieff's own. He had attended an esoteric school, where his teacher was none other than his grandfather Achuthan, a greatly renowned scholar of mathematics and Hindu astrology. In the 1840s when Achuthan died, the teenager forsook his former life and retreated into the jungle to meditate on enlightenment. There he would remain in total seclusion for 25 years. The seasons and years blended into one and he lost all track of time, until one day he was struck by a bolt of green and black lightning and thereupon he beheld a vision of total realisation. With it came 'samadhi', the yearned-for mystical state of total union with the divine. True to the dying wish of his grandfather, he resolved to keep his promise to become a wandering sannyasin and to walk across the world. His travels took him to Afghanistan where he met with the Agha Khan who invited him to stay, which for a while he did. Accounts of his travels are not for the fainthearted. One such journey took him across the perilous Arabian desert, whose searing sands he successfully traversed without the benefit of either camel or map. He was received in Mecca where he became one of the only non-believers ever to lay eyes on the holy-of-holies, the Kaaba or Black Stone so revered by the Sabean culture who venerated Hubal there long before the rise of Islam. Here the saint went into deep meditation.

While in Italy he was received by the Pope and although the Vatican did not allow open access to those outside the Catholic faith, Shivapuri Baba was granted unique admission to their precincts. On his travels across Europe he was entertained by the Kaiser, and during time in America he was entertained by President Theodore Roosevelt. On meeting Einstein the elderly Sadhu gave the physicist a few pointers in mathematics: "Absolutely speaking, only God exists", he said, "so the question of adding one thing to another cannot be entertained. Relatively speaking, no two things or beings are homogeneous. So, to say $1 + 1 = 2$ is convenient, definitely, but not correct."

During his travels in England Shivapuri Baba received a Royal invitation to meet with Queen Victoria who was so greatly impressed by his transcendent presence that she duly installed him at Buckingham Palace as an advisor. It should come as no surprise he instructed the Indian nationalist Bal Tilak, who identified the home of the Vedas as the North pole. To climbers seeking to scale Everest he revealed the best route up to its majestic peak, having walked that way from China. It is on his advice that the British climber Lord John Hunt and his party made their celebrated ascent in 1953.

It cannot fail to stimulate some wonder that he visited so many stone sites, Mecca, Jerusalem, Athens, even Lake Titicaca in South America, as he walked down from the USA. We can only guess if he was privy, like Gurdjieff, to an ancient method of Neolithic navigation.

His final home after a journey of epic proportions was a mountain called Siva Puri, Kathmandu, whose name he adopted. Yet still he remained peripatetic, taking regular pilgrimages on foot to the sacred city of Varanasi on the banks of the Ganges in India.

What remains instructive about Shivapuri Baba's conversations with Bennett is his reference to 'eternal laws', resonant with Gurdjieff's own teachings as recounted to his student Bennett. Using his 'ray of creation' and step diagram,

Gurdjieff explained that there are 48 natural laws that mankind is bound by while living in a physical body. Halving the influence of those laws is a necessary step towards inner freedom and the development of the so-called 'higher emotion centre', or astral body. Through further work, man can reduce the total number of laws governing him to just six, and thereby come to live in the 'higher intellectual body', at which point free will is realised in the individual. The last state is of course liberation of the fully realised being, represented by the number seven in Gurdjieff's system. Gurdjieff often said of these states that the Absolute is the source of everything and everything is one. Shivapuri Baba hinted at the advanced sciences when he said that a man had to decide whether life was real. Gurdjieff said as much himself in the title of his book, *Life is Only Real Then, When "I Am"*.

Without knowing anything about Gurdjieff or his system, Shivapuri Baba referred to living under just three such laws. By living a simple existence and being bound by so very few of the influences usually exerted upon the average human being, he was effectively declaring himself to be operating at the level of pure being, at one with the bio-luminous Unified Field. How this elderly man was able to navigate vast tracts of the Earth without the use of maps, travel great distances on foot often in harsh conditions and with his simple wisdom come to influence so many world leaders in the political, religious and civic realms defies all modern pronouncements or explanations of such things. Shivapuri Baba finally departed the physical plane in January 1963 at the age of 137. It is said that he made a final announcement; "Live right life, worship God. That is all. Nothing more." At that he took a last sip of water before saying "Gaya" (I am gone), lay down and passed away.

Whether the mysterious Lama G whom we first met at the beginning of this book ever existed is not known, yet to simply brush aside the idea of wise or holy men bearing messages of hope to humanity is not only to disparage Gurdjieff, but to disenfranchise oneself from a potential source of perennial wisdom. It is clear the very idea of enlightened beings working with a Unified Field, a life-affirming energy of benefit to all beings, will soon become the most exciting area in scientific discovery and therefore vital to our collective future.

Bibliography

Chapter 1

Bennett, J.G. (2018). *The Masters of Wisdom*. Petersham, Ma: J. G. Bennett Foundation.

Bisher, J. (2009). *White Terror : Cossack Warlords of the Trans-Siberian*. Abingdon: Routledge.

Brunton, P. (2014). *A Search in Secret India*. United States: Merchant Books.

catalog.loc.gov. (n.d.). *Journal de Saint Petersburg 1901*. [online] Available at: https://catalog.loc.gov/vwebv/search?searchCode=LCCN&searchArg=sn%20 85020116&searchType=1&permalink=y [Accessed 2 Apr. 2022].

French, P. (1995). *Younghusband : The Last Great Imperial Adventurer*. London: Flamingo.

Gurdjieff, G.I. (2011). *Beelzebub's Tales to His Grandson*. England: Aziloth Books.

Hannigan, T. (2019). *Murder in the Hindu Kush : George Hayward and the Great Game*. Cheltenham: History Press.

Hopkirk, P. (2006). *The Great Game : on Secret Service in High Asia*. London: John Murray.

Chapter 2

Anderson, M. (1991). *The Unknowable Gurdjieff*. Harmondsworth, Middx.: Arkana.

Anthony Blake (n.d.). *Website of Anthony Blake*. [online] www.anthonyblake. co.uk. Available at: https://www.anthonyblake.co.uk/ [Accessed 2 Apr. 2022].

Beekman Taylor, P. (2020). *G.I. Gurdjieff : A Life*. Utrecht, Netherlands: Eureka Editions.

Beekman Taylor, P. (n.d.). *Inventors of Gurdjieff*. [online] www.gurdjieff.org. Available at: https://www.gurdjieff.org/taylor1.htm [Accessed 2 Apr. 2022].

Bennett, J.G. (1975). *Witness : the Autobiography of John G. Bennett*. London: Turnstone Books.

Bennett, J.G. (2006). *Long Pilgrimage : the Life and Teaching of Sri Govindananda Bharati, known as The Shivapuri Baba*. Kathmandu, Nepal: Giridhar Lal Manandhar.

Bennett, J.G. (2018). *The Masters of Wisdom*. Petersham, Ma: J. G. Bennett Foundation.

Dreyfus, G. (2006). *Reflections on the History of Tibetan Scholasticism. Journal of International Buddhist Studies*.

French, P. (1995). *Younghusband : the Last Great Imperial Adventurer*. London: Flamingo.

George, J. (n.d.). *Gurdjieff Heralds the Awakening of Consciousness Now*. [online] www.gurdjieff.org. Available at: https://www.gurdjieff.org/george1.htm [Accessed 2 Apr. 2022].

George, J. (2020). *SEARCHING FOR SHAMBHALA*. [online] The Chronicles of Chögyam Trungpa Rinpoche. Available at: https://www.chronicleproject.com/searching-for-shambhala/ [Accessed 2 Apr. 2022].

Gilbert, A. (1996). *Magi : the Quest for a Secret Tradition*. London: Bloomsbury.

Gurdjieff, G.I. (2011). Beelzebub's tales to his grandson. England: Aziloth Books.

Lefort, R. (1998). *The Teachers of Gurdjieff*. Cambridge, Ma: Malor Books.

Mayhew, B. and Kohn, M. (2005). Tibet. Melbourne Etc.: Lonely Planet Publications.

Moore, J. (1993). *Gurdjieff : the Anatomy of a Myth : a Biography*. Shaftesbury ; Rockport, Mass.: Element.

Murray, M.A. (1954). *The Divine King in England, a Study in Anthropology*. London: Faber And Faber.

Omar Michael Burke (1993). *Among the Dervishes : an Account of travels in Asia and Africa, and Four Years Studying the Dervishes, Sufis and Fakirs by Living Among Them*. London: The Octagon Press.

Ouspensky, P.D. (2020). *In Search Of The Miraculous*. S.L.: Albatross Publishers.

Peters, F. (1986). *My Journey with a Mystic*. Laguna Niguel, Ca: Tale Weaver Pub.

Shah, I. (1964). *The Sufis*. New York, N.Y. Doubleday.

Snellgrove, D.L. (2019). *INDO-TIBETAN BUDDHISM : Indian Buddhists & Their Tibetan Successors*.

Snelling, J. (2002). *Buddhism in Russia : the Story of Agvan Dorzhiev, Lhasa's Emissary to the Tzar*. London: Vega.

Tapsell, J. (2014). *Ameth : the Life and Times of Doreen Valiente*. London, England: Avalonia, May.

Thomas De Hartmann, Olga De Hartmann and T A G Daly (2011). *Our Life with Mr. Gurdjieff*. Sand Point, Idaho: Moonlight Press.
Wilson, C. (2005). *G.I. Gurdjieff : the War Against Sleep*. London: Aeon.
Wilson, C. (2020). *Mysteries*. London: Watkins.
Information also taken from direct discussions with Bert Sharp, John Flores and Nicholas Ternenshenko.

Chapter 3
Aleksandr Ivanovič Andreev (2014). *The Myth of the Masters Revived : The Occult Lives of Nikolai and Elena Roerich*.
Allen, C. (2000). *The Search for Shangri-La : A Journey into Tibetan History*. London: Abacus.
Andrew, T. (1977). *Shambhala : Oasis of Light*. London: Sphere.
Bernard, R.W. (2017). *The Hollow Earth: The Greatest Geographical Discovery in History Made by Admiral Richard E. Byrd in the Mysterious Land Beyond the Poles – the True Origin of the Flying Saucers*.
Bernbaum, E. (2001). *The way to Shambhala : A Search for the Mythical Kingdom Beyond the Himalayas*. Boston: Shambhala.
Blavatsky, H.P. (1910). *Studies in Occultism (1910) : volumes 1-3*. Montana: Kessinger Pub. Co., 199.
Blavatsky, H.P. (1963). *Secret Doctrine: The Synthesis of Science, Religion, and Philosophy*.
Blavatsky, H.P. (2018). *Isis Unveiled : A Master Key to the Mysteries of Ancient and Modern Science and Theology*. Pantianos Classics.
Chapple, C. and Venkatesananda, S. (1984). *The Concise Yoga Vasistha*. Albany: State University Of New York Press.
Charroux, R. (1979). *Lost Worlds : Scientific Secrets of the Ancients*. Fontana/Collins.
Chögyam Trungpa (2001). *Great Eastern Sun : The Wisdom of Shambhala*. Boston, Mass. London: Shambhala.
David-Neel, A. (2020). *Magic And Mystery In Tibet*. S.L.: Aziloth Books.
El Morya, Kuthumi, Sinnett, A.P., Blavatsky, H.P., Tiruvalum Subba Row, Mavalankar, D.K. and A Trevor Barker (1926). *The Mahatma letters to A.P. Sinnett from the Mahatmas M. & K.H.* London: T. Fisher Unwin.
Fabrice Midal and Monk, I. (2012). *Chogyam Trungpa : His Life and Vision*. Boston: Shambhala.
Henry, A. (1898). *In the Forbidden Land : An Account of a Journey in Tibet, Capture by the Tibetan Authorities, Imprisonment, Torture, and Ultimate Release. Vol. I.* London Heinemann.

History of Islam. (2009). *Akbar, the Great Moghul.* [online] Available at: https://historyofislam.com/contents/the-land-empires-of-asia/akbar-the-great-moghul/.

Hite, K. (2013). *The Nazi Occult.* Botley, Oxford, UK: Osprey Publishing.

J Douglas Kenyon (2015). *Paradigm Busters : Beyond Science, Lost History, Ancient Wisdom.* Livingston, Mt: Atlantis Rising.

Lachman, G. (2012). *Madame Blavatsky : The Mother of Modern Spirituality.* New York: Jeremy P. Tarcher/Penguin.

Lachman, G. (2021). *The Dedalus Book of the 1960s : Turn off Your Mind.* Sawtry: Dedalus ; Gardena, Ca.

Lepage, V. (2000). *Shambhala : The Fascinating Truth Behind the Myth of Shangri-la.* Varanasi: Pilgrims Pub., Ca.

Liam Matthew Brockey (2014). *The Visitor : André Palmeiro and the Jesuits in Asia.* Cambridge, Massachusetts: Harvard University Press.

Lomas, R. (2009). *The Invisible College : The Royal Society, Freemasonry and the Birth of Modern Science.* London: Corgi.

Namkhai Norbu and Enrico Dell'angelo (2012). *The Lamp that Enlightens Narrow Minds : The Life and Times of a Realized Tibetan Master, Khyentse Chökyi Wangchug.* Berkeley, California: North Atlantic Books.

Nicoll, M. (1970). *Psychological Commentaries on the Teaching of G.I. Gurdjieff and P.D Ouspensky / 1-3 v.* London: Stuart And Watkins.

Ossendowski, F. (2018). *Beasts, Men And Gods.*

Ouspenskii, P. (1977). *In Search of the Miraculous : Fragments of an Unknown Teaching.* New York: Harcourt Brace Jovanovich.

Ouspenskii, P. (1986). *The Fourth Way : A Record of Talks and Answers to Questions Based on the Teaching of G.I. Gurdjieff.* London: Arkana.

Reigle, D. and N. (n.d.). *The Lost Kalacakra Mula Tantra on the Kings of Sambhala.* www.academia.edu. [online] Available at: https://www.academia.edu/6423778/The_Lost_Kalacakra_Mula_Tantra_on_the_Kings_of_Sambhala [Accessed 2 Apr. 2022].

René Guénon, Fohr, H.D. and Fohr, S.D. (2004). *Symbols of Sacred Science.* Hillsdale: Sophia Perennis, Cop.

Roerich, N. (2001). *Altai-Himalaya : a travel diary.* Kempton, Ill.: Adventures Unlimited.

Roerich, N. (2017). *Shambhala The Resplendent.*

Stasulane, A. (2005). *Theosophy and culture : Nicholas Roerich.* Roma: Pontificia Università Gregoriana.

studybuddhism.com. (n.d.). *Study Buddhism – an extensive source of Buddhist teachings.* [online] Available at: https://studybuddhism.com/en [Accessed 2 Apr. 2022].

Tapsell, J. and Newton, T. (2013). *London's Mystical Legacy*. Brutus Media.
tibetanbuddhistencyclopedia.com. (n.d.). *In Search of Shambhala by Mary Sutherland - Tibetan Buddhist Encyclopedia*. [online] Available at: http://tibetanbuddhistencyclopedia.com/en/index.php/In_Search_of_Shambhala_by_Mary_Sutherland [Accessed 2 Apr. 2022].
tibetanbuddhistencyclopedia.com. (n.d.). *Red Star Over Shambhala - Tibetan Buddhist Encyclopedia*. [online] Available at: http://tibetanbuddhistencyclopedia.com/en/index.php/Red_Star_Over_Shambhala [Accessed 2 Apr. 2022].
Tomohiko Uyama (2014). *Asiatic Russia : Imperial Power in Regional and International Contexts*. London: Routledge.
Wilson, C. (1989). *Beyond the Occult*. New York: Carroll & Graf.
Wilson, C. (1995). *The Occult : A History*. New York: Barnes & Noble.
www.blavatskyarchives.com. (n.d.). Blavatsky Study Center: *Website on Helena Petrovna Blavatsky & Theosophy including Blavatsky Archives*. [online] Available at: https://www.blavatskyarchives.com/ [Accessed 2 Apr. 2022].
Yumpu.com (n.d.). *Madame Blavatsky, Buddhism and Tibet by Leslie Price*. [online] yumpu.com. Available at: https://www.yumpu.com/en/document/read/4415203/madame-blavatsky-buddhism-and-tibet-by-leslie-price [Accessed 2 Apr. 2022].

Chapter 4

Bellezza, J.V. (2017). *DAWN OF TIBET : the Ancient Civilization on the Roof of the World*.
Bernbaum, E. (2001). *The Way to Shambhala : A Search for the Mythical Kingdom Beyond the Himalayas*. Boston: Shambhala.
Black, J. (2010). *The Secret History of the World*. London: Quercus.
Brennan, J.H. (2002). *Occult Tibet : Secret Practices of Himalayan Magic*. St. Paul, Minn.: Llewellyn Publications.
China Society (1965). *Nine Dragon Screen : Being Reprints of Nine Addresses and Papers Presented to the China Society, 1909-1945*. China Society.
Churchward, J. (1960). *The Sacred Symbols of Mu ... Illustrated*. Neville Spearman: London; Printed in U.S.A.
Churchward, J. (2007). *The Lost Continent of Mu*. Kempton, Ill.: Adventures Unlimited Press.
Churchward, J.E. (2014). *The Stone Tablets of Mu*. Huntsville, Ar: Ozark Mountain Publishing.
Dashu, M. (2010). *Xi Wangmu, the Shamanic Goddess of China*. www.academia.edu. [online] Available at: https://www.academia.edu/4075136/Xi_Wangmu_the_shamanic_goddess_of_China [Accessed 2 Apr. 2022].

Dotson, B. (2008). *Complementarity and Opposition in Early Tibetan ritual.* www.academia.edu. [online] Available at: https://www.academia.edu/6522536/_ Complementarity_and_opposition_in_early_Tibetan_ritual_ [Accessed 2 Apr. 2022].

Dotson, B. (2011). *'Theorising the king: Implicit and Explicit Sources for the Study of Tibetan Sacred Kingship.'* www.academia.edu. [online] Available at: https:// www.academia.edu/6522539/_Theorising_the_king_implicit_and_explicit_ sources_for_the_study_of_Tibetan_sacred_Kingship_ [Accessed 5 Apr. 2022].

Frazer, J.G. (2017). *GOLDEN BOUGH : a Study in Magic and Religion.*

Gardiner, P. and Osborn, G. (2007). *The Serpent Grail : the Truth Behind the Holy Grail, the Philosopher's Stone and the Elixir of Life.* London: Watkins.

Gyatso, G.T. and Dorji, G.T. (2009). *The Treasure of the Ancestral Clans of Tibet.* Translated by Y. Dhondup. Dharamsala, H.P Library Of Tibetan Works And Archives.

Hopkins, J. (2012). Okar Research: *Shambhala: Tribes, Clans and Castes.* [online] Okar Research. Available at: http://balkhandshambhala.blogspot. com/2012/11/balkhtribes-clans.html [Accessed 2 Apr. 2022].

Joseph, F. (2005). *The Atlantis Encyclopedia.* Franklin Lakes, Nj: New Page Books.

Kong-Sprul Blo-Gros-Mtha-Yas and Dorje, G. (2013). *The Treasury of knowledge. Book six, Parts One and two, Indo-Tibetan Classical Learning and Buddhist Phenomenology.* Ithaca, N.Y.: Snow Lion ; Enfield.

Lepage, V. (1996). *Shambhala : The Fascinating Truth Behind the Myth of Shangri-la.* Wheaton, Ill.: Quest Books.

Paul, R.A. (1989). *The Sherpas of Nepal in the Tibetan Cultural Context : (the Tibetan Symbolic World: a Psychoanalytic Exploration).* Delhi Motilal Banarsidass.

Rossi, D. and Norbu, N. (2013). *A History of Zhang Zhung and Tibet / Volume One the Early Period.* Berkeley, Calif.: North Atlantic Books.

Stein, R.A. (n.d.). *Tibetica Antiqua.*

Temple, R. (2000). *The Crystal Sun : Rediscovering a Lost Technology of the Ancient World.* London Arrow.

White, D.G. (2001). *Tantra in Practice.* Delhi: Motilal Banarsidass.

Wilensky-Lanford, B. (2011). *Paradise Lust : Searching for the Garden of Eden.* New York: Grove.

Wilson, C. (2006). *Atlantis and the Kingdom of the Neanderthals : 100,000 Years of Lost History.* Rochester, Vt.: Bear & Co.

Wilson, C. (2007). *From Atlantis to the Sphinx.* London: Virgin.

Chapter 5

Allen, C. (2000). *The Search for Shangri-La : A Journey into Tibetan History*. London: Abacus.

collab.its.virginia.edu. (n.d.). Home. [online] Available at: https://collab.its.virginia.edu/wiki/renaissanceold/home.html [Accessed 2 Apr. 2022].

Dakpa, N. (2005). *Opening the Door to Bön*. Ithaca, N.Y.: Snow Lion Publications.

Gardner, A. (2012). *Drenpa Namka, Bon Master – Treasury of Lives | Tricycle*. [online] Tricycle: The Buddhist Review. Available at: https://tricycle.org/trikedaily/treasury-lives-bon-master-drenpa-namka/ [Accessed 2 Apr. 2022].

Guenther, H.V. (1996). *The Teachings of Padmasambhava*. New York: E.J. Brill.

Gyatso, G.T. and Dorji, G.T. (2009). *The Treasure of the Ancestral Clans of Tibet*. Translated by Y. Dhondup. Dharamsala, H.P Library Of Tibetan Works And Archives.

Jestice, P.G. ed., (2004). *Holy People of the World : A Cross-Cultural Encyclopedia*. Santa Barbara, Calif. ; Oxford: Abc-Clio.

Kapstein, M. (2002). *The Tibetan Assimilation of Buddhism : Conversion, Contestation and Memory*. New York ; Oxford: Oxford University Press.

Rossi, D. and Norbu, N. (2013). *A History of Zhang Zhung and Tibet / Volume One the Early Period*. Berkeley, Calif.: North Atlantic Books.

Snellgrove, D.L. and Richardson, H. (2003). *A Cultural History of Tibet*. Bangkok: Orchid Press.

The Treasury of Lives. (n.d.). *The Treasury of Lives: A Biographical Encyclopedia of Tibet, Inner Asia and the Himalayan Region*. [online] Available at: https://treasuryoflives.org/ [Accessed 2 Apr. 2022].

Vessantara (2007). *Meeting the Buddhas : a Guide to Buddhas, Bodhisattvas and Tantric Deities*. Delhi: Motilal Banarsidass Publishers.

Chapter 6

Abbas, Dr.S. (n.d.). Iran Chamber Society: *History of Iran: Persian Affinities of the Licchavis - a Review*. [online] www.iranchamber.com. Available at: https://www.iranchamber.com/history/articles/persian_affinities_licchavis_review.php [Accessed 2 Apr. 2022].

Ahmad, H.M.G. (2018). *Jesus In India*.

Allen, C. (2000). *The Search for Shangri-La : a Journey into Tibetan History*. London: Abacus.

Bellezza, J.V. (2017). *DAWN OF TIBET : the Ancient Civilization on the Roof of the World*.

Bennett, J.G. (2018). *The Masters of Wisdom*. Petersham, Ma: J. G. Bennett Foundation.

Eisenman, R.H. and Wise, M. (2001). *The Dead Sea Scrolls Uncovered*. London: Vega.

Ernst, C.W. (2004). *Eternal Garden : Mysticism, History, and Politics at a South Asian Sufi Center*. New Delhi: Oxford University Press.

Farooq, A. (2011). *Jesus and Moses in India*. Iuniverse Inc.

Ferrier, J.P. (2002). *History of the Afghans*. Translated by W. Jesse. Lahore: Sang-E-Meel Publications.

Gibson, D.J. (n.d.). *Eden*.

Kriwaczek, P. (2003). *In Search of Zarathustra : the First Prophet and the Ideas That Changed the World*. London: Phoenix.

Magi | Scripture, Traditions, & Importance. (2019). In: Encyclopædia Britannica. [online] Available at: https://www.britannica.com/topic/Magi.

Martin, D. (2001). *Unearthing Bon Treasures : Life and Contested Legacy of a Tibetan Scripture revealer, with a General Bibliography of Bon*. Leiden ; Boston: Brill.

Mountcastle, W.W. (2008). *The Secret Ministry of Jesus : Pioneer Prophet of Interfaith Dialogue*. Lanham, Md.: University Press of America.

Ni'mat Allāh (2013). *History of the Afghans : Translated from the Persian of Neamet Ullah*. Translated by B. Dorn. New York: Cambridge University Press.

Nottingham, T.J. (2011). *The Wisdom of the Fourth Way: Origins and Applications of A Perennial Teaching: 1 (Gurdjieff and the Fourth Way Teachings)*. U.S.A.: Theosis Books.

Rosenmueller, K. and Morren, N. (1836). *The Biblical Geography of Central Asia*. Edinburgh.

Schumacher, R. (n.d.). *The King Makers: A Look at the Magi*. [online] blogos. org. Available at: https://www.blogos.org/compellingtruth/magi.php [Accessed 2 Apr. 2022].

Székely, E.B. (1988). *The Teachings of the Essenes from Enoch to the Dead Sea Scrolls*. Saffron Walden, Essex: C.W. Daniel Co.

the Guardian. (2010). *Pashtun clue to lost tribes of Israel*. [online] Available at: https://www.theguardian.com/world/2010/jan/17/israel-lost-tribes-pashtun#:~:text=%22Pathans%2C%20or%20Pashtuns%2C%20are [Accessed 10 Apr. 2022].

The New American Bible. (2011). Huntington, Indiana: Our Sunday Visitor Publishing Division, Our Sunday Visitor, Inc.

Wilson, C. and Flem-Ath, R. (2005). *The Atlantis Blueprint*. London: Time Warner Books.

www.attalus.org. (n.d.). Excerpta Latina Barbari - Translation. [online] Available at: http://www.attalus.org/translate/barbari.html#:~:text=The%20 names%20of%20the%20Magi [Accessed 2 Apr. 2022].

Yule, H. (1903). *Hobson-Jobson: Being a Glossary of Anglo-Indian Colloquial Words and Phrases, and of Kindred Terms ; etymological, historical, geographical, and discursive*. London: John Murray.

Chapter 7

Anon, (n.d.). *Orientalia, Nova Series, Vol. 63(No. 2), pp.68–83*.

Blavatsky, H.P. (1963) *The Secret Doctrine: The Synthesis of Science, Religion, And Philosophy*.

Brophy, T.G. (2002). *The Origin Map : Discovery of a Prehistoric, Megalithic, Astrophysical Map and Sculpture of the Universe*. New York: Writers Club Press.

El Daly, O. (2016). *Egyptology : the Missing Millennium : Ancient Egypt in Medieval Arabic Writings*. London ; New York (N.Y.): Routledge.

El Daly, O.N. (2003). *Ancient Egypt in medieval Moslem/Arabic writings*. [online] discovery.ucl.ac.uk. Available at: https://discovery.ucl.ac.uk/id/ eprint/10103492/ [Accessed 2 Apr. 2022].

Elukin, J. (2002). *Maimonides and the Rise and Fall of the Sabians: Explaining Mosaic Laws and the Limits of Scholarship*. Journal of the History of Ideas, [online] 63(4), pp.619–637. Available at: https://www.jstor.org/stable/3654163 [Accessed 2 Apr. 2022].

Forwood, A.K. (2011). *They Would Be Gods*. Raleigh, N.C.: Lulu Pub.

Green, T.M. (1992). *The City of the Moon God : Religious Traditions of Harran*. Leiden: E.J. Brill.

Grierson, R. and Munro-Hay, S.C. (2000). *The Ark of the Covenant*. London: Phoenix.

Gzella, H. (2012). *Languages from the World of the Bible*. Boston: De Gruyter.

Hancock, G. (2017). *Magicians of the Gods*. New York Thomas Dunne Books.

Hatcher Childress, D. (2002). *Lost Cities & Ancient Mysteries of Africa & Arabia*. Stelle, Ill.: Adventures Unlimited Press.

Herodotus (n.d.). *An Account of Egypt*. Translated by G.C. Macauley.

Jones, P.S. (1957). *Recent Discoveries in Babylonian Mathematics 1: Zero, Pi, and Polygons*. The Mathematics Teacher, [online] 50(2), pp.162–165. Available at: https://www.jstor.org/stable/27955350 [Accessed 2 Apr. 2022].

Kramer, S.N. (2008). *The Sumerians : Their History, Culture, and Character*. Chicago, Ill: University Of Chicago Press.

Manley, D. and Peta Rée (2001). *Henry Salt : Artist, Traveller, Diplomat, Egyptologist*. London: Libri.

Martinez, S.B. (2013). *The Lost History of the Little People : Their Spiritually Advanced Civilizations around the World*. Rochester, Vt.: Bear & Co.

Martinez, S.B. (2016). *The Lost Continent of Pan : the Oceanic Civilization at the Origin of World Culture*. Rochester, Vermont: Bear & Company.

Massey, G. (1995). *A Book of the Beginnings : Containing an Attempt to Recover and Reconstitute the Lost Origins of the Myths and Mysteries, Types and Symbols, Religion and Language, with Egypt for the Mouthpiece and Africa as the Birthplace*. Baltimore, Md: Black Classic Press.

McKim Malville, J. (2014). *Astronomy at Nabta Playa, Southern Egypt*. Handbook of Archaeoastronomy and Ethnoastronomy, [online] pp.1079–1091. Available at: https://link.springer.com/referenceworkentry/10.1007%2F978-1-4614-6141-8_101 [Accessed 18 Oct. 2021].

Monges, M.M.-K.-R. (2002). *The Queen of Sheba and Solomon*. Journal of Black Studies, 33(2), pp.235–246.

Powell, A.E. (1971). *The Solar System*. Mokelumne Hill Pr.

Springett, B.H. (1922). *Secret Sects of Syria and the Lebanon, a Consideration of Their origin, Creeds and Religious Ceremonies, and their Connection with and Influence Upon Modern Freemasonry*. London: G. Allen And Unwin.

Tamdgidi, M.H. (2012). *Gurdjieff and Hypnosis : a Hermeneutic Study*. New York (Ny): Palgrave Macmillan, , Cop.

Wallis Budge, E.A. (2003). *An Egyptian Hieroglyphic Dictionary : with an Index of English words, King list, and Geographical List with Indexes, List of Hieroglyphic characters, Coptic and Semitic Alphabets, etc*. Whitefish Mt: Kessinger Publishing.

Webb, J. (1987). *The Harmonious Circle : the Lives and Work of G.I. Gurdjieff, P.D. Ouspensky, and Their Followers*. Boston: Shambhala.

Wilson, C. and Flem-Ath, R. (2005). *The Atlantis Blueprint*. London: Time Warner Books.

Chapter 8

Frankel, V.E. (2015). *The Symbolism and Sources of Outlander : the Scottish Fairies, Folklore, Ballads, Magic and Meanings That Inspired the Series*. Jefferson, North Carolina: Mcfarland & Company, Inc., Publishers.

Gardiner, P. and Osborn, G. (2007). *The Serpent Grail : the Truth behind the Holy Grail, the Philosopher's Stone and the Elixir of Life*. London: Watkins.

Hancock, G. (2017). *Magicians of the Gods*. New York Thomas Dunne Books.

Hayes, M. (1994). *The Infinite Harmony: Musical Structures in Science and Theology*. London: Weidenfeld & Nicolson.

Jacobs, A. (2010). *Eutopia : the Gnostic Land of Prester John : a Novella*. Winchester, UK ; Washington, USA: O Books.

Johnson, K.P. (1995). *Initiates of Theosophical Masters*. Albany, N.Y.: State University Of New York Press.

Pace, A. (2004). *The Hal Saflieni Hypogeum*. Midsea Books Ltd,Malta.

Rosenthal, L. (n.d.). *The Sound of Gurdjieff*. [online] www.gurdjieff.org. Available at: https://www.gurdjieff.org/rosenthal1.htm [Accessed 2 Apr. 2022].

Shirley, J. (2004). *Gurdjieff : an Introduction to His Life and Ideas*. New York: J.P. Tarcher/Penguin.

Thomas De Hartmann, Olga De Hartmann and T A G Daly (2011). *Our Life with Mr. Gurdjieff*. Sand Point, Idaho: Moonlight Press.

Vesco, R. and Hatcher Childress, D. (2007). *Man-made UFOs : WWII's Secret Legacy*. Kempton, Ill.: Adventures Unlimited.

Von Däniken, E. (2020). *The Gold of the Gods*. Kempton, Illinois, USA: Adventures Unlimited Press.

Chapter 9

Abbas, Z. (2002). *Atlantis : The Final Solution : A Scientific History of Humanity over the Last 100,000 Years*. San Jose: Writers Club Press.

Allen, C. (2000). *The Search for Shangri-La : a Journey into Tibetan History*. London: Abacus.

Bangdel, D. and Huntington, J.C. (2003). *The Circle of Bliss : Buddhist Meditational Art ; [in conjunction with the Exhibition The Circle of Bliss: Buddhist Meditational Art ; Los Angeles County Museum of Art, October 5 - January 11, 2003, Columbus Museum of Art, February 6 - May 9, 2004]*. Chicago, Ill: Serindia Publications, C.

Bhāgavata Purāna 3.32.8-10.

Charroux, R. (1974). *The Gods Unknown*. New York: Berkley Pub. Corp.

China Society (1965). *Nine Dragon Screen : Being Reprints of Nine Addresses and Papers Presented to the China Society, 1909-1945*. China Society.

Churchward, J. (1960). *The Sacred Symbols of Mu ... Illustrated*. Neville Spearman: London; Printed in U.S.A.

Doyle, C.C. (2014). *The Mahabharata Secret*. Noida, Utta Pradesh, India: Om Books International.

Georg Bühler (1903). *On the Indian Sect of the Jainas*. Translated by J. Burgess. London Luzac.

Hancock, G. (1995). *Fingerprints of the Gods*. New York: Three Rivers Press.

Hatcher Childress, D. (2003). *The Anti-Gravity Handbook*. Kempton, Ill.: Adventures Unlimited Press.

Johnson, B. (2011). *What the Blank Do We Know about the Bible: A Journey of Discovery*. Rainier, Wa: Living Free Press.

Lepage, V. (2000). *Shambhala : The Fascinating Truth Behind the Myth of Shangri-La*. Varanasi: Pilgrims Pub., [Ca.

Loewenstein, Prince, J. (1965). *Swastika and Yin-Yang*. London.

Noorbergen, R. (2014). *Secrets of the Lost Races : New Discoveries of Advanced Technology in Ancient Civilizations*. Teach Services.

Pramanik, M. (n.d.). *Dwarka: India's Submerged Ancient City*. [online] www.bbc.com. Available at: https://www.bbc.com/travel/article/20220113-dwarka-indias-submerged-ancient-city.

Ramachandra Dikshitar, V.R. (1999). *War in Ancient India*. New Delhi Cosmo Publ.

Ramesh, C. (2014). *Thought-forms and Hallucinations : Some Curious Effects of the Holographic Mind Process*. Chidambaram Ramesh, Charleston, Sc.

Sanderson, I.T. and Hatcher Childress, D. (2001). *Vimana Aircraft of Ancient India & Atlantis*. Kempton, Il: Adventures Unlimited.

Singh, M.R. (1972). *Geographical Data in the Early Purānas; a Critical Study*. Calcutta Punthi Pustak.

Stookey, L.L. (2004). *Thematic Guide to World Mythology*. Westport, Conn.: Greenwood Press.

Tilak, B.G. (2011). *The Arctic Home in the Vedas : Being Also a New Key to the Interpretation of Many Vedic Texts and Legends*. London: Arktos.

Wilson, C. (2007). *From Atlantis to the Sphinx*. London: Virgin.

Wilson, C. (2020). *Mysteries*. London: Watkins.

Wilson, C. and Flem-Ath, R. (2005). *The Atlantis Blueprint*. London: Time Warner Books.

Index

Also by Jonathan Tapsell

Ameth: The Life and Times of Doreen Valiante
Avalonia Books | ISBN 978-1-905297-70-2
AMETH is the first definitive biography of Doreen Valiente (1922-1999), an English Witch who became known as 'the Mother of Modern Witchcraft'. Based on the author's work collating her artefacts, interviewing people who knew her, reading and researching numerous personal magical documents and correspondence bequeathed by Doreen, this book gives unparallelled insight into her magical life.

London's Mystical Legacy
(with Toyne Newton)
Brutus Media | ISBN 978-0-9574061-5-5
This book's findings and research about the founding of London have finally been vindicated – it is now a scientific fact that London is far older than conventional histories have taught us. The legend of Brutus of Troy laid the foundation of the nation state whose idea is incorporated into the City Of London (the Crown) based in the square mile, quite distinct and far more powerful than any monarch, president or government. But could the Brutus myth be something far-reaching in light of the recent archeological discovery in London? For the past 5,000 years London has held its secrets close within its ancient framework. Is this now time for a new dawn in this most timeworn of cities?

The Psychic Jungle
Lilith Mandrake Books | ISBN 978-0-9934628-0-1
The Psychic Jungle is a personal journey into a world hitherto unknown. A high-octane tale, with a body count to match. The book features Nazi Satanists, with links to government-sponsored terrorists, remote viewers battling with intelligence agents, Witches who meet secretly with the Royal family, and assassins with ties to the Vatican – all of whom wish to control or influence our society. Strange powers and perceptions leap out in every corner of this unparalleled journey; a journey which is one of true crime and psychic detection at great personal risk to the author.

About the author

Jonathan Tapsell archived the world's collection of Wicca (Doreen Valiente) and has physically explored several of the sites mentioned in this book. He helped Bert Sharp found the World Gurdjieff Conference 'All and Everything' and hosted his Work group with John Flores.

Lightning Source UK Ltd.
Milton Keynes UK
UKHW020615270822
407756UK00007B/216

9 780957 406179